Traveling
Michigan's Thumb

Traveling
Michigan's Thumb

Exploring a Shoreline
of Small Pleasures and
Unexpected Treasures

by Julie Albrecht Royce

Thunder Bay Press

Holt, Michigan

Thunder Bay Press, Holt, MI 48842

Traveling Michigan's Thumb
Exploring a Shoreline of Small Pleasures and Unexpected Treasures

Photographs by Robert Royce except as otherwise credited.
Book and Cover design by Julie Taylor.
Front Cover Image:
Lake Huron, Photo Courtesy of Susan Jurkiewicz
Back Cover Images:
Petoskey Stones, Photo Courtesy of Robert Royce
Hip Roof Barn, Photo Courtesy of Robert Royce
Marine City Lighthouse, Photo Courtesy of Judy White, Marine City Chamber of Commerce
Sea Captain at the Maritime Days Parade, Photo Courtesy of Judy White, Marine City Chamber of Commerce
Croswell Swinging Bridge, Photo Courtesy of Susan Jurkiewicz
Port Sanilac Lighthouse, Photo Courtesy of Joe Jurkiewicz

First Thunder Bay Press printing, April 2008
ISBN 10: 1-933272-10-4
ISBN 13: 978-1-933272-10-8

Dedicated to Mick Albrecht
-he was born in the Thumb
-grew up in the Thumb
-raised his family in the Thumb
-worked in the Thumb
-and in 2003,
died in his beloved Thumb.

There was no place he would have rather been,
and he was what the Thumb is really about – its wonderful people.

Table of Contents

Overview

Welcome to the Thumb. Welcome to a multitude of unexpected pleasures as you explore this peninsula within a peninsula. Get away to a place where the pace is relaxed, the people friendly, the views spectacular, and the water is waiting with an invitation to endless fun. Take your insiders' guide, *Traveling Michigan's Thumb*, along for the trip.

My husband, Bob, summed up the Thumb Experience shortly after we began this project. We were standing at the counter in a small restaurant in Algonac waiting for coffee. We had just returned from Harsens Island and had a few minutes to spare while waiting for the Ferry to take us to Walpole Island. Wondering if he was bored, I asked, "Are you having fun?" His response was, "Well, it's not roller-coaster kind of fun, but I am enjoying myself." That is the Thumb. There are no mega-amusement parks, but you will not miss the long lines and huge crowds. There are no four or six lane highways, but you will not feel a need to rush anywhere. Deadlines will seem blissfully unimportant.

This guidebook is set up as a continuous route north from New Baltimore and around the tip of the Thumb to Caseville, with a couple of options for your return trip. You will be traveling the shoreline of M-29 and M-25 and you will not need a map for most cities and villages along the way. An overview map of the entire route and basic maps of Port Huron and Sarnia are included; as well as the address and telephone numbers for the various Chambers of Commerce where you will find friendly people willing to help answer any questions. Whether you follow the entire route or choose spots along the way, you are sure to enjoy your visit to the Thumb.

Several Canadian cities (Sombra, Mooretown and Sarnia) are included in this book because they are just minutes from Thumb cities via ferry or the Blue Water Bridge. They make pleasant side trips from Algonac, Marine City or Port Huron. *Do Not Forget a Passport.* In the past a driver's license has been adequate identification for crossing into Canada but that is changing.

Part One of *Traveling Michigan's Thumb* provides detailed information in a straightforward format for each city or village in this guide. It will help you plan a day trip, weekend getaway or summer-long holiday. You can explore beautiful parks, enjoy miles of sandy beaches, tour unique museums, take a diving or snorkeling trip, fish for salmon or trout, shop at antique stores, boutiques or quaint gift shops, play a round of golf, or embark on a day cruise. Along the way you can dine on everything from local favorites to upscale cuisine.

Prices for hotels, motels, B&B's, and restaurants are intentionally not included in this guide book. Lodging prices vary based upon season and specials and restaurant prices vary based upon whether you order a light snack or a full entrée. Most of the descriptions, however, will tell you whether an establishment is "upscale" or "down home" or provide other indications of whether the prices are on the high end or a real bargain.

There is no doubt this guide will miss certain places and maybe include a few others that you feel should not be here. This is not an advertising guide and no one has been solicited or paid to be included. These are simply my choices. If you find an error, a store or restaurant that has closed, or something you feel should be included or omitted next time, please bring it to my attention at: P.O. Box 127, Lexington, MI 48450, or *royce@msu.edu.* Your input is welcome.

While I have done everything I can to ensure the information was correct when this book went to press, things change. Stores go out of business and hours are modified. I recommend you call to confirm anything that is especially important to your trip.

Part Two of *Traveling Michigan's Thumb*, "*A Bit of History and A Bit of Fun*," takes you beyond the typical guide book. It will provide you with a compelling background and history of the Thumb and a unique flavor of the area to savor on your journey. Learn about the Great Lake herself in *My Love Affair with Lake Huron*, or read about the Thumb's first residents in *Native Americans in Michigan's Thumb*. Discover great shipwrecks and a few monsters in *What Lies Beneath*. Explore historically significant lighthouses in *Beacons Lighting the Way*, or check out some of the Thumb barns and discover why they are painted red in *Barns*. Shiver and smile as you read *Ghost Stories for around the Campfire*. Read about the treasures you can find along the shore in *Walking the Beach*. Finally, learn about the major disasters that forever changed the Thumb in *The Great Fires of 1871 and 1881* and *The Big Blow, the Storm of 1913*.

I hope you enjoy your travels through the Thumb and that you come back often.

Acknowledgements

I am deeply grateful to my husband, Bob, without whom this book would not have been possible. He offered his enthusiastic encouragement each step of the way. He played chauffeur to every excursion I took during the collection of information. He enjoyed the restaurants (Oh, how he enjoyed the restaurants), offered his subtle comments ("I would never stay in a dump like that."), and helped proofread the numbers. He is the computer expert and was always ready to help bail me out of any technical problem I encountered. Nearly all of the photos without a credit line were taken by my husband.

Bob is a traveler at heart. He will go anywhere and I have only to start a sentence with "Let's go…" and before I finish he has already answered with an emphatic, "We can do that." While this project was a labor of love, and one I would have enjoyed under any circumstances, his company along the way made it more fun.

I am indebted to Courtney Phillips and Ofer Elitzur for reading the draft and offering their many valuable editing suggestions.

Much of the historical data that I incorporated into the city backgrounds came from the Chambers of Commerce in each town. I wish to specifically thank the following individuals and Chambers of Commerce for their suggestions and assistance: Lisa Edwards/Greater Algonac, Judy White/Marine City (Ms. White also provided several photos for the Marine City Section of the guide), Patricia Bark/St. Clair, Laura Crawford/Marysville, Marci Fogal/Port Huron, Seth Stapleton/Bad Axe, Dana Miller/Port Austin, Anne Clark/Caseville and Libby Alexander/Bay Port. I am indebted to Lesley Woods and Michael Lawley at Tourism Sarnia-Lambton for providing helpful information and several photographs for this guide. The Port Sanilac Historical Society kindly allowed me to use their background material. Julie Taylor, my editor at Thunder Bay Press, provided maps and offered more helpful suggestions than I can count.

I am grateful to the many people I met along the way and who, in one way or another, helped me with this project: Pam Semp, Bobbie Ramsey, William McCain, John DeMuch, John Brockman, Francis Sampier, Bill Bonner, Sue Kuhlman, Janice Dubay, Bonnie Albrecht, Linda Cutler, Jeanie Linington and Jennifer Boyce to name a few. And, to the myriads of unnamed others who offered a bit of information or a kind word, you have my gratitude.

A special thanks is owed to Susan and Joe Jurkiewicz who not only offered much needed support during the project and provided tips for new places to consider, they also took several great pictures included in the guide. Susan's picture of Lake Huron is on the front cover.

Part One

A Guide to Traveling Michigan's Thumb

Map of the Thumb Route

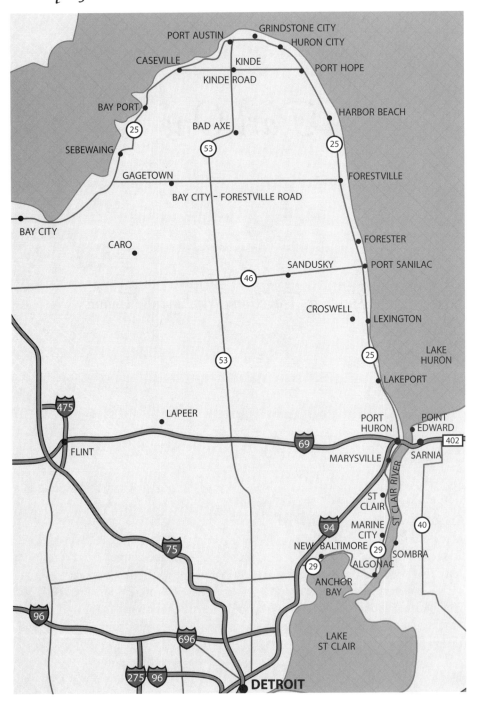

Introduction to Informational Listings

The route around the shoreline of the Thumb, with wide vistas of Lake Huron's sparkling blue water, provides spectacular views and a wealth of things to see and do. The journey starts in New Baltimore on Lake St. Clair and follows the St. Clair River on its path to Lake Huron. We will take a few trips onto the Canadian shore of the St. Clair River. The ease of crossing into Canada in a matter of minutes from Algonac, Marine City and Port Huron, as well as the interesting stops beckoning from the Canadian side, make it worthwhile for Thumb travelers to consider making these short side trips. We will also make a few stops to inland Thumb towns; but primarily Lake Huron's shore will be our map.

Note:

M-29 and M-25 will be the route you travel. These two lane roads will also have local names. For instance, you will start on Dixie Highway which will become Pointe Tremble in Algonac, River Road in St. Clair, Fort Gratiot in Marysville, Military, Huron and Pine Grove in Port Huron, Lakeshore in Lakeport, etc. Do not let the name changes confuse you. It is hard to get too lost in the Thumb and you can generally find your way back to M-29 or M-25 pretty easily.

There are two spots along the journey where you should consider following the side roads because they offer better views of the shoreline. Those deviations will be suggested at the appropriate point.

The St. Clair River

The St. Clair River is the part of the St. Lawrence Seaway connecting Lake St. Clair to Lake Huron. Both Lake St. Clair and the St. Clair River are dotted with many islands including: Harsens Island, Russell Island, Squirrel Island, Dickenson Island, Bassett Island, Seaway Island, and Walpole Island. There is also Gull Island, site of the Jobbie Nooners (See description under Algonac). The River has three channels: the North, South and Middle Channel, each winding its way into some of the loveliest lakeshore in the United States.

The South Channel is about 10 miles long and empties into Lake St. Clair. The North Channel, which flows past Algonac, is about 6 miles long and ends at Anchor Bay. The Middle Channel, approximately 3 miles from Algonac, runs a distance of 7 miles to Muscamoot Bay.

The St. Clair River is 39 miles long and has depths ranging from 40 to 50 feet and in certain areas even 90 feet deep. It also has shallow spots that could prove dangerous to an inexperienced freighter captain. Watching freighters is addictive along the St. Clair River, primarily because they get so up-close-and-personal. The River is narrow and at times it seems you can reach out and touch a passing ship. Nowhere else will you get such a spectacular view of these huge vessels. They come from all over the world, as they make their way from Lake Huron to her sister lakes, transporting their cargo. The shoreline is dotted with benches where locals and tourists wile away their time watching the action and listening to the freighters' horns.

In local marshes you will sight swans, herons and ducks. The area is home to 150 species of birds. The wildlife, as well as the opportunities for fishing, and recreational boating, make this area a natural for summer activity. Fishing is an angler's dream come true. Walleye is arguably the best game fish in Michigan, although many local restaurants proclaim Lake Perch their house specialty. Both are easily caught, even by an amateur. The lake and river are filled with salmon, bass and trout. The spring smelt run is always popular.

Experienced divers enjoy the challenge of the St. Clair River near Port Huron. It is an exciting dive spot where the speeds of the swift waters can exceed four knots. The river can be seductive with its lure of shipwrecks and other artifacts, but at times, it can also be treacherous. Divers should not tackle these waters without appropriate training, as the waters will test both diving expertise and physical stamina. Because this narrow channel is one of the busiest waterways in the world, divers must also be savvy and skilled at diving in an area of extremely heavy boat traffic.

Furthermore, the river has special rules: It is one of the only spots in Michigan where a diver is not required to tow a dive flag: Boats have the right of way. Instead, divers must put out two flags, one at the point of entry and one at the exit point of their dive. Because of the often congested boat traffic, divers treat this area as an overhead environment dive, surfacing near their point of entry.

On good days the underwater visibility can be up to 80 feet and the ecosystem is one of the most diverse found in the Great Lakes. Although winter diving would seem to be out of the question, there are always a few courageous souls who brave the frigid waters - just for the bragging rights attendant the thrill of diving into the St. Clair River during the bitter Michigan winter.

New Baltimore *(Also includes Anchor Bay and Fair Haven)*

Population: 11,000.

Directions:

From Detroit: I-94 East towards Port Huron (28 miles). Take Exit 243 (New Baltimore/M-29), turn right on 23 Mile Road (M-29), 3.7 miles to New Baltimore.

From Flint: I-475/I-75 South 40 miles, take exit 77A/Utica onto M-59 and continue 20 miles (M-59 becomes Hall Road and then William P. Russo Highway) to I-94 E 2.9 miles to exit 243 New Baltimore/M-59 to right on M-29, 3.7 miles to New Baltimore.

Background and History

Located on the north coastline of Lake St. Clair, New Baltimore was originally called Ashleyville. It got its first post office on September 20, 1851, was incorporated as a village in 1867 and as a city in 1931. As early as 1796 French settlers chose the waterfront for their farms and homes.

The city's location on the waterfront connected it to the region's navigable transportation system and allowed it to operate port facilities with piers extending a hundred feet or more into Lake St. Clair. Its economic base included lumber and building materials, creamery products, barrels, brooms, bricks and coffins.

When the automobile changed the state's transportation patterns the city began catering to resorters by offering hotels, salt baths, taverns, and even an opera house.

New Baltimore may not technically be "Thumb" but since you will likely have to pass through there to begin your journey, a few places are listed to make your trip more enjoyable.

Food/Restaurants

The Glass Onion, 35611 Green Street (586) 716-5320. The cook works 24/7 to create the homemade Polish specialties you can enjoy at this new restaurant. They serve huge pirogies. Open Mon to Sat 11:00 am to 10:00 pm. Stops serving at 9:00 pm on Sun. Breakfast 9:00 am to noon Sat and Sun.

The New Green Street Tavern, 37700 Green Street, (586) 725-6700. This Irish Pub has changed ownership but remains a local favorite. They make outstanding burgers, and like many of the restaurants in this area they do Lake Perch like it really should be done! Open Mon to Fri 11:00 am to midnight, Sat and Sun noon to midnight.

Jiggers Bar and Grill, 8367 Dixie Highway, Fair Haven, (586) 725-4644. Burgers, nachos, sandwiches, and entrees including fresh, never frozen, chicken. The décor is pretty plain but the brews are cold. In the summer they have barbecues and Luaus and other special events. Also has a Sunday Brunch. Open for breakfast at 7:00 am every day. Usually does not close before 2:00 am.

The Raft, midway between New Baltimore and Algonac on M-29 in Fair Haven, (586) 725-9100. The mushroom/Swiss burger is delicious paired with a cold beer. The homemade chicken soup was also excellent. Open Mon to Thurs 9:00 am to midnight, Fri and Sat 9:00 am to 1:00 am and Sun noon to midnight.

Stahl's Bakery, 51005 Washington Street, (586) 716-8500. The building is as interesting as the baked goods are delicious. Built in 1868 of local bricks it has been a department store among other things. Stahl's originated in Detroit and moved to New Baltimore in 1978. They have 75 years of hand baking experience. Their brick, oven-baked breads are worth the trip. You cannot leave without having one of their famous belly-button cookies. Open Mon to Sat 7:00 am to 7:00 pm and Sun 10:00 am to 3:00 pm.

The Tin Fish, 10069 Dixie Highway (2½ miles northeast of New Baltimore), (586) 725-7888. Great restaurant with a full menu and bar service. On a nice day the patio is the place to be. Boat accessible. Summer entertainment Monday to Wednesday; inside and on patio. Open seven days in summer, 11:00 am to 1:00 am, reduced hours in the winter or off-season.

The Town Pump, 51110 Bedford Street, (586) 725-5505. A local favorite where the Pumpburger rules. Full menu with dinners including: perch and fried chicken, or quesadillas, wet burritos or pizza. Hours: Mon to Thurs 11:00 am to midnight, Fri and Sat 11:00 am to 2:00 am, Sun noon to 10:00 pm.

Museums

The Grand Pacific House Museum, 51065 Washington Street, (586) 725-4755. Frederick Losh used locally made bricks to construct this building in 1881 and it was first operated as an Italianate hotel. Losh did well catering to the tourists drawn to the small city. His hotel was later converted to a boarding house that remained open until 1986 when it was sold to the New Baltimore Historical Society and opened as a museum. Wed to Sun 11:00 am to 5:00 pm.

Antiques and Other Shopping

Geri's Gift Boutique, 51261 Washington Street, (586) 725-0881, *gmuthler@ comcast.net*. Something new every day and almost all of it handmade. Geri carries gourmet food items, towels, baby clothes, shawls, candles, purses and much more. Open Mon to Sat 10:00 am to 6:00 pm and closed Sun.

Plum Hollow, 50935 Washington Street, (586) 725-5900. You can find a variety of interesting home accent pieces including candlesticks, picture frames, lamps and plates. Summer hours June to August, Tues to Sat 10:00 am to 5:00

pm, Sun noon to 4:00 pm, closed Mon. Call for winter hours.

Washington Street Station Antiques and Collectibles, 51059 Washington Street, (586) 716-8810. Find vintage, modern, deco '40s, '50s, '60s and '70s furniture and all kinds of antique items. Next door to the museum. Open Wed to Sun 11:00 am to 5:00 pm, closed Mon and Tues.

Parks and Beaches

Walter and Mary Burke Park. End of Washington Street on the water, (810) 725-0291. Swimming beach, fishing, changing area, restrooms, boat launch, picnic area, grills, indoor & outdoor pavilions, swings, and a playscape that will delight the little ones.

Marina

Schmidt Marina, 50725 Taylor Street, (586) 725-9192. Full service marina, generally with about 10 transient slips available.

Festival

• The Bay-Rama Fish Fly Festival, June.

Contact

The Anchor Bay Chamber of Commerce, (586) 725-5148, *www. anchorbaychamber.com.*

Algonac

Population: 4613.

Directions:
From New Baltimore follow M-29 east thirteen miles to Algonac.

Background and History
Algonac refers to itself as the Venice of Michigan because of its vast waterway system of rivers and channels. As early as the mid-1600s, the French Sulpicion priests, Dollier de Casson and Gallinee, explored this area around Lake St. Clair and the St. Clair River. Adrien Joliet paddled along the St. Clair River's shores about 1669. His trip met with disaster when his canoe overturned and he lost all of the maps and information he had been collecting. In 1697 another French Priest, Father Hennepin, traveled to this area and named the river St. Clair because he landed on the feast day celebrating Santa Clara.

After these early explorers paved the way, fur traders began making repeated voyages in search of pelts. Beaver pelts were especially popular with affluent French society. Michigan became a territory in 1805, but the earliest permanent residents in the Algonac area settled around 1815. In 1821 there were only four taxpayers in the area which later became Algonac. These taxpayers lived a solitary life in their log cabins, and it is not likely they raised a great deal of revenue for the young government. By 1836 there were farmers in the Algonac area, which was then known as Manchester or Pointe Du Chene, the latter meaning Point of the Oaks. In the spring of 1836 the settlers organized the "Algonac and Pointe Du Chene Company" and plotted out the village of Algonac. Their plotting became official in 1843.

Henry Rowe Schoolcraft, an agent in charge of Native American affairs, named the city in honor of the Algonquin tribe living in the area. Translated from the French, the word Algonac means place of the Algonquin.

For over half a century Algonac was home to a world-wide boating empire built by Christopher Columbus Smith and his four sons. It was appropriately, if not imaginatively, named the Chris Smith and Sons Boat Company. The Chris Craft plant employed many local residents and became a leader in building power boats. Algonac was, and remains, famous for its many speed-boating events and fishing contests. Its location on the St. Clair River has helped define the city. For related stories see the Ghost of Morrow Road and The Old South Channel Range Lights, both in Part Two of this guide.

Jobbie Nooner: No discussion of Algonac would be complete without mention of the *Jobbie Nooner*. Sue Kulman, an Algonac librarian, describes it as a huge biannual party currently held on Gull Island. It creates monstrous problems for local law enforcement officials, as well as for the United States Army Corps of Engineers, responsible for Gull Island.

It all began in 1975 when Lee O'Dell, a jobber in the auto industry, decided he wanted to take his co-worker and friend, Lee Wagner, out for a birthday celebration. They decided to ditch work for the afternoon or pull a *nooner*. They, and some of their friends, got together on their boats and started to party. That was about thirty-years ago and the party continues. It has grown from seventeen men to nearly five thousand people taking their boats to Gull Island for "*The Mardi Gras of the Midwest*" with all of the revelry, music and partying that is synonymous with the New Orleans' version. The original *Jobbie Nooner* was in Anchor Bay. Only later was Gull Island, an uninhabited island at the entrance to the South Channel, determined to be a better site for this popular party. In recent years the waters around Gull Island have been crowded with an estimated one-thousand boats for the occasion; so if you are going, you might want to be there early, although by definition, the party starts at noon. There are two *Jobbie Nooners* each year. The first is usually held the last Friday before the auto industry's July Shutdown. The second is usually held on a Saturday in late August or early September. If you go, take lots of sunscreen, no glass bottles and pick up after yourself. Leave the children home; this rowdy event is not suitable for them.

Food/Restaurants

Cheers Tavern on the Marsh, 6211 Pointe Tremble Road, (810) 794-4500. Features seafood, steak and chops with an impressive wine selection. Kitchen open daily from 11:00 am to 10:00 pm, and the bar remains open until 2:00 am.

Club Capri, 6343 Pointe Tremble, (810) 794-7431. Upscale Italian dining on the waterfront. All pasta is homemade and the Fettuccine Alfredo and the Lasagna would both be excellent choices. Accessible via Sassy Marina. All-you-can-eat cod on Fridays. Kitchen open Sun to Thurs noon to 9:00 pm, Fri and Sat noon to 11:00 pm. Bar open later. Entertainment Wed, Fri and Sat.

Coney Island, 1065 St. Clair River Drive, across from Ferry Dock in Algonac, (810) 512-5184. Nothing pretentious but a good place to grab a bite any time of the day. A favorite with locals. Open Mon to Sat 7:00 am to 9:00 pm and Sun 7:00 am to 8:00 pm.

The Galley, 2430 Pointe Tremble Road, (810) 794-4844. Family dining with steaks, lake seafood, Italian and Mexican specialties. Friday all-you-can-eat cod. Open Mon to Thurs noon to 10:00 pm, Fri to Sun 11:00 am to 10:00 pm. The hours may change slightly each year.

Harbour Club Bar and Grill, 1999 Pointe Tremble Road, located in the center of the Algonac Harbour Club Marina on M-29, (810) 794-0880, *www. algonacharbourclub.com,* for the current menu and additional information. Seasonal hours.

Hook, Line and Sinker Bar and Grill, 8094 Dixie Highway, Ira, (586) 725-6099. Place to get a good steak dinner at a reasonable price. In the winter you will enjoy the large natural fireplace. Open Mon to Sat 10:00 am to 2:00 am and Sun noon to 2:00 am (closes earlier depending upon business).

McRae's Big River Grille, 9715 St. Clair River Drive, (810) 794-3041. Enjoy beautiful views of the St. Clair River while dining on "South Florida" style grilled foods. Casual atmosphere. All you can eat pickerel (walleye). Open seven days for lunch and dinner, Mon to Thurs 11:30 am to 10:00 pm, Fri and Sat 11:30 am to 11:00 pm, and Sun noon to 9:00 pm.

Sand Bar Restaurant, 7479 Dyke Road (M-29) as you drive into Algonac from New Baltimore, (586) 725-2100. Enjoy the view of sunset over Lake St. Clair. Anything from a snack to a full dinner and local bands to entertain you. Accessible by boat. Open year around.

Stroh's Ice Cream Parlour, 430 Pointe Tremble Road, (810) 794-2930. Drive-thru restaurant for ice cream treats. Order malts, shakes, floats, deluxe banana splits, sundaes, strawberry shortcake, hot fudge ice cream puffs, and more. You can also get quarts and gallons to go. Stroh's has been there for 18 years. Seasonal, closes in October. During the season open noon to 10:00 pm, seven days.

Lodging (see also parks, campgrounds and marinas)

Linda's Lighthouse Inn B&B, 5965 Pointe Tremble Road (M-29), (810) 794-2992. Offers four rooms, each with private bath. Air conditioned. Extras: complimentary bicycles, 300 feet of private deck with hot tub. Boat dockage available at no additional cost (the B&B is accessible by boat, as well as by car). Hearty breakfast. The B&B overlooks Dickinson Island.

River's Edge Motel, 703 St. Clair River Drive, (810) 794-5467. Great location and superb views, close to shops and restaurants. Friendly staff to help you any way they can.

Museums

Algonac/Clay Township Historical Society Community Museum, 1240 St. Clair River Drive, (810) 794-9015, *www.algonac-clay-history.com*. The museum is housed in the Bostwick Building, which was built in 1849 in the Greek Revival style. It houses exhibits about local history, local schools, boat building (including Chris-Craft), boat racing, hunting, fishing, and military. Open Sat and Sun 1:00 pm to 4:00 pm and Wed 7:00 pm to 9:00 pm during June, July and August. It will also open for special requests.

Log Cabin Museum, 4710 Pointe Tremble Road. (For additional information call the Algonac/Clay Township Historical Society Community Museum at (810) 794-9015). Authentic log cabin from the 1800s featuring crafts and exhibits. After 1882 the cabin was owned by the Bedford family. It is believed to have been a school prior to that. At some point its exterior was covered with siding to make it look more modern. The exterior gave no clue to what lay beneath. During demolition, the log cabin was discovered. It is built of hand-hewn logs, some more than a foot in diameter. The logs are notched on the ends so they fit together without nails.

Shopping
The Shop The Shop, 4930 Pointe Tremble, (810) 794-4227. The Shop The Shop has been open for 26 years and has a large selection of women's evening wear, sportswear (casuals), swimwear (available year around) and accessories. It also carries a small selection of men's clothing, as well as brass gift items and floral arrangements. You can browse a garden section and consider their select antiques. Open year round, Mon to Sat 9:30 am to 5:30 pm, Sun 11:00 am to 4:00 pm.

Parks, Beaches and Campgrounds
Algonac State Park. This park is actually located in Marine City. 8732 River Road, Marine City, (810) 765-5605. (See Park Listing under Marine City for details.) This great park is also a place to pick up the Bay to Bridge Trail. (See description under St. Clair.)

Marinas, Water Sports, Boat and Jet Ski rentals
Anchor Bay Scuba Training Center, 8655 Dixie Highway (M-29) between New Baltimore and Algonac, (586) 725-1991, *www.anchorbayscuba.com*. Air-fills, equipment rental, nitrox and training. River guided dives available. Accessible by water and has both summer and winter hours.

Algonac Harbour Club, 1999 Pointe Tremble Road (M-29), (810) 794-4448, (Also has Harbour Club Bar and Grille and the outside Tiki Bar), *www.algonacharbourclub.com*. Summer wells available, two heated swimming pools (one with hot tub), bath houses, laundry rooms and recreational activities.

Riverview Campground and Marina, 4175 Pointe Tremble Road (M-29), (810) 794-0182. Hosts Janet and Bill Welser. Located on the St. Clair River's North Channel and offering great fishing, boating, bike trail and full hookup. Clean showers and bathroom.

Other Things to See and Do
Colony Tower, Pointe Tremble (M-29). This steel framed water tower is a local landmark built in 1925 by the Chicago Bridge and Iron Works. It held the main water supply for the "Colony on the St. Clair," a secluded residential community, established outside Algonac during the early 1920s. The tower, which resembles a lighthouse, is 136 feet tall, and once held a 60,000 gallon water tank. A light on top helped guide aircraft and boat navigation in the area from 1925 through 1937, at which time lighting the tower became cost prohibitive.

St. John's Wet Prairie, Clay Township, (just outside Algonac). Six tenths of a mile east of the Colony Tower on the north side of the road. Gravel parking lot. Peaceful 87 acres of lakeplain prairie. This globally imperiled ecosystem is perfect for canoeing, fishing (no motorboats), nature study, photography, hunting and bird watching. Lakeplain prairies are relatively flat, occurring on sand ridges overlaying clay. High water tables fluctuate seasonally, and over periods of years, with the rise and fall of the Great Lakes. Fires were also important for maintaining lakeplain prairies. It is estimated there are as many as 160 different kinds of plants, including blazing star and tall sun flower as well as grasses such as big blue stem and Indian grass found in this marshy area. You can watch great blue herons glide to the ground or search for rarer species of birds.

Harsens Island

The Champion Ferry, (810) 748-3757, will take you for the short ride to Harsens Island located at the top of Lake St. Clair at the mouth of the St. Clair River.

Perhaps the greatest attractions of the island, which is rather secluded and isolated, are its freshwater deltas, wildlife, and the opportunity for freighter watching. Sportsmen are attracted to the hunting and fishing offered on the island. There is a Hunt Club on the island and a private airport. In its early days visitors boarded the Tashmoo, a steamship which carried passengers from Detroit to any one of the luxury hotels on the island. Today, none of these hotels remain standing, most the victim of various fires over the years. *Lynn's B&B,* located at 2732 South Channel Drive about ¼ mile from the Corner Store, offers rooms, (810) 748-8834. It is the only place to stay on the island.

The island has approximately 2,000 full-time residents and many other summer-only residents. The island is a cross between rural America and a luxury resort community. Until 1960, it was called Sans Souci, a name given to it by its first postmaster. The loose translation from French is "carefree" or "serenity with your surroundings."

While on the island you will want to drive to San Souci Landing and perhaps have lunch at the *Island Grill* and browse the *Crown Studio and Gallery*. The grill is open Mon to Wed 8:00 am to 3:00 pm, Thurs to Sat 8:00 am to 9:00 pm, and Sun 8:00 am to 4:00 pm.

The Crown Studio and Gallery features nautical and maritime works and owner, George Crown, might even share a bit of the island's interesting history with you, such as the story he shared with me about an innocuous ghost who is said to routinely unmake beds in one of the homes on the island. Everyone can use a ghost to blame for less than perfect housekeeping. See related story about another Harsens Island Ghost in Part Two

Across the street from the gallery is the *Riverfront Shoppe*, 3061 South

Channel Drive (810) 748-3623, which offers a selection of nautical gifts, home accessories, and "penny candies"- which make great treats for grandchildren. The shoppe is open Mon to Thurs 10:00 am to 5:00 pm, Fri and Sat 10:00 am to 7:00 pm and Sun 10:00 am to 5:00 pm. Next to the *Riverfront Shoppe* you can sit on a park bench and enjoy the freighter traffic. It is the only public place on the island to freighter watch.

Walpole Island, Canada

(519) 627-1475, *www.bkejwanong.com*. Take the Walpole-Algonac Ferry, (519) 677-5781, for an eight minute ride to this First Nation Village called Bkejwanong, meaning "where the waters divide." *You should take your passport.* The village is located between the United States and the Canadian mainland on the North Shore of Lake St. Clair. It has been occupied by aboriginal peoples for over 6,000 years and continues to be home to the Ojibwa, Pottawatomie and Odawa. With a common heritage, these three tribes formed the Council of Three Fires which survives to the current time as a political and cultural council. This island possesses one of the richest and most diverse wetland areas remaining in the Great Lakes Basin. There are oak savannas, tallgrass prairies and Carolinian forests. The wildlife is plentiful and guides are available for a waterfowl hunt. You can enjoy bird-watching (on your own or with a guide), or take guided nature tours. Walpole Island attracts hunters and fishers from many parts of North America. The Web site, above, provides a listing of places where you can get your hunting and fishing licenses. The Walpole Island Heritage Center or Nin.da.waab.jib (meaning "those who seek to find") was founded in July 1989 as the research arm of the Walpole Island First Nation. The Bkejwanong Territory was not included in any of the eighteenth or nineteenth century land surrenders or treaties, and Walpole Island First Nation continues to assert and exercise Aboriginal title to its territory, unceded lands and waters. The island's lure is its nature areas and you would be well-advised to call before going and to consider hiring a guide.

Wallaceburg, Canada

If you take the ferry from Algonac to Walpole Island, continue through the island and cross the bridge you will find yourself in Ontario, Canada, on Highway 40 (also Dufferin Avenue).

Baldoon Golf Course is located at 7018 Dufferin Avenue (just minutes from the bridge off Walpole Island), (519) 627-2366, *www.baldoongolf.com*. This 18-hole golf course offers casual dining with a course view.

The town of Wallaceburg is less than three miles beyond the golf course. It is strategically located along the banks of the scenic Sydenham River which flows directly into the St. Clair River. In Wallaceburg you can visit the *Wallaceburg and District Museum* (519) 627-8962. Wallaceburg was originally a Scottish settlement named Baldoon. Among its important artifacts, the museum has pieces of a barn dating to the 1790s. It is displayed in the Museum's Log Cabin. There is also a 1913 Model-T Roadster and an original Lee-Enfield rifle prototype from 1878. You will view an impressive collection of industrial artifacts including hand blown glass pieces produced in Wallaceburg, which was once dubbed Canada's *Glasstown*. The museum is open Mon to Sat 10:00 am to 4:00 pm.

Snyeview Farm Market is located on RR #4, (519) 677-5656, just after you cross the bridge from Walpole Island. This market not only offers traditional fruits and vegetables, but also bagged pinto beans, green split peas, cranberry beans, baby lima beans, white pea beans, lentils, and kidney beans, as well as maple syrup, suckers, candy and butter.

Algonac Festivals
- Jobbie Nooner
- Algonac Clay Offshore Races, June.
- Algonac Pickerel Festival, July.
- Greater Algonac Chamber Classic Car Show, September.
- Yard Sale Trail, August. Starts in New Baltimore and goes to Sebewaing.
- Annual Art Fair, Labor Day Weekend.

Cruises and Ferries
The Walpole Algonac Ferry Line, (519) 677-5781, *www.walpolealgonacferry. com*. A two ferry operation (12-car and 9-car) runs daily according to traffic with a boat arriving or leaving about every fifteen to twenty minutes. Operates seven days a week 6:40 am to 10:00 pm.

Champion Ferry, (810) 748-3757. Operates between Algonac and Harsens Island. 24-hour service.

Contacts
Algonac Historical Society, (810) 794-9015.

The Algonac Chamber of Commerce, (810) 794-5511, *www.algonacchamber. com*.

Blue Water Area Convention and Visitors Bureau, (800) 852-4242, for dates of Festivals, *www.bluewater.org*.

Marine City

Population: 4652.

Directions:
Located on M-29 approximately 3 miles north of the city of Algonac. From I-94 take Exit 294 and travel northeast 19 miles.

Background and History
Marine City occupies a central location along the St. Clair River District. It is one of three international crossings to Canada in the St. Clair River. A quick ferry trip allows a visitor to step off in Sombra, Ontario.

Marine City is a former lumbering town with lovely Victorian homes (drive Main Street and you will see several worthy of note), churches, registered historical sites (like Holy Cross Church), and the "Nautical Mile" (one of the best places on the St. Clair River to watch freighters and other marine traffic).

In the 1800s Marine City was a prominent shipbuilding community. In 1818 Sam Ward traveled from the East Coast, teamed up with Reverend Gabriel Richard of Detroit and bought land north of Bridge Street. They wasted no time in establishing a shipyard at the foot of what is now Broadway Street. For half a century Marine City's primary industry was shipbuilding and at one time there were five shipyards along the Belle River. Together the men built some of the finest ships to sail the Great Lakes. It has been estimated that 250 boats were built in the city during its shipbuilding heyday.

Today parks dot the shoreline and their numerous benches make great spots to choose an inviting book and fritter away the afternoon. The Belle River calmly winds through the city and presents the perfect opportunity for canoeing.

Freighter passing Nautical Mile in Marine City
Photo Courtesy of Judy White, Marine City Chamber of Commerce

Lovely Victorian on Main Street

Marine City Lighthouse
Photo Courtesy of Judy White
Marine City Chamber of Commerce

This area of the Thumb was settled first by the French who were followed by German farmers. Today more than 30 percent of the population can trace its heritage to the hardworking German immigrants.

Marine City celebrates the end of its cold winter with the annual Spring Salmon Festival. Summer brings many additional festivals and draws antiques enthusiasts from significant distances. Buses pull up regularly to the Marine City Antiques Warehouse which has been a stopping off place for visitors for many years. If you are traveling this route in the fall you will have the opportunity to enjoy the magnificent change of colors. Marine City describes itself as a quaint town in a bustling world. Its downtown boasts turn-of-the-century street lamps, fine and casual dining with great river views, shops to explore and the Peche Island Rear Range Lighthouse with its bold letters proclaiming its location: *MARINE CITY*. (See related story in Part Two of this guide.)

Food/Restaurants

AJ's on the River, 7493 River Road between Algonac and Marine City, (810) 765-2800. A nice place to stop for a drink and to watch the river. This bar has casual dining and features oven-baked sandwiches and pizza, but also offers seafood, steaks, chops, and ribs. A pool table stands ready to test your skill, but you may find the view distracting. Kitchen open seven days 11:00 am to 11:00 pm, bar remains open until 2:00 am.

Anita's Place, 341 South Water Street, (810) 765-7177. Mexican and

American food. Nachos are a favorite here. Great view of the river. Open Mon to Sat 10:00 am to 10:00 pm (Fri the kitchen stays open later), Sun noon to 10:00 pm with the bar open later. Anita now has an ice cream shop next door, so stop and get an ice cream cone to eat as you walk along the water.

The Little Bar, 321 Chartier, (810) 765-8084. This was a haunt of Henry Ford Sr. Burgers, fish, barbecue and steaks. Open seven days from 3:00 pm.

Louie's Corner Restaurant, 137 North Parker Street, (810) 765-8133. Family style restaurant featuring steak and seafood. Mon to Sat 7:00 am to 8:00 pm and Sun 7:00 am to 2:00 pm.

Morelli's Café, 147 South Water Street, (810) 765-5202. A great location to enjoy good food and good company for either breakfast or lunch. Food is tasty and the service is fast. Morelli's has been owned and operated by the same family for years and started as a bait and boat livery where new customers asked for coffee which led to making breakfasts and eventually the restaurant turned out to be a better business for the family than the more seasonal bait and boat business. Open seven days, 6:00 am to 2:00 pm.

Oak Room Grill, 7200 South River Road, (810) 765-3210. This restaurant offers creative American cuisine and features fresh seafood, steaks, pasta and chops. Prime Rib is a special and the homemade soups are excellent. Also offers daily specials and catering services. Occasional entertainment. Open Mon to Wed 11:00 am to 10:00 pm, Thurs to Sat 11:00 am to 1:00 am, and Sun noon to 10:00 pm.

Riviera Restaurant, 475 South Water Street, (810) 765-9030. Next to the ferry dock at the start of the walking trail (the Nautical Mile). Offers a wide variety of food choices including fresh pickerel (walleye). They are known for their fish-and-chips dinner which they claim is St. Clair County's most popular dish. Open Sun to Thurs 7:00 am to 9:00 pm, Fri and Sat 7:00 am to 10:00 pm.

Yumme Designs Restaurant, 602 Market Street, (810) 765-9862. Offers breakfast, lunch, and early dinners. Sandwiches, salads, chicken, fish, and pasta. Open Tues to Fri 8:00 am to 6:00 pm, Sat 11:00 am to 6:00 pm and Sun and Mon 8:00 am to 2:00 pm.

Lodging (see also parks and campgrounds)

The Heather House B&B, 409 Main Street, overlooking Ontario, Canada, across the St. Clair River, (810) 765-3175, *www.theheatherhouse.com*. A lovely Queen Anne structure built in 1885 for William Sauber who was the chief engineer for a fleet of Great Lakes steamers. The B&B has five bedrooms, each with private bath and porch. Two suites have hot tubs and the Huron Room has a small sitting-room overlooking the river. A spacious parlor also overlooks the river, and guests can enjoy a reading room in the home's turret. A large breakfast is served in the formal dining room. A public beach and shopping are close by.

Museums and Galleries

Picture This Art Gallery and Gifts, 220 South Water Street, (810) 765-1310. Local artists, artist of the month, and limited editions. Open Tues to Fri 9:30 am to 5:00 pm, Sat 9:30 am to 3:00 pm.

Pride and Heritage Museum, 405 South Main Street, (810) 765-5446. Exhibits include artifacts from Marine City's nautical history and a fully-equipped blacksmith shop. The museum attempts to bring Marine City to life with three distinct displays: the Maritime, the Lifestyle and Business, and the Commercial Gallery. The highlight of the exhibits is a 4½ by 36 foot diorama showing life on the Belle River in 1885, when five shipyards engaged in producing the finest ships on the Great Lakes. The museum has designed complete, furnished rooms dating back 150 years. Open Sat and Sun 1:00 pm to 4:00 pm.

Antiques and other Shopping

Back Alley Antiques, 413 Broadway, (810) 580-9910. Eclectic assortment of antiques, art and vintage items. Call for hours.

The Book Blues Bookstore, 102 Broadway, (810) 765-8111, *www. thebookblues.com*. Gently used and new books. Great little bookshop that features author signings, wine tasting and other events. Open 10:00 am to 8:00 pm daily, except Wed open noon to 6:00 pm and closed Sun.

Broadway Antiques and Treasures, 311 Broadway, (810) 765-5550. Open Fri to Sun 11:30 am to 4:30 pm.

Great Lakes Arts & Antiques, 425 Broadway, (810) 765-5593. You can browse housewares, cameras, coins & primitive items. As the name suggests this store also showcases Great Lakes art photos. Additionally they provide photography services, consignment and eBay sales. Open Thurs to Mon 11:00 am to 6:00 pm or by chance or appointment.

Lighthouse Books N Brew, 324 South Water Street, (586) 549-5137, *www. lighthousebooksandbrew.com*. Specialty coffees and granitas (slushies) and a few snacks. Also carries used books. Open Mon to Fri 11:00 am to 8:00 pm and Sat and Sun 11:00 am to 5:00 pm.

Marine City Antique Warehouse, 105 Fairbanks (M-29), (810) 765-1119. This is the *granddaddy* of all antique places in Michigan's Thumb. If you are looking for antiques, you have to stop here. They offer three floors with over 15,000-square-feet of just about anything you can imagine and a whole lot of stuff you never even thought about. This is the antiques store that brings in tour buses. The inventory includes furniture, china, glass, clocks, tins, jewelry, primitive, sports, paper, prints, paintings, pottery, American art, toys, nautical, stained glass, clothing accessories, silverware, musical instruments, linens, lace, mirrors, rugs, tools, books, dolls and more.

This place will draw you to the area for antiques and if you happen to find some of the smaller shops open at the time of your trip, so much the better. Open

Mon to Sat 10:00 am to 5:00 pm, Sun noon to 5:00 pm.

At the west end of the Marine City Antique Warehouse is a "Used Furniture Warehouse."

My Sister's Closet, 204 South Water Street, (810) 765-6923. A resale shop carrying wedding gowns, after-five (evening wear), glittering evening clutches and other clothing. Open Mon to Fri 11:00 am to 6:00 pm, Sat 10:00 am to 5:00 pm, reduced winter hours.

Nepenthe, 338 South Water Street, (810) 765-6843. Open by chance or appointment.

Old Times 'n' Such, 213 Broadway Street, (810) 765-9577. Call for hours.

Ship to Shore Antiques and More, 242 South Water Street, (810) 580-1215. Merchandise to satisfy a wide variety of tastes with emphasis on model ships and nautical art. Generally open during the summer season from 11:00 am to 6:00 pm, seven days, but wise to call first. Reduced hours non-season.

Snuggery Antiques, 8540 River Road, (810) 765-4737. An ever-changing inventory that features furniture, dishes, toys, trains, and collectibles. They displayed a wonderful Tiffany floor lamp with a price definitely reflective of its beauty.

Trendy Tots, 416 South Water Street, (810) 765-1450. Cute resale clothes for infants through size 16. Also maternity clothes. Open Mon to Sat 11:00 am to 5:00 pm.

Vera Grace Emporium, 214 Broadway, (810) 650-5576. Vintage items and works of art by local artisans. Open seven days 11:00 am to 5:00 pm.

Water Street Antiques Mall, 412 South Water Street, (810) 765-4822. Nautical, shabby chic, and a lot of "guy stuff." Open Mon to Sat 10:00 am to 5:00 pm and Sun 2:00 pm to 5:00 pm.

Enjoying the sunshine and water at Marine City Beach
Photo Courtesy of Judy White
Marine City Chamber of Commerce

Parks Beaches and Campgrounds

Algonac State Park, 8732 River Road, Marine City, (810) 765-5605. A place to indulge in long walks and enjoy the lakeplain prairies and oak savannas that are considered globally significant. These special habitats include nineteen species on the state endangered, threatened, and special concern lists. Prairies and oak savannas require periodic burning to remain healthy.

The park is home to some of the rarest natural communities in Michigan. The Blazing Star Prairie across from the archery range is the best place to view prairie plants, birds, and butterflies. The park contains approximately 1,500 acres and has a half mile of St. Clair River frontage. It is open all year, offering a variety of activities including: hiking, trap shooting, small and big game hunting (during the fall and winter seasons), and cross-country skiing. From the park you can also spend an enjoyable day watching the freighters move along the St. Clair River.

Facilities: The park has 296 modern campsites located in two campgrounds. It has three modern toilet/shower buildings, electric service and a sanitation station. The day use area has a picnic facility with shelter and restroom facilities.

The Algonac State Park is a place to pick up the Bay to Bridge Trail. (See description under St. Clair listing.)

Marine City Beach, end of South Water Street. The place where crowds gather on a hot day.

Other Things to See or Do

Drake Park Amphitheater, Water Street at St. Clair Street. This will be the site of concerts, plays, readings and maybe even movies. The Historical Society can be thanked for this wonderful amphitheater.

Holy Cross Catholic Church

Sea Captain alongside his freighter at the Maritime Days Parade
Photo Courtesy of Judy White, Marine City Chamber of Commerce

Nautical Mile. Take a stroll along the Nautical Mile walkway on Huron Street. You can access the walkway at the ferry landing.

Holy Cross Church, 610 Water Street. This grand old church has a historic-site designation. It is located on a piece of land long known as Catholic Point. This land was given to the church by President John Quincy Adams. The current structure was built in 1903.

Take a 10 minute Ferry ride to Sombra, a quaint little town in Ontario.

Festivals

- Maritime Days Parade, May.
- Antique and Yard Sale Trail, August.
- Vintage Tour of Homes, September/October.
- Santa Parade, December.

Cruises and Ferries

Bluewater Ferry, for transportation between Marine City and Sombra, Ontario, Canada, (519) 892-3879. Runs seven days a week beginning, at 6:40 am in Sombra. $6 for a car, $5 additional for a trailer and $1 for a bicycle.

Contacts

Historical Society of Marine City, (810) 765-3567.

The Marine City Chamber of Commerce, PO Box 38, Marine City, MI 48039, (810) 765-4501, *www.marinecitychamber.org*.

Blue Water Area Convention and Visitors Bureau, (800) 852-4242. Also check *www.visitmarinecity.org*.

Sombra, Ontario, Canada

Population: Very small. One source indicates 250 residents.

Directions:

The Bluewater Ferry from Marine City takes you to Sombra in minutes, (519) 892-3879. Runs daily, weather permitting, beginning at 6:40 am. **Take your passport.**

Currency:

Traveling to Canada is made easier because we share the language and for the most part the currency designations are the same, although the value changes with the exchange rate. You will find the same coins (penny, nickel, dime and quarter) with just slightly different looks. Likewise the bills look very similar and are easy to handle. You may, however, initially be confused by the loonie and the toonie. As one traveler told me, she ordered a cup of coffee, paid with a ten dollar bill and got a five dollar bill and coins as change. She knew the coffee had been less than two dollars and was certain she had been short-changed. She did not realize a loonie is worth a dollar and a toonie is worth two dollars.

Background and History

The Spanish word for shade or shady place is *sombre*; and that was the inspiration for naming this tiny hamlet. Early surveyors found themselves in such dense forest that the sun could not shine through. The original people in the area were Shawnee. Sombra was first recognized as a municipal entity in 1826, and for many years, due to a lack of adequate drainage, was called Mudtown. Do not let that prior dismal appellation dissuade you from visiting this charming little village, with its bird's eye view of the St. Clair River. You will likely consider it one of the gems of your trip.

Food/Restaurants

The Aft Cabin, 167 King Street, (519) 892-3651. Offers a screened garden patio and casual, upscale dining. Reservations are recommended. Enjoy the quiche of the day or maybe a wild salmon burger. If you are enjoying dinner at the Aft Cabin, consider the pickerel (walleye) or fresh lake perch. Save room to top off your meal with Caribbean Rum Cake made on the premises using amaretto and caramel. Lunch: Mon to Sat 11:00 am to 2:00 pm. Dinner: Fri and Sat 5:00 pm to 10:00 pm.

The Fry Truck, Main intersection of Sombra by Ansell's. Place to buy French fries to eat as you meander through town. Summer only.

Riverview Restaurant, 3465 St. Clair Parkway, (519) 892-3311. Specializing in home-cooked meals and pastries. The interior is decorated early truck-stop style, but the food is substantial and it is a place locals enjoy. The crossing guard from Walpole Island was eating there although there were certainly closer places he could have chosen. He recommended the butter tarts. They were better than anywhere else. There must be a secret to the flaky, buttery crust. If you are feeling hungry enough for a hearty meal, try the pork chops. Open seven days, year round, Mon to Fri 7:00 am to 7:00 pm, Sat 8:00 am to 1:00 pm, Sun 9:00 am to 7:00 pm. Closed long weekends.

Village Bakery and Pizza Café, St. Clair Parkway (Next to Three Sisters Gift and Art Gallery), (519) 892-3935. Serves breakfast all day. The fresh baked cinnamon buns are a must, but they also have muffins, croissants and cookies. Choose a daily luncheon special or an Open Face Sandwich, wrap, chili or just soup. The pizza is excellent, or you can always opt for an Angus Beef Steakburger. If you are looking for a healthy alternative to a burger and French fries, consider a salad or the trans-fat-free oven fries with a sub. Open seven days 8:00 am to 7:00 pm.

Whittington's Tea Room and Boutiques, 156 King Street, (519) 892-3991. In addition to an interesting menu, this charming tea room offers many gourmet items for purchase. Try the grilled pear, sugared walnut, Roquefort and mango salad, and if your appetite permits, the garlic and herb crusted turkey breast served on rosemary focaccia bread with creamy Havarti, sprouts, and cranberry garlic rum preserve. Open Tues to Sun 11:30 am to 4:00 pm.

Whittington's Tea Room and Boutiques

Lodging (also see Campgrounds below)

Bogey's Inn and Suites, 2845 St. Clair Parkway, (519) 867-3999. Double French doors lead into the rooms. Open all year. On the waterfront with seasonal mooring up to 50 feet.

Sheboane Bed and Breakfast, 2955 St. Clair Gardens (beside Cathcart Park), (519) 892-3389, *www.sheboane.ca*. Full breakfast available. Rooms ensuite with whirlpool tubs and three piece bathroom. Private balconies afford a view of the St. Clair River. Open year round. Check their Web site for room pictures.

Sombra Bed and Breakfast, 160 Smith Street, Sombra (519) 892-3311. Historical Victorian home on the St. Clair Parkway. Open year round. Rooms are restored with antiques and offer either two single or two double beds. The second floor has a sitting room and deck with view of the river. It is one block from the Marine City ferry.

Museums

The Sombra Museum, 3490 St. Clair Parkway (downtown in the village of Sombra), (519) 892-3982. Housed in a turn-of-the-century Victorian in the heart of Sombra, this museum was originally the Bury home, built in 1881. It is presented today with eight rooms furnished as they would have been in the late 1800s. You can experience the hominess and warmth of the kitchen, and the elegance of the dining room which displays silver, crystal and china from the period. The Parlour and Music Rooms offer a peek at the entertainment of the time. Even the children's bedroom is filled with toys and clothing of the era. The home provides an excellent example of Victorian architecture and the furnishings make it feel authentic. The museum also features a maritime heritage exhibit which illustrates the importance of the St. Clair River and the Great Lakes to the history of the area. There is an Agricultural and Technology Room which highlights tools used in farming, smithing, logging, cooperage, photography and butter making. A Reference Room has archives, cemetery records and photos of businesses, ships, schools, and churches in the area. The 1930 log cabin characterizes the lifestyle of early Sombra pioneers. There is a small selection of gifts, including books on local history. Open Victoria Day and the remainder of May to September 1:00 pm to 3:00 pm, July and August expanded hours 11:00 am to 4:30 pm. By appointment at other times.

Shopping

Sombra has several unique one-of-a-kind shops, many located in old Victorians which enhance their charm.

Ansell's, 159 King Street, (519) 892-3904, or toll-free (800) 678-7094. Offers Canadian-made souvenirs, a selection of moccasins and Canadian maple nut fudge, as well as other gifts, currency exchange, maps and nautical items.

This was a pretty laid-back place: The clerk was sitting on the porch with several cronies and came sauntering in as customers browsed. Open year round. Summer hours: Mon to Sat 9:00 am to 8:00 pm, Sun 10:00 am to 8:00 pm, Winter hours: Mon to Sat 9:00 am to 5:00 pm and Sun 10:00 am to 5:00 pm.

Barnacle Bill's Beach Shoppes, 200 King Street, (519) 892-3882, or (519) 352-4541. This little shop near the shoreline carries Woolrich brand men and women's clothing, as well as Cotton Reel men's clothing. It had a lovely selection of wool sweaters and in the summer has a large selection of bathing suits. Open January to April, Sat and Sun 10:00 am to 5:00 pm, and May to December daily 10:00 am to 5:00 pm.

The Hummingbird/Grape Expectations, 3502 St. Clair Parkway (a few doors down from King Street), *humbird6@hotmail.com,* (519) 892-3245, or toll-free (888) 293-9250. This wine making establishment allows you to become a vintner. They supply everything you need including one hundred and eighty grape selections from around the world. You can make nearly any kind of wine. Call ahead to make sure they have your preferred grape selection available and to book an appointment time to start your batch. You will be given a mini-tour of the process, and it will take about five minutes to start the batch. The wine is then set aside under proper conditions for the appropriate number of weeks. You will receive a telephone call to set up a second appointment to bottle your wine. The next step, where the wine is bottled and corked, takes about twenty-five minutes. You can provide your own bottles and labels, or you can purchase them from Grape Expectations. To transport your batch to the U.S. you can expect to pay an IRT tax of approximately $6.50 per batch.

Three Sisters Gifts and Art Gallery, 3486 St. Clair Parkway, (519) 892-3934. The shop is brimming with unusual gifts to fit every budget including Native American crafts from across North America. Browse the assortment of dream catchers, sun catchers, hand-beaded moccasins, mukluks and mitts, hand-crafted chief's ceremonial spoons, corn husk dolls, glacier pearl jewelry, British Columbian jade, stonewashed sweatshirts, jackets and scarves that come with cards describing the design, original artwork, hand-painted Christmas ornaments, and much more. The gallery is owned by Sue Walliser and she features the original art of her younger sister and the trade bead bracelets and porcupine quill earrings of her older sister. Open Tues to Sat 10:00 am to 5:00 pm and Sun noon to 5:00 pm, Spring to Christmas.

Whittington's, 156 King Street, (519) 892-3991. Located in a gracious old home which is also the site of Whittington's Tea Room. The various rooms of this shop feature boots, shoes, purses, bath and soap items, candles, rugs, towels, giftware and items for the house. A bejeweled candle lighter caught my eye, not terribly practical, but so elegant. The shop is open seven days a week 10:00 am to 5:00 pm.

Parks, Beaches and Campgrounds
   Branton Cundick Park, (519) 862-2291. Waterfront park with a boat ramp. It also has a playground, camping, sports field, picnic area, and restrooms.
   Cathcart Park, St. Clair Parkway, (519) 892-3342. The campground has seventy-three sites, electric, water, showers and a playground for children. It also has restrooms and a picnic area.
   Reagan Park and Sombra Park, (519) 862-2291. Offer only picnic areas.
   The St. Clair River Trail, (519) 867-2655. Follows the banks of the St Clair River connecting a series of beautiful waterfront parks. Perfect for walkers, runners and bicyclers. There are restrooms at points along the way. Maps available on the Internet site, *www.stclairrivertrail.com*.

Mooretown

   Moore Museum, 94 Moore Line Road, Mooretown, Ontario, Canada, (519) 867-2020. Mooretown is less than 10 miles north of Sombra and easily accessible by the Marine City (Bluewater) Ferry followed by a short drive north on St. Clair Parkway. The museum grounds contain a historic riverside village. It is another undiscovered gem that tourists visiting the Thumb should not miss if they are crossing into Canada. Among other buildings, the village includes a one-room schoolhouse with rows of one-arm school desks reminiscent of Michigan's early country schools. The village's historic Trinity St. Clair Chapel was built in 1919 and was formerly the Trinity Anglican Church. The church highlights the importance of religion in the community and appears fully ready to serve with its wooden pews and stained glass windows. The village has a functional blacksmith shop demonstrating the essential need for a smithy's skills in the early communities. A Rear Range Light (lighthouse) from 1890 is preserved on the grounds - retired after guiding ships up the St. Clair River for 92 years. You can also visit the original Mooretown Railroad Station. The Reilley Victorian Cottage introduces you to the home life of a bygone day. It features a sitting porch for enjoying the river breezes. The village's more modest Log Cabin shows the home of a settler in the 1800s and displays handmade quilts and a kettle for dipping candles. The exhibit buildings house a wide variety of artifacts ranging from a ten-thousand-year-old mastodon bone to a store front and miscellaneous marine equipment. The museum is a pleasant walk back in time. Open March and April with variable hours (call for details), May and June Wed to Sun 11:00 am to 5:00 pm, July and August seven days 11:00 am to 5:00 pm and September to December 15, Mon to Fri 9:00 am to 5:00 pm.

Other Things to See or Do
   St. Clair Parkway Golf Course, 132 Moore Line, Mooretown, (519) 867-2810, or toll-free (877) 362-3344. This 18-hole, par 72 golf course has the largest greens in southwestern Ontario. It also has a pro shop and driving range.

St. Clair

Population: 5802.

Directions:

An hour north of Detroit or 20 miles south of Port Huron on M-29.

(See note under Marysville to take the more scenic route between St. Clair and Marysville.)

Background and History

The name St. Clair pays tribute to General Arthur St. Clare who was governor of the Northwest Territory which included Michigan before it gained statehood.

Actual settlement of the area began under the British flag in the 1700s. Development was significantly aided by the area's location on the St. Clair River; and St. Clair became the site of a local fort. There are historical landmarks and many of the homes of the early seafaring families remain standing today. The marina has one hundred slips if you plan to arrive by boat. The visitor to St. Clair has a choice of competing activities including: the Alice W. Moore Woods, the Imagination Station playground for children, a stop at the St. Clair Historical Museum or the Art Association Gallery, and a very spectacular walk along the river on the longest freshwater boardwalk in the United States. All are waiting to make your visit a pleasant one.

Salt may be Michigan's least publicized natural resource and St. Clair County lies on a sheet of salt. About 600,000,000 years ago, during the Paleozoic Era and up through about 230,000,000 years ago, seawater flooded the Michigan basin many times. The seawater would recede or simply evaporate, leaving behind mineral deposits known as rock-salt (halite), liquid brines, lime and sandstone. Early settlers used salt to preserve game. It was critical to survival on the Michigan frontier. It is believed that man was preceded in the use of salt by four legged creatures, including mastodon and musk oxen. Their remains are often found at sites where there are salt seeps. Native Americans used salt as a form of money to barter between tribes.

As Michigan entered the twentieth century, it led the country in the production of salt and many natural salines. It is not surprising that these resources created wealth for local citizens and even caused cities to sprout in certain areas.

The city of St. Clair has the distinction of being the leading salt producer in the world. Next winter when you pull out the bucket of salt to de-ice your driveway, or anytime you reach for the salt shaker to flavor your popcorn, remember you owe a debt of gratitude to St. Clair.

At Port Huron, St. Clair and Detroit hot water is pumped into the salt to form artificial brines which are then pumped and used in the manufacture of salt and in the chemical industries. There are no longer any active salt mines in Michigan. All salt is obtained by the hot water pumping method. In 1886 Diamond Crystal Salt opened a factory in St. Clair. Akzo Salt Company bought Diamond around 1990 and the current owners, Cargill Salt, bought the business from Akzo.

Food/Restaurants

Achatz Riverview Restaurant, 201 North Riverside, Riverview Plaza, (810) 329-4913. Home-style, casual family dining with carry-out available. Breakfast served anytime, and they have a breakfast special that will satisfy the hungriest customer. Also open for lunch and dinner.

Crumbs Pastry Pantry, 201 North Riverside, Riverview Plaza, (810) 329-5773. Fabulous delicacies from Sweetheart Bakery: donuts, cookies, brownies, muffins, cakes and cheesecake. Opens at 5:00 am, seven days.

London's Ice Cream Parlor, 201 North Riverside, Riverview Plaza, (810) 329-2995. Place for a great hand-dipped ice cream cone to enjoy as you wander the River Walk.

Murphy Inn, 505 Clinton Avenue, *www.murphyinn.com*, (810) 329-7118. Either a great Italian grinder or an Oriental chicken salad would make a nice lunch after a leisurely stroll along the river. If you are looking for a bit heartier fare, they also offer full dinners, including lake perch and steaks. Sunday all-you-can-eat, roasted, fried or barbecued chicken. Kitchen open seven days, Sun to Thurs 11:00 am to 10:00 pm, Fri and Sat 11:00 am to 11:00 pm. Often open later on summer weekends when they may have live entertainment.

Pepper Joe's Restaurant, 119 Clinton Avenue, (810) 326-1710. Great lunches of fajitas, wraps, salads, soups and bread bowls. Open Sun to Thurs 11:00 am to 10:00 pm, Fri and Sat 11:00 am to 11:00 pm.

River Crab, 1337 North River Road, (810) 329-2261, or toll-free (800) 468-3727. Next door to the Bluewater Inn, this restaurant offers river views and features items such as Salmon Rockefeller and Macadamia Encrusted Mahi Mahi, along with twenty other varieties of fresh fish, beef, and chicken entrees. Open lunch Mon to Sat 11:30 am to 4:00 pm, Sun brunch 10:00 am to 2:00 pm. Dinner Mon to Thurs 4:00 pm to 10:00 pm, Fri and Sat 4:00 pm to 10:30 pm, Sun 3:30 pm to 9:30 pm.

River Watch Restaurant at the St. Clair Inn, 500 North Riverside, (810) 329-2222. Several dining rooms including the South Porch and North Porch which were originally part of the open Veranda and overlook the St. Clair River. The River Lounge also offers views to go with the cocktails and food. Extensive lake and sea specialties including Potato Encrusted Pickerel. Also a full selection of steaks, chops, and ribs. Breakfast, lunch and dinner are served daily. Also daily specials. Open for breakfast Mon to Sat 8:00 am to 11:00 am, lunch Mon to Sat 11:00 am to 4:00 pm, and dinner Mon to Thurs 4:00 pm to 9:00 pm, Fri and Sat 4:00 pm to 10:00 pm and Sun noon to 8:00 pm.

Sue's Coffee House, 201 North Riverside, Riverview Plaza, (810) 326-1212. Specialty coffee drinks, tea, smoothies and pastries. Open Mon to Thurs 6:00 am to 9:00 pm, Fri 6:00 am to 11:00 pm, Sat 7:00 am to 11:00 pm and Sun 8:00 am to 5:00 pm.

The Voyageur, 525 South Riverside, (810) 329-3331. This sports bar (bowling) and restaurant is located on the river and provides diners with great views that, even from the parking lot, are worth the trip. Lunch Mon to Sat 11:00 am to 4:00 pm. Dinner Mon to Thurs 4:00 pm to 9:00 pm, Fri and Sat 4:00 pm to 9:30 pm, and Sun noon to 8:00 pm.

Lodging (see also parks and campgrounds)

Bluewater Inn, 1337 North River Road, (810) 329-2261, or toll-free (800) 468-3727. Every room is your own private space for viewing the St. Clair River. Each of the twenty-one rooms reflects a different theme. The Georgian Bay Room, with its white wicker furniture, is a favorite. For a more masculine taste, the Schooner Room, furnished with a brass cannonball bed, might be more appropriate.

Murphy Inn, 505 Clinton, *www.murphyinn.com*, (810) 329-7118. The Murphy Inn is an old colonial inn that, according to one traveler staying there, "feels like going back to grandmas." The inn opened in 1836 and has earned the right to call itself one of Michigan's oldest inns. Its seven guest rooms are on the second floor. (The Irish pub and dining room described under Food above occupies the first floor.)

St. Clair Inn, 500 N. Riverside, (810) 329-2222. A mid-west landmark since it was built, today it is also an official national landmark. The St. Clair Inn combines a picturesque waterfront setting on the St. Clair River with the cozy warmth and hospitality of an English country inn. The inn provides seventy-nine rooms and can accommodate business functions as well as the pleasure traveler. Great rooms and good food.

Museums and Galleries

Alice W. Moore Center for the Arts, 201 North Riverside, Riverview Plaza, *www.stclairart.org*, (810) 329-9576. Home of the St. Clair Art Association. You will find photographs, prints, original paintings, sculptures, jewelry, glass art, handbags, and other items of art for sale. Occasional speakers and programs, changing exhibits and workshops. Open Tues to Sat 10:00 am to 5:00 pm.

St. Clair Historical Museum, 308 South Fourth Street, (810) 329-6888. This Romanesque style building, originally a Baptist church, was given to the city in 1974, and currently serves as the community center and museum. The museum contains a collection of old pictures from St. Clair's early days and it has a

First Baptist Church, Currently St. Clair Historical Museum

Diamond Crystal room. (See above for history of St. Clair's relationship to her salt industry.) The museum is currently creating an old train depot that will be housed in a separate building. Open Sat and Sun 1:30 pm to 4:30 pm.

Antiques and other Shopping

Antiques and Collectibles Antique Mall, 201 North Riverside, Riverview Plaza, (810) 329-3173. You can spend some serious time exploring the 6,000 square feet of space occupied by dealers offering a variety of antiques from several periods and specialties. Open Tues to Sat 10:00 am to 5:00 pm, Sun noon to 4:00 pm.

Chocolate Harbor, 201 North Riverside, Riverview Plaza, (810) 329-7779. Features chocolates and gifts for all occasions. The toffee was terrific. They carry gourmet coffees in addition to their selection of hand-dipped chocolates. Mon to Sat 9:30 am to 5:30 pm. Closed Sun.

The Red Geranium, 212 South Third Street, (810) 329-3610, *theredgeraniumllc@att.net*. A specialty gift boutique where you will find everything from home accessories to the perfect evening bag and nearly everything in between: lamps, clocks, accent furniture, home accessories, WoodWick® candles, seasonal items, jewelry, scarves, bookends, picture frames, table linens, personal spa items, dishware, baby and children's clothing and toys, and gourmet food. The Red Geranium also plans to open the GEM Tea Room by the time this guide is published, hours will be based upon demand.

Store open Mon to Fri 10:00 am to 6:00 pm and Sat 10:00 am to 4:00 pm, Sun open during special events weekends, usually noon to 4:00 pm. Winter hours December 26 to March 31, Mon to Sat 10:00 am to 4:00 pm.

Parks, Beaches and Campgrounds

Greig Park, 547 North Carney. This is a city park with a great play area called Imagination Station. Also has restrooms and picnic area.

St. Clair River Walk. If you have traveled to St. Clair, it would not be right to leave without walking the longest freshwater boardwalk in the United States.

Marina

St. Clair Boat Harbor, 902 South 2nd Street, toll-free (800) 447-2757. Floating docks, fish cleaning station, launch ramp, shuttle, gas, diesel pump-out, showers, restrooms, TV, electric, water, WiFi, canoe, kayak, bike rentals, grills fifty-one seasonal slips and sixty-nine transient slips.

Other Things to See and Do

Alice W. Moore Woods Nature Sanctuary, Second and Hawthorne. This is a pleasant, wooded, walking, nature trail.

Avoca Rail Trail, (810) 989-6960, *www.stclaircountyparks.org*. This trail was purchased by the St. Clair County Parks and Recreation Commission from the CSX Railroad in 1999. It offers 9.82 miles of paths for walkers, hikers, bicyclists and horseback riders. There are both paved and unpaved sections. The Mill Creek Railway Bridge, once used for trains, is now a pedestrian walkway and the highlight of the Avoca Rail Trail.

Bridge to Bay Trail, 547 North Carney, (810) 989-6960 *www. stclaircountyparks.org*. This trail runs along the shoreline of St. Clair County and is diverse in style and landscape. The trail takes you past state and municipal parks, museums, gazebos, and lighthouses. It starts in Algonac State Park and ends with continuous travel to Greig Park in St. Clair. Further sections will be added including: Marysville, Port Huron, and Fort Gratiot Township. It will eventually go as far as the Blue Water Bridge. It connects community to community for walkers, joggers, strollers, inline skaters, and bicyclists of all ages. Various sections include boardwalks, river walks, rail trails, safety paths, and bike paths. The trail is a cooperative program involving the Parks and Recreation Commission and cities and townships located along the St. Clair County Shoreline. To access the trail in St. Clair (which has approximately 5 miles finished) turn from Riverview onto Brown. The trail starts at Brown and Carney or you can access it at Greig Park.

KM Ranch, 6277 Fred Moore Highway, 4.5 miles west of St. Clair, (810) 329-7364, *www.kmranch.net*. You can learn horseback riding during your summer vacation. Lessons are offered in all aspects of western horsemanship, but you must pre-schedule. Ages six and up. They also offer farm tours, parties, day camps, and "life-on-a-horse-farm" day and half-day packages where the student learns everything from mucking stalls and feeding, to basic riding and handling skills as they work along side a staff member.

Festivals
- St. Clair Craft Show, June.
- St. Clair Art Fair, June.
- Off Shore Power Boat Race, July.
- Antique Show, July.
- Off Shore Power Boat Race, August.
- Antique Yard Sale Trail, August.
- Women's League Home Tour, September/October.
- Art and Craft Show, September/October.

Golf
Pine Shores Golf Course, 515 Fred W. Moore Highway, (810) 329-4294. Club house and carts. Municipal golf course open to the public.

Rattle Run Golf Course, 7163 St. Clair Highway, (810) 329-2070, *www. rattlerun.com*. Golf Digest 4-Star Place to Play. 18-hole public course, par 72.

Contacts
Blue Water Area Convention and Visitors Bureau, *www.bluewater.org*, (800) 852-4242 for information concerning festivals.

The St. Clair Chamber of Commerce, 201 North Riverside, Riverview Plaza, (810) 329-2962.

Home Tour and Juried Art Show, (810) 329-4764, *www.stclairriverviewplaza. com*.

Marysville

Population: 9684.

Directions:

About 5 miles south of Port Huron

Note: Less than a mile north of Newman Road, as you drive from St. Clair to Marysville, you may wish to follow the more scenic River Road to the right rather than staying on M-29. River Road will take you into Marysville and past the lovely Huron Park and Marysville museums. You can also access River Road by taking a right on Huron and then a left onto River Road. River Road comes back to M-29 just before Port Huron and you will turn right into Port Huron. About a half mile after your turn onto M-29, however, the road becomes Gratiot Boulevard and at that point it is M-25.

Background and History

The city of Marysville was incorporated as a city on October 28, 1919. Its original name was Vicksburg after E.P. Vickery, who built a saw mill in Marysville in the 1840s. Sometime in the 1860s, Mr. Vickery sold his mill and the town renamed the mill for the new mill owner's wife, Mary. In this lumbering era, the mill was an extremely important part of existence and naming the town after the mill owner (or his wife) was a significant honor.

Marysville, like St. Clair, is situated on a salt flat. Visitors can enjoy Marysville's fifty-eight acre Huron Park on the beautiful St. Clair River.

Food/Restaurants

Junction Buoy, 1415 River Road, (810) 364-5730, *www.junctionbuoy.com.* Riverfront restaurant offering casual dining and spirits with a complete lunch and dinner menu. They have an especially nice selection of salads, and like many restaurants in the area, excellent perch dinners plus daily lunch and dinner specials. It is open seven days a week all year. Enjoy the outside deck when weather permits. Sometimes offers entertainment. Open Mon to Thurs 11:00 am to 10:00 pm, Fri and Sat 11:00 am to 11:00 pm, Sun noon to 10:00 pm. Bar open later and winter hours are reduced.

Seros Restaurant, 925 Gratiot Boulevard, (810) 388-9311, ***The Four Star Restaurant***, 1835 Gratiot Boulevard, (810) 364-6950 and ***The Pelican Cafe***, 2825 Gratiot Boulevard, (810) 364-6383, are all family restaurants offering decent food, hefty portions and good prices. Gratiot Boulevard also has chains (Big Boy and Tim Horton) Pizza joints (Little Caesar's, Pizza Hut, and Goodfella's

Grill) and fast food (McDonald's, Taco Bell, Burger King, Long John Silvers, and KFC). All are located close to the Super 8 Motel.

Lodging
Super 8 Motel Marysville, 1484 Gratiot Boulevard, (810) 364-7500, *www.super8.com*. Offers seventy rooms and suites. Extras: indoor pool, spa, and fitness room.

Museums
Marysville Historical Museum, 887 East Huron Boulevard, (810) 364-5198 or (810) 364-6613, *www.marysvillemuseum.org*. The museum displays several rooms, each with a single theme, such as Pioneer's Parlor, Marine Room, Indian History, and Fashion Display. Open Sat and Sun 1:30 pm to 4:30 pm.

Wills Sainte Claire Auto Museum, 2408 Wills Street, about a half mile off Busha Highway in an industrial park, (810) 388-5050, *www.willsautomuseum.com*. Look for the pyramid shaped building on the corner of Busha and Wills, and watch for the Flying Goose signs out front. The museum provides a history of the Wills Sainte Claire automobile that was manufactured in Marysville. About twelve thousand vehicles of this model were produced from 1921 to 1926. Mr. Wills retired from Ford Motor Company in 1919 and decided to build his own car. It featured a Flying Goose radiator emblem and was the first car to have backup lights. Chrysler Corporation purchased the factory property in 1935. The museum was the result of a donation of the building on Wills Street to house actual Wills Sainte Claire automobiles (currently six to eight of them), as well as related memorabilia. Open June, July and August the second and fourth Sunday of the month from 1:00 pm to 5:00 pm; from September to May the second Sunday of the month from 1:00 pm to 5:00 pm or by appointment for groups.

Parks Beaches and Campgrounds
Marysville City Park, Huron Boulevard and Riverview. This is a lovely, treed park with playground, zero depth splash pad for tots, picnic tables, restrooms, grills, two boat launches, beach with changing rooms and terrific views from the 1.2-mile boardwalk along the river.

Festivals
- Village Green Plaza Craft Show, May.
- Marysville Days Festival, June.
- Blue Water Volleygrass, July.
- Art in the Park, July.
- Village Green Plaza Sidewalk Sales, July.
- Antique Yard Sale Trail, August.
- Village Green Plaza Craft Show, September/October.
- Santa Visit and Parade, First Saturday in December.

Golf

Golf Country, 4730 Smiths Creek Road (off Range Road), (810) 364-9160 or toll-free (888) 860-9160, *www.golf-country.com*. Open year round with a complete pro shop and practice range. Golf instructions for adults and juniors. A place to buy anything in the line of golf equipment and accessories; they also do repairs and custom clubs.

Marysville Golf Course, 2080 River Road, (810) 364-4653. A par 72, 18-hole golf course, rated 3½ stars by Golf Digest of Places to Play. It features level lies along a wooded terrain with open, green complexes and understated bunkering. It has a pro shop, putting green, and club rental. Its location along the scenic St. Clair River makes it a great place to golf.

Contacts

Marysville Chamber of Commerce, for information concerning community events, call (810) 364-6180 or check the web at *www.marysvillechamber.com*.

The Blue Water Area Convention and Visitors Bureau, toll-free (800) 852-4242, *www.bluewater.org,* for information concerning festivals.

Map of Port Huron and Sarnia

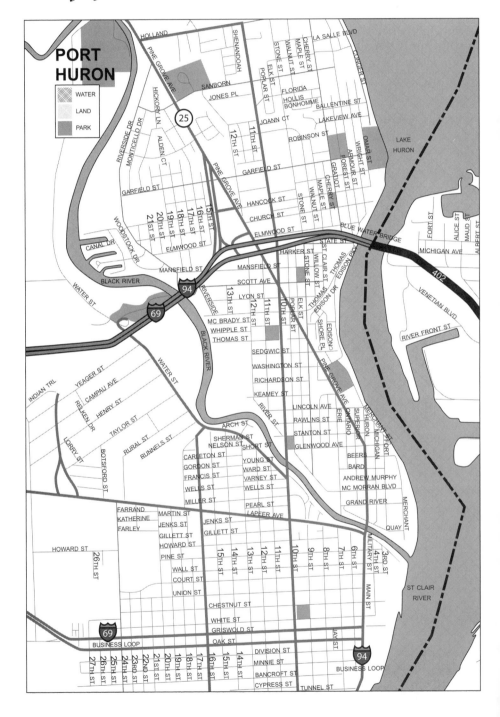

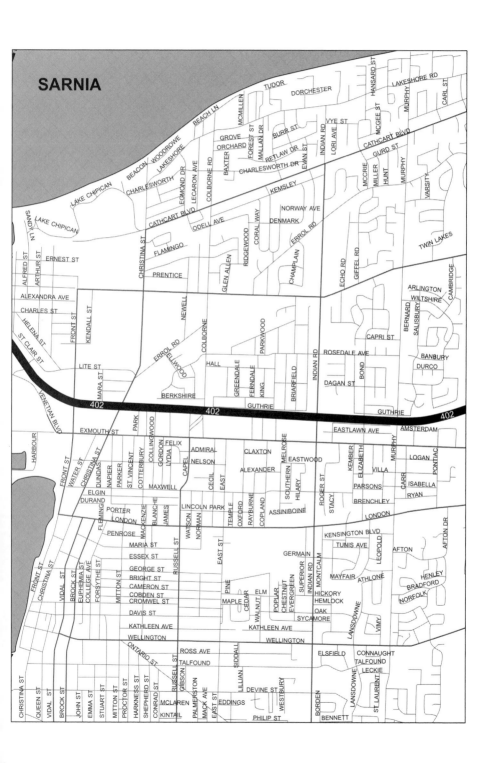

Port Huron/Fort Gratiot

Population: Port Huron 32,500; Fort Gratiot 14,626.

Directions:
Five miles north of Marysville on M-25. Sixty-five miles east of Flint on I-69. Sixty miles northeast of Detroit on I-94. At the point you enter Port Huron from the South, M-29 has become Gratiot which is also M-25 and from this point on you are following M-25.

Note: M-25 will take you past the Seaway Terminal and the interesting old Victorian homes. Past the drawbridge, M-25 will become Huron. Just beyond the downtown area you will come to a fork in the road; M-25 veers to the left and is called Pine Grove, Huron continues to the right. By staying to the right on Huron, rather than following M-25, you will wind past Pine Grove Park and the Lightship Museum. (Keep following the river.) You will have better views of the waterway along the St. Clair River and the Blue Water Bridge. When you get to the Thomas Edison Depot Museum (just under the bridge), turn left on State Street, and then right on Gratiot, which will eventually hook up again with M-25. This alternate route will avoid the congestion of the shopping mall, franchise food places and other less scenic areas.

Background and History
Port Huron bills itself as the Maritime Capital of the Great Lakes, which gives you insight into the city's self-image and its global role. The waterways, including the St. Clair River, Black River and Lake Huron, give Port Huron a strategic role in shipping commerce. Port Huron has also been designated one of Michigan's All-American "Cool" cities.

This history of Port Huron will include the history of Fort Gratiot because the two are closely entwined. Locals from the Thumb will say they are going to Port Huron, when their intention is really to shop at the Birchwood Mall, Wal-Mart, Barnes and Noble, or Meijer's, or to have lunch at Red Lobster or the Olive Garden. All of these places are actually in Fort Gratiot.

The construction of a small fur trading fort may have been the earliest European involvement in the area now known as Port Huron and/or Fort Gratiot. Fort St. Joseph was built by the French in 1686 to protect against possible British interference with the French fur trade. It was a timbered block house that stood at the site of what is now Bistro 1882.

Prior to that, the area was inhabited by Native Americans and a few French families living in settlements along the Black River. Canoes glided almost silently along river banks lined with tall pine forests. Tribes met in the area for various ceremonies and to settle disputes. Burial mounds have been found between the river and the area south of Water Street.

In 1814 Charles Gratiot brought a group of men to the area and built a small military post that was named in his honor. Fort Gratiot occupied the land between Mansfield Street and Scott Avenue, from the St. Clair River to the Black River. It was established to protect the waters of Lake Huron against the British in the war of 1812. By 1822, the fort was abandoned, and by 1826, it lay in ruins, only to be rebuilt in 1829. The most lethal attack against the fort was not by man, but by disease. The fort was forced to withstand an outbreak of cholera that resulted in many deaths. Soldiers, fearful for their lives, fled the fort to escape the epidemic. Their bodies were found along local roads where they dropped as the plague caught up with them.

In 1866 there was a murder committed at Fort Gratiot. Two men went fishing. Only one returned and he told a story of how his companion fell overboard. When the body washed up on the shore the bullet hole told a different tale. This old-time, CSI-type drama resulted in a charge of murder against the surviving fisherman, who was hanged for his crime.

The fort was open for a period of time to enlist men for the Civil War but was permanently closed in 1879. The land was split up and sold and became many businesses in the area. The city received twenty acres for Pine Grove Park. It is believed that the first street developed in Port Huron was Water Street. Some of the earliest buildings were constructed along Water and Military. The earliest residents of the city of Port Huron can be traced to 1790.

Saw mills began springing up along the Black River in the early 1800s, heralding the era of the lumber baron. Two fires in the Thumb and the resultant elimination of much of the forest bounty brought the end of the lumber mills. (See The Days the Thumb Burned in Part Two of this guide.) The last existing mill was the Howard and Son Mill, located just east of the railroad bridge. It burned in 1903. The Black River became quieter without boats carrying lumber, but the lake remained active with the great freighters carrying ore.

In 1886 initial plans began for a tunnel connecting the United States and Canada—Port Huron to Sarnia—but it was August 30, 1926, before the tunnel under the St. Clair River was completed. Steam whistles and honking automobile horns signaled the news and the city went crazy in celebration. The tunnel has been subject to two sabotage attempts, one that was foiled, and the other so ineffective it did no damage. Seven hundred men worked seven days a week in three eight-hour shifts to build the tunnel. The tunnel caused several deaths, as men were overcome by fumes when they attempted to reconnect cars that had become uncoupled. One child was born in the tunnel. Unfortunately, passenger trains no longer run through the tunnel and it is only used for freight trains. If you are standing aboard the Bramble in the Seaway Terminal when a train goes underneath, you will be able to hear and feel it.

The Blue Water Bridge also connects the United States with Canada, Port Huron to Sarnia. The initial bridge was built in 1938. When the second span was added in 1997, extensive renovation took place on the original span as well. The Blue Water Bridge is the only bridge owned jointly by Michigan and Canada. The second span opened to traffic on the morning of July 22, 1997 – a time and date that had been kept secret to avoid people lining up to be the first to cross. The bridge is an architecturally magnificent backdrop to the waters of the St. Clair River and Lake Huron. International Flag Plaza offers the perfect place to sit and admire its structural beauty.

Today the Black River and Lake Huron are fishing and recreational bodies of water. They enrich the lives of both those who live in Port Huron and those who visit. Port Huron/Fort Gratiot boasts a lighthouse and a famous lightship. (See related stories in Part Two of this guide.)

As you drive into Port Huron from the south, note the beautiful Victorian homes that remain along the waterway between the Seaway Terminal and the drawbridge. If traffic is moving too fast to allow you to appreciate the old architecture, consider parking your car and walking along these few blocks.

Port Huron offers something to suit everyone's tastes: from shopping to dining, from fishing charters to sightseeing, from theatre to museums, and everything in between.

Food/Restaurants

Bistro 1882, 2333 Gratiot Avenue, (810) 966-6900. Not the biggest restaurant in Port Huron, but the intimate ambiance and interesting menu make it a worthwhile stop. It is located about a block from the International Flag Plaza, almost under the Blue Water Bridge. The name "1882" comes from the fact that various owners have operated businesses, including a grocery store and an antique furniture store, at this location since that year. Originally, a trading post stood at this location. Because of its rich history, Bistro 1882 was spared demolition when the area was cleared for a second span of the Blue Water Bridge. At lunch you can sit and reflect a bit on the area's colorful background while you enjoy the Reuben Quesadillas, the San Francisco Crab Melt, or perhaps the Michigan Cherry Chicken Croissant with an accompaniment of sweet potato salad. The menu changes three times a year. The dinner menu offers Pistachio Encrusted Chicken and you can always order a filet mignon or New York strip steak. Open Mon to Sat 11:00 am to 10:00 pm, Sun brunch 10:00 am to 2:00 pm and then open until 10:00 pm. Depending on the day and season, reservations might be a smart idea.

The Brass Rail, 410 Huron Avenue, (810) 982-4592. The Brass Rail is a Port Huron landmark, opening and remaining in the same location since 1937. During the early period of its life, it was an ice cream bar. The cooler and top of the bar are solid mahogany. The side columns are solid onyx with cast iron trim.

Beautiful mirrors and Tiffany lamps add to the richness of this bar. Stop in and try the house drink specialty: a Tom and Jerry. The Brass Rail is a favorite with locals and visitors alike. It does not have a full kitchen or grill, but does offer nachos and snacks. Open seven days noon to 2:00 am.

Catch 22, 1229 7th Street, (810) 984-1437. Lovely Victorian restaurant with intimate dining rooms that can serve up to forty-five diners. The pub downstairs has original fieldstone walls surrounding the bar which can accommodate another twenty. The bar was originally a cutting table from a former mercantile store in old Downtown Port Huron. Chef and owner, Stephen Wilhelm, was born in Port Huron. Seafood is the specialty and the wine list is impressive. Live entertainment on Friday night. Outdoor patio when weather permits. Reservations recommended. Open Mon to Thurs 11:00 am to 9:00 pm, Fri and Sat 11:00 am to 10:00 pm, and closed Sun.

Cavis Grill, 401 Quay Street, (810) 982-2192. A little, hole-in-the-wall restaurant that serves up a hearty breakfast. Locals recommend it to out-of-towners who want good food and nothing pretentious. The omelets have been written up and recommended in local publications; the fresh ingredients make them special. Open daily at 6:00 am.

Chan's Buffet, 4165 24th Avenue, Fort Gratiot, (810) 385-3838. All-you-can-eat buffet including a salad bar, a dessert bar, and both American and Chinese food. Open Mon to Thurs 11:00 am to 9:30 pm, Fri and Sat 11:00 am to 10:00 pm, Sun noon to 9:30 pm.

Copper Lantern, 902 Military Street, (810) 966-9555. Cute coffee shop with sandwiches, soups, and salads, including a great spinach salad. Not open for dinner or most week-ends. Open Mon to Fri 8:00 am to 3:00 pm.

Fogcutter, 511 Fort Street, (at the top of the Fogcutter Building), (810) 987-3300, *www.fogcutterrestaurant.com*. In the heart of Downtown Port Huron for over 35 years. The view is its ambiance, and you can watch boat traffic passing between the St. Clair River and Lake Huron. Years ago there was a dress code, but today they welcome you in blue jeans. You would probably still feel more comfortable in something a bit dressier for dinner. They specialize in seafood, and the Lake Perch is always a sure thing. The onion soup was perfect: thick and cheesy. Open Mon to Thurs 11:00 am to 9:00 pm, Fri 11:00 am to 10:00 pm, Sat noon to 10:00 pm, and Sun noon to 8:00 pm.

The Huron Athletic Club, 319 Huron Avenue, (810) 987-9090. Original tin ceilings and brick wall, sports memorabilia, and big screen TVs set the ambiance for this pleasant two-level bar and restaurant. They claim to have the best burgers in town and say they have the customers to prove it. You have to save room for the Apple and Wild Berry Cobbler with Amaretto Cream. Drinks are one dollar off during Happy Hour. Open Sun to Wed 11:00 am to 9:00 pm, Thurs 11:00 am to 10:00 pm, Fri and Sat 11:00 am to midnight.

Palms Krystal Bar and Restaurant, 1535 Pine Grove Avenue, at the intersection of Pine Grove, Stone and Thomas Streets, (two stop lights south of the Blue Water Bridge on Pine Grove), (810) 985-9838. This place is home to Chicken-in-the-Rough and has been a local tradition for more than fifty years. At one point, Chicken-in-the-Rough had more than a hundred franchises. Whether the chicken is as good as the hype is for you to decide. If chicken is not your dish, the ribs run a close second as the favorite of customers. Open Mon to Thurs 11:00 am to 10:00 pm, Fri and Sat 11:00 am to 11:00 pm, Sun 11:30 am to 9:00 pm.

Powers Diner, 1209 Military Street, (three blocks south of the Military Street Drawbridge on the west side of the street), (810) 985-5130, or (810) 985-5029. This little restaurant looks as though it is made of tin or aluminum and at first glance more closely resembles a shiny trailer than your average sandwich joint. It was opened in 1934 by Dale Powers for whom it is named. The current owners, after viewing a documentary on diners, decided it was time to replace the old building with the current, shiny structure. They serve a variety of panini sandwiches (all made to order), hot-baked subs, roll-up sandwiches, and more. They also serve breakfast anytime. Open Sun to Wed 7:00 am to 9:00 pm, Thurs 7:00 am to 10:00 pm, Fri and Sat 7:00 am to 11:00 pm.

Quay Street Brewing Company, 330 Quay Street, (driving north, Quay Street is the first street after the drawbridge), turn right on Quay, and the restaurant is towards the water, (810) 982-4100. This microbrewery has six popular house brews served year-round and additional seasonal brews. They also have a delicious root beer for the designated driver. For lunch, a good choice is the house specialty, grilled lamb-burger topped with cucumber sauce. For dinner you might consider the Parmesan and Herb Crusted Lake Trout. The restaurant is open Mon to Thurs 11:30 am to 9:00 pm, Fri and Sat 11:30 am to 10:00 pm and Sun (seasonal) from noon to 8:00 pm. The bar is open Mon to Wed 11:30 am to 11:00 pm, Thurs to Sat 11:30 am to 1:00 pm, and Sun (seasonal) noon to 8:00 pm.

The Raven, 932 Military, (810) 984-4330, *www.ravencoffeehouse.com*. Located in an 1870s building with gargoyles, this coffee shop claims you will love their food as much as their atmosphere. The hype is true, and the Raven is a Port Huron favorite. In addition to great coffee and tea, they have wonderful soups and salads. The sandwiches carry such interesting names as Masque of Red Death or The Tell Tale Heart. Additionally, there is Internet access and eclectic music. You will enjoy the experience. Open Mon and Tues 7:30 am to 10:00 pm, Wed to Fri 7:30 am to 11:00 pm, Sat 8:30 am to 11:00 pm, and Sun noon to 10:00 pm.

The Red Pepper Mexican Restaurant, 1735 24th Street, (Near Griswold), (810) 966-4991. For good Mexican food, this is the restaurant that several locals recommended. It is a bit off the beaten path, if you are using the suggested route in this guide. You will, however, drive by their second location in Lakeport as you are traveling north from Port Huron/Fort Gratiot and may prefer to stop at that location (7116 Lakeshore Road, (810) 385-7088). The exterior will not wow you, but the parking lot was crowded at 2:15 in the afternoon, well after what would be considered the regular lunch rush. The food is inexpensive and there are daily specials. The combination plate with one corn taco, one small beef and bean burrito, and one cheese enchilada lets you avoid making difficult decisions. It is a good choice for anyone who can not make up his or her mind.

Roche Bar, 405 Quay Street, (810) 982-7464. Friends describe this as a "local, divey bar they enjoy stopping at." There is no offense intended and it is included because every travel guide should offer some local hang-outs and joints.

Rum Runnerz, 400 Quay Street on the water, (810) 984-2326, *www.rumrunnerz.com*. A decent menu including entrees like delicious Blackened Mahi-Mahi as well as sandwiches and lighter fare. The specialty drinks will grab your attention. For example: they offer six kinds of martinis – one the regular classic version and the other five worthy of consideration, although a purist would never agree they are true martinis. You have to be intrigued by the Swedish Massage Martini made with Skyy Vodka, peach schnapps, cream de cacao, and heavy cream. Who needs dessert? Deck for outdoor eating. Open Mon to Thurs 11:00 am to midnight (kitchen closes at 10:00 pm), Fri and Sat 11:00 am to 2:00 am (kitchen closes at 10:00) and Sun noon to 8:00 pm.

Thomas Edison Inn Ivy Dining Room, 500 Thomas Edison Parkway, (at the foot of the Blue Water Bridge), (810) 984-8000, *www.thomasedisoninn.com*. A combination of the excellent food and great views of the Blue Water Bridge and the waterfront make this the place for a special occasion. It is equally appropriate for an ordinary day when you just feel like giving yourself a treat. You can enjoy a delicious meal and watch the freighters wind their way along the river. It is a favorite place for Sunday brunch with a selection of food that is overwhelming. You could pack on a lot of pounds if you went very often – unless, of course, you can exercise remarkable restraint. You will find restraint difficult to muster when faced with such a wide array of tempting entrees and desserts. The restaurant serves breakfast, lunch, and dinner, in addition to the Sunday brunch. Breakfast: Mon to Sat 7:00 am to 10:30 am, Sunday Brunch: 11:00 am to 2:00 pm, Lunch: Mon to Sat 11:30 am to 4:00 pm. Dinner: Mon to Thurs 5:00 pm to 10:00 pm, Fri and Sat 5:00 pm to 11:00 pm, Sun 3:00 pm to 9:00 pm.

Vintage Tavern, 103 Michigan Street (one block off Main, downtown Port Huron), (810) 982-1866. Small plate dinners with wonderful choices including Seared Sashimi Tuna, Three Cheese Tapas Platter, and Teriyaki Salmon. The Sweet Potato Chips have become a hit. The tavern retained the original tin ceilings and wood floors of the old building. A men's clothing store originally occupied the space and then in turn: Kresge's, Grayson's Department Store, and Arden's. With the coming of the mall, Arden's closed and the building sat empty (other than a short stint as a bridal shop) until the current owners saw its inner beauty and created Vintage Tavern. The fireplace adds a cozy note in chilly weather. They have an extensive wine cellar, and it is fun to try their "wine tasting" which offers you 1½ ounces of each of four white or red wines. Open Mon to Thurs 11:30 am to 2:00 am, Fri and Sat noon to 2:00 am and Sun 2:00 pm to 8:00 pm. May close a bit earlier during the week if no customers.

White Castle, 2852 Pine Grove Avenue, (810) 985-5863. It may seem a bit incongruous to be listing White Castle immediately after describing the Thomas Edison Inn's Ivy Room and the upscale Vintage Tavern, but in an alphabetical guide this is where it comes. All variations of food are included in this guide, because sometimes you want steak with gourmet trimmings, but other times a burger and fries are what you crave. Fort Gratiot has one of the few remaining White Castles. This little drive-thru has those greasy, onion-flavored, miniscule burgers you may fondly remember. The frozen ones just are not the same. If you have not been to a White Castle lately and want a dozen (Has anyone ever eaten just one?), this is your chance.

Fast Food, Family Dining, Chain Restaurants

Traveling Michigan's Thumb, for the most part, does not include fast food establishments or large chains – those you can get at home. However, the following list is included, without specific details, for anyone who is shopping at the Birchwood Mall or just needs a fix from a favorite fast food joint:

- Arby's 3502 Pine Grove Avenue, (810) 984-3557.
- Big Boy, 3961 24th Avenue, (810) 985-9691.
- Burger King, 3584 Pine Grove Avenue, (810) 987-6799.
- Cheap Charlie's, 4495 24th Avenue, (810) 385-5511.
- Coney Island North, 4425 24th Avenue, (810) 385-8880.
- Daybreak Café, 3910 24th Avenue, (810) 966-5000. (Good place for breakfast).
- Golden Corral, 4783 24th Avenue, (810) 385-3855.
- McDonald's, 2509 Pine Grove Avenue, (810) 987-3374.
- Olive Garden, 4210 24th Avenue, (810) 385-5694.
- Red Lobster, 4220 24th Avenue, (810) 385-8773.
- Ruby Tuesday, 4280 24th Avenue, (810) 385-8966.
- Subway, 4845 24th Avenue, (810) 385-3470.
- Taco Bell, Birchwood Mall, (810) 385-4439.
- Ted's Coney Island, 3950 24th Avenue, (810) 987-2960.
- Tim Hortons 3829 Pine Grove Avenue, (810) 982-4047.
- Wendy's, 1700 Hancock Street, (810) 982-0688.

Lodging

Best Western, 2282 Water Street, (Exit 274 off I-94), (810) 987-1600. Extras: heated indoor pool and exercise room.

Catch 22, 1229 7th Street, (810) 984-1437. This lovely new restaurant in town (described above) also offers weary travelers two rooms with turn-of-the-century charm and modern amenities. One queen room and one deluxe suite available.

Comfort Inn, 1700 Yeager Street, Exit 274 off I-94, (810) 982-5500. Extras: heated indoor pool, whirlpool, fitness equipment, game room, and breakfast. Golf packages available for the nationally ranked USGA Championship Black River Country Club.

Davidson House B&B, 1707 Military Street, (810) 987-3922, *www. davidsonhouse.com*. Located in the Military Historical Homes District, this opulent Queen Anne home was designed in 1888 and took two years to construct. It is twenty rooms large with seven fireplaces and was the first home in Port Huron to be electrified. It offers four guest rooms, two with fireplaces. It is located across from the St. Clair River.

Days Inn Port Huron, 2908 Pine Grove Avenue, (810) 984-1522. Located one mile from downtown, the historical district, the business district, and the freeway. Free continental breakfast. Extras: seasonal pool and tennis courts.

Fairfield Inn by Marriott, 1635 Yeager Street, (Exit 274 off I-94), (810) 982-8500. Extras: small, heated indoor pool, whirlpool, fitness room, sun deck, game room, and continental breakfast.

Hampton Inn, 1655 Yeager Street, (Exit 274 off I-94), (810) 966-9000. Extras: heated indoor pool, whirlpool, fitness room, complimentary continental breakfast, two telephone lines in every room, voice mail and data port.

Hill Estate B&B, 602 Lakeview Avenue, (810) 982-8187, or toll-free (877) 982-8187. An 1884 Victorian with two rooms, each with private bath. The Bridgeview Room has a private hot tub. The B&B is within walking distance of the beach.

Holiday Inn Express, 1720 Hancock Street, (at the foot of the Blue Water Bridge, Business Loop I-69 at I-94 East), (810) 987-5999. Extras: heated indoor pool, whirlpool, fitness room, playroom, video game room, and deluxe complimentary continental breakfast.

Sage House B&B, 829 Prospect Place, (810) 984-2015, or toll-free (866) 585-0622, *www.sagehouse.net*, *sagehouse@sbcglobal.net,* or *sagehouse@ comcast.net*. Historic Queen Anne style home across from Pine Grove Park. View of ships traveling the St. Clair River. Three rooms with private baths. Resident cat.

Thomas Edison Inn, 500 Thomas Edison Parkway, (810) 984-8000, *www. thomasedisoninn.com*. An English Tudor style inn with a heated indoor pool, sauna, whirlpool, and area transportation. The inn also has a nice gift shop and the Ivy Room Restaurant (see above under restaurants). The boardwalk along the water passes in front of the inn, and you can watch the activity or take a relaxing waterfront stroll. A great place to stay in Port Huron.

The Port Huron Museum

Galleries and Museums

Cap'n Jim's Gallery, 211 Huron Avenue, (810) 987-0767, *www.jclary. com*. Jim Clary is a renowned marine artist, but he is also somewhat of a local historian. He has written several books about the Great Lakes, as well as a Pulitzer-nominated volume about the sinking of the Titanic entitled, *The Last True Story of the Titanic*. Inside the shop, Jim's brother shared the story of a customer who complained he bought a "Clary" at a garage sale for $35, and here was that same "Clary" on sale in the shop for $28. The disgruntled customer swore he had been robbed. It was quietly pointed out to him that the shop price was $2800, not $28; we can only imagine the stories that lucky garage-saler had for his next dinner guests.

Carnegie Center/Port Huron Museum, 1115 6th Street between Court and Wall Streets, (810) 982-0891, *www.phmuseum.org*. The museum was built in 1904, and originally served as the city library. Andrew Carnegie, the famous philanthropist, provided the money for this beautiful classical building. It became a museum in 1968. Inside you will find permanent and traveling displays.

The museum is home to over fifteen-thousand objects and archival items relating to the history, pre-history and culture of the Blue Water Area. There is also genealogical information, and you can tour a pilot's house. The second floor contains marine artifacts of the Great Lakes

Outside on the museum grounds you will find several anchors, and you can visit a log cabin house built in the late 1850s by Conrad Kammer. The cabin was originally built in Casco Township southwest of Port Huron. Several generations of Kammers lived in it. In 1981 the cabin was purchased by new owners who were intent on tearing it down and rebuilding. By that time, the exterior had been covered with layers of siding. When the treasure beneath was discovered, the

Kammer House/Log Cabin

owner donated it to the museum and it was moved to its current location. Open seven days a week from 11:00 am to 5:00 pm.

Coast Guard Cutter Bramble Museum, at Seaway Terminal on M-25, (as you enter Port Huron from the south), (810) 982-0891, *www.phmuseum.org*. Built by the Zenith Dredge Company in Duluth, Minnesota, the Bramble was commissioned on April 22, 1944. The original cost for the hull and machinery was $925,464. The Bramble's missions were to serve as an aid to navigation, marine environmental protection, search and rescue and domestic ice breaking. Your tour of the cutter will provide you with its interesting history and a bit of Coast Guard information. Open seven days, Memorial Day to Labor Day 11:00 am to 5:00 pm. Open September through December and April through May, Thurs to Mon 11:00 am to 5:00 pm. Closed January through March.

Fort Gratiot Lighthouse, at the foot of Garfield Street at Gratiot near the Blue Water Bridge. It is worth a climb to the top to look out at the mouth of Lake Huron. This is Michigan's oldest working lighthouse. (See Part Two of this guide, Beacons Lighting the Way for additional information.) Tours are available Friday through Monday 11:00 am to 5:00 pm (last tour begins at 4:00 pm), May through September, weather permitting.

Huron Lightship Museum, docked in Pine Grove Park, (810) 982-0891, *www.phmuseum.org*. When retired from active service in 1970, the Huron was the last lightship on the Great Lakes. (See Part Two of this guide for additional information.) Open seven days a week Memorial Day to Labor Day 11:00 am to 5:00 pm. Open September through December, and April through May, Thurs to Mon 11:00 am to 5:00 pm. Closed January through March.

The Knowlton Ice Museum, 1665 Yeager Street, at Water Street next door to the Hampton Inn, (off Exit 274 of I-94), (810) 987-5441, or (810) 984-3369.

This is an unexpected little treasure. You may be wondering how interesting an ice museum can be? You will be pleasantly surprised. It chronicles those earlier times when families had no refrigerator, but only an "ice" box. The museum contains a large collection of ice-industry artifacts, including its century-old ice delivery wagon. It also houses a large collection of classic photos documenting ice harvesting on the Black River in the late 1800s. It has a rare film of the ice business in the early 1920s showing an ice harvest in Wisconsin. If that was the extent of its exhibits, it would still be a worthwhile place to spend an hour, but the Knowlton Ice Museum also has a large license plate collection, antique vehicles, and surprisingly, a doll and baby buggy room – a little something for everyone. Open June to September, Thurs to Sat 1:00 pm to 4:00 pm. Tours by appointment all year.

Studio 1219, 1219 Military Street, (810) 984-ARTS, *www.studio1219.com*. Studio 1219 houses the largest public art gallery in Michigan's Thumb and is a cooperative of more than 150 artists who use the space to create art, share their visions, and also help run the gallery. This studio is unique in that it is an "arts incubator." Small retail shops are "incubated" to become successful, independent businesses that will eventually "graduate" into the Port Huron business community. Classes are offered year-round in the large upstairs classroom or in the Citizen's First Pottery Studio that is equipped with two electric and one gas kiln. The pottery studio also has a cooperative of potters and glass artists. The three main galleries are an impressive 1700 square feet with an additional 600 square feet in the Van Gogh Gallery. Every month the Van Gogh Gallery features a different artist or group of artists. The 130-year-old building has been renovated most recently from a furniture store and includes a second floor balcony that overlooks Mainstreet and the waterfront development of Desmond Landing. The retail stores are occupied by Artistic Images (portrait artist and art supplies), Oftbeat Percussion (ethnic percussion, accessories, music, instruction, and assorted gift items), K&F Photography (portrait photographer) and the Bluewater Musician Network (dealing in pre-owned musical instruments and music lessons). Major events at the studio include the Renaissance Roam in May, for which area homes are set up as galleries. The trolley takes visitors from one site to the next. The Themed Annual Fundraiser occurs every October and a Holiday Gallery in November and December offers beautiful and unique gifts. Space is available to rent for social events or gatherings. The gallery hours are Wed and Sun from noon to 5:00 pm and Thurs, Fri, and Sat from noon to 8:00 pm, and closed Mon and Tues.

Thomas Edison Depot Museum, just underneath the Blue Water Bridge on the Edison Parkway, (810) 982-0891, *www.phmuseum.org*. The Edison Depot Museum chronicles the life and history of Port Huron's most notable and perhaps favorite son. Thomas Edison spent his childhood years in Port Huron. The museum is housed in the Grand Trunk Western Railroad Fort Gratiot Depot, a

Thomas Edison Museum

building included on the National Register of Historic Places. Trains connecting at this depot carried people and freight between Port Huron and Detroit, Port Huron and Sarnia, and Port Huron and other destinations. In its time it was Port Huron's link to the greater world. Twelve-year-old Thomas departed the depot daily on the Port Huron to Detroit run and sold newspapers and snacks to finance his burgeoning quest for knowledge. Edison, who loved experimenting, marked all of the vials in his lab, "POISON," so no one would disturb them. The building was constructed in 1858 and became a major stop for immigrants. In 1881 more than seventy-seven thousand arrivals from other countries took their first steps into the United States here. The museum's exhibits demonstrate Edison's history of invention, family ties, the problems he had to overcome, and his ultimate triumph as one of the greatest – if not the greatest – inventor of his time. The museum has several hands-on, interactive displays and its own small theater. Open seven days a week, Memorial Day to Labor Day, 11:00 am to 5:00 pm, Thurs to Mon the rest of the year.

Antiques and Other Shopping

The two-block area of Huron Street (M-25) in downtown Port Huron still merits a bit of your time, although many local residents still mourn its loss of Sperry's and the Diana Sweet Shop from years gone by.

Backyard Soaps and More, 331 Huron Avenue (810) 985-SOAP, or toll-free (866) 985-SOAP, *www.backyardsoaps.com*. They claim fun never smelled so good. The clerks are friendly, helpful, and knowledgeable of the product and the store. Their product line is made on the premises, and you can see the production taking place in the back room. Products include: body scrubs, butters, lotions, lip balms, hand soaps, liquid soaps, room deodorizers, and more. They will create a gift basket for a special occasion or help you choose party favors for showers and other events.

Forget-Me-Not Paper Arts, 215 Huron Avenue, (810) 966-9664. Carries handmade greeting cards and a variety of paper goods. Offers classes in card making and other paper arts. Open Tues and Wed 11:00 am to 5:00 pm, Thurs 11:00 am to 7:00 pm and Fri and Sat 11:00 am to 5:00 pm.

Grand River Antiques, 411 Grand River Avenue (about a half block off the downtown shopping area), (810) 982-9400. Art, linens, mission-style furniture, pottery, stained glass, and miscellaneous antiques. Open Wed to Sat 11:00 am to 5:00 pm or by appointment.

Green Gable Antiques, 1507 Military Street (M-25), (810) 985-8397. Only a couple of blocks from the downtown shopping area, this gracious old home was built in the 1890s. The merchandise includes: mission, Victorian, art deco, stained and beveled glass and architectural pieces. Open summer Fri and Sat 10:00 am to 5:00 pm, Sun noon to 4:00 pm, or by appointment. The owners are in the process of adding a Victorian atrium which will offer ice cream, pastries, soups, salads, and sandwiches. There will also be dinner specials. The interior of the atrium will be from one-hundred-year-old salvaged architectural pieces.

The Irish Rose, 207 Huron Avenue, (810) 982-5487, *theirishroseco@prodigy. net*. This charming store carries a wide selection of linen and embroidered pieces. It claims to have the largest assortment of Irish merchandise in the area. It also carries a beautiful assortment of heavy knit sweaters in great colors and patterns. If you fall in love with Ireland while shopping here, they will even arrange a tour for you to visit the Emerald Isle through their travel business. Open Tues to Sat 10:00 am to 5:00 pm.

Karen's Kornucopia, 201 Huron Avenue, (810) 989-9858. New upscale resale and consignment shop in the heart of Mainstreet. Open Mon to Fri 10:00 am to 6:00 pm, Sat 10:00 am to 5:00 pm and by appointment on Sun.

Yesterday's Treasures, 4490 Lapeer Road, (810) 982-2100. Pocket watches, coins, and military items. Open Wed to Sat 10:30 am to 5:00 pm.

Shopping beyond Downtown Port Huron

The Big Red Barn Flea Market, 4189 Keewahdin Road. Originally a dairy barn, this flea market has been selling treasures for at least twenty years. You will find eggs and pies and a wide assortment of merchandise. It has about thirty venders and fall and winter Saturday nights offers auctions. Open Sat 10:00 am to 7:00 pm, Sun 10:00 am to 5:00 pm. Also has the Milkhouse Ice Cream and Coffee Shop open Wed to Fri 4:00 pm to 9:00 pm, Sat 10:00 am to 10:00 pm and Sun 10:00 am to 9:00 pm.

The Birchwood Mall on M-25 in Fort Gratiot. This is a typical mall, so not much more needs to be said. If you are looking for a relaxing trip filled with little pleasures, you are probably avoiding the mall experience. On the other hand, if you have a teenager eager to get to a mall, it is the only one you will find along the route. The stores are the typical collection, anchored by Younkers, Macy's,

International Flag Plaza

Target, Sears, and J.C. Penney's. There is a food court with a carousel.

Parks, Beaches and Campgrounds

International Flag Plaza, located under the Blue Water Bridge. It begins a river walkway and provides great views of the water traffic. The park honors those who respond to 911 calls in the United States and Canada.

KOA Campground of Port Huron, 5111 Lapeer Road, (Kimball) (810) 987-4070, *www.koa.com*. Features wooded RV and tent sites and 117 Kamping Kabins, 2 Kamping Kottages, and 6 lodges. Also has 7 playgrounds and 2 swimming pools.

Lakeside Park on Gratiot has a swimming beach, picnic tables, a nice playground area, and restrooms. Great place to watch the freighters and other water traffic.

Lighthouse Park, 3002 Conger, (at Gratiot). Provides a playground, swings, picnic area, sandy swimming beach, grills and restrooms. This is an interesting park because the Fort Gratiot Lighthouse is next door, and the Blue Water Bridge is in view. Like most of the parks in Port Huron/Fort Gratiot, it also has scenic views of the river's marine activity.

Lincoln Park at Electric and Military, between North and South Boulevard, is a favorite with those who like gardens. It is a lovely spot for a summer stroll. The park also gets winter use because its "natural bowl" provides a good place for sledding.

Pine Grove Park, 1204 Pine Grove, is described as one of the jewels of the Port Huron area, with its sweeping 1,500 feet of river view. It offers picnic areas, playground equipment, and shuffleboard courts. It is across the street from the Huron Lightship Museum.

Port Huron Township RV Park, 2301 Water Street, (810) 982-6765. One hundred thirty sites, close to town with flat, level sites and lots of grass. Small playground but not much for children to do. Most sites have sewer hookup. Laundry and clubhouse.

Water Sports, Marinas, Boat and Jet Ski Rentals

The City Marina, (810) 984-9745. Offers the largest marina facilities operated by a city in the state of Michigan. The slips, located at Quay and River Streets, are downtown and are used almost exclusively for transient boat traffic. They are open twenty-four/seven from May 1 to October 15. The City Marinas at other locations offer only seasonal service, and marina operations include two boat launch facilities on the Black River.

Dive Inn Watersports, 3858 24th Avenue, (810) 987-6263, *diveinn@advnet. net*. Offers scuba lessons for beginner through technical, and also instructor certification in their private indoor pool. They have dive charters during the summer months, and they have a large rental department. Open Mon to Fri 10:00 am to 6:00 pm, Sat 9:00 am to 3:00 pm, and closed Sun.

Fort Street Dock, Quay Street, offers twenty slips as well as electric and water dockside facilities. (See City Marina above.)

Municipal Marina, Water Street close to the I-94 ramp. Dockside facilities include electric, water, ice, laundry, restrooms, and showers.

River Street Marina, River Street at the end of Stone Street, behind St. Clair County Community College. This marina has ninety-five slips and dockside facilities including electricity, water, RV, charts, ice, restrooms, and showers. The location is close to downtown shopping and restaurants.

For additional Harbor information call the Port Huron Harbormaster at (810) 984-9745.

Other Things to See or Do

Blue Water Entertainment and Sports Dome, (also known as the Birchwood Sports Dome), 2851 Keewahdin Road, (810) 385-3663, *www.bwsportsdome. com*. Sports, entertainment, and fun for everyone. It aims to give visitors a wide variety of activities to share with their family. They offer a climbing wall, the largest arcade in Port Huron (still not very big), roller hockey, soccer, football, basketball, skating, and volleyball. You can leave children (generally not under ten years old and depending upon maturity) and maybe catch a quiet dinner while the kids are entertained. A five dollar pass will give you access to everything except the climbing wall (which is ten dollars).

Fort Gratiot Bike Path and Nature Trail, Access at Keewahdin Road Beach. Miles of paved pathways perfect for walking, biking and rollerblading. There are also several non-paved hiking tails throughout the marshland and a forty-acre preserve where you can watch swans, marsh hawks, geese, mallard ducks and other animals. A floating observation deck is located on the east side of the pond and is a great place to watch wildlife.

Great Lakes Maritime Center at Vantage Point, at the confluence of the Black and St. Clair Rivers, (810) 985-4817, *www.achesonventures.com* or *www. boatnerd.com.* Acheson Ventures is revitalizing and transforming a mile of waterfront property along the St. Clair River and working to improve the quality of life for residents of the area and create an interesting area for locals and travelers to visit. Previously this stretch was industrial property that failed to capitalize on the fabulous views. The current work is sponsored by Dr. James Acheson, a local philanthropist. At the south end of the property is the newly renovated Seaway Terminal, home of the tall ship *Highlander Sea* and the decommissioned *USCG Cutter Bramble.* The Great Lakes Maritime Center opened in 2006 and has a long wall of windows offering a clear view of river traffic. Inside the Coffee Harbor you will find a comfortable place to sit and enjoy a variety of coffees, soft drinks, deli sandwiches, and salads. Along the waterfront you can get fries at the French Fry Truck or a hand-dipped ice cream cone from the Ice Cream Trailer. There is a fishing pier and a promenade. The center offers a variety of activities and opportunities to learn about the maritime history of our spectacular Great Lakes. Information is provided through displays, speaker programs, and videos; *www.boatnerd.com* is the most widely used Web site for Great Lakes maritime information and GLMC is the world headquarters for the site. A live underwater camera feed lets you view activity under the surface of the St. Clair River and a live display of ship movements can be followed. There is an outside observation deck for sunny summer days or an inside viewing room for days when weather is less than optimal. You can even bring your fishing gear and see if you can catch dinner from the pier. Open daily, 6:00 am to 8:00 pm. (See Acheson Ventures below under cruises.)

Jim's Garage/Tourist Information Center, Corner of Griswold and Pine Grove. This restored Standard Oil Gas Station is a good place to see the historical display of Port Huron's South Side. Acheson Ventures has video cameras and monitors set up to allow visitors a view of marine traffic. Open weekends in the summer.

McMorran Tower, 701 McMorran Boulevard, (810) 985-6166, *www. mcmorran.com.* The tower was the last addition to the three-building complex that is the site for many local entertainment events. It was completed in October 1965. A climb up the 188 stairs to the observation deck (150 feet above the ground) allows you to survey the entire Port Huron area. You can view the double spans of the Blue Water Bridge and the surrounding city and countryside. You can see the Black River, and if you give free rein to your imagination, you can almost picture canoes and maybe even a Native American ceremonial meeting. For those with less vivid imaginations, it is interesting to pick out local landmarks from this high perch. Wear shoes with a good grip as the stone steps get slippery. In fact, the tower is open only in the summer because the moisture

The McMorran Tower

and snow of the winter make it too dangerous to climb. It is a very worthwhile exercise in more ways than one.

Port Huron Civic Theatre, *www.phct.com*, founded in 1956 as Port Huron Little Theatre, this ensemble does shows at McMorran Auditorium. Brad Rowell of Port Huron is the president of the group and can be contacted via e-mail at *bradphct@gmail.com* or called at (810) 984-4014 for current information.

Port Huron Trolley, (810) 987-7373. You might not be able to get a cup of coffee for a thin dime, but ten cents is all it will cost you to ride the Port Huron Trolley. The trolley will provide you with a unique tour, recapturing the past of public transit, and it will also give you an overview of many Blue Water Area sights. The tour lasts about an hour and is a real bargain. It takes you past forty points of interest including: the Huron Lightship, Old Fort Gratiot Trading Post, Thomas Edison Depot, McMorran Arena and Tower, the Museum of Arts and History, and many more. That is a deal and a half! The starting point for each run is downtown at 331 Huron Avenue. The trolley runs hourly from June to September, Mon to Sat 11:00 am to 4:00 pm, Fri to 5:00 pm.

Sawmill City, 5055 Lapeer Road, (5 miles from Port Huron, next to KOA camp), (810) 982-5090. A fun-park with go-carts, adventure golf, batting cages, paintball, bank-shot basketball, hippo wet/dry slide, giant jumping pillow and bumper-boats. Seasonal, opening in April.

Victorian Homes on Military. Driving north into Port Huron on M-25, between the Seaway Terminal and the Jim's Garage/Tourist Information Center, you will see many beautiful Victorian homes. Take time to enjoy them. A few that are noteworthy:

Green Gable Antiques

1501 and 1503 Military. This old house has been turned into rentals but retains much of its original charm.

1507 Military. Currently Green Gables Antiques. Since this Queen Anne style home has been turned into an antiques shop, you are afforded the opportunity to go inside. The house was constructed in 1893. It has an interesting history, serving as home to a former Speaker of the House of Representatives and a speakeasy – not at the same time of course.

1617 Military. The Lohrstorfer House. This is not a Victorian, but it is elegant nonetheless. It was built by Dr. Fred Lohrstorfer for his wife, Alice, who was apparently spoiled, rich, and ungrateful. She thought the home was below

The Lohrstorfer House

The Davidson House   **The Thompson House/The Castle**

the level of elegance that she deserved. The marriage failed and the Port Huron papers had ample fodder for many juicy stories out of the rather public divorce.

1623 Military. No history available but worth a look.

1707 Military. The Davidson House B&B. An 1888 Queen Anne style home with seven fireplaces as well as jeweled and leaded glass windows. This elegant home has loads of ornate woodwork and is listed on the National Register of Historic places.

1719 Military. The Castle, as it is called (in fact bears a small placard to that effect), is a monster three-story, also known as the Thompson House. It was built by Mr. John Thompson who made his money in the coal business. Construction began after Mr. Thompson returned from his honeymoon in France. He and his wife, Ida, lived in the castle with their only daughter Mary who was thrown a very splashy, society wedding in the home.

1723 Military. Currently used by United Way. Not an ornate Victorian but still an interesting old home.

1806 Military. This home features lots of bric-a-brac, a turret, leaded glass, and rounded-rooms common in Victorian architecture.

1905 Military. Lots of gingerbread, 2003 Yard-of-the-Year, and another home built in the Queen Anne style. The home was constructed in 1885 for a cost of $6000. For several years it was the Catholic League House, and is currently being restored by its owners.

1906 Military. This home was built in the 1890s and its earliest known resident was Charles Thompson, a furniture dealer. Like the other Victorians in this area it is built in the Queen Anne style.

1806 Military

1905 Military

1909 Military. Leaded glass and a great front porch are noted characteristics of this lovely old home. It was awarded the 2005 Yard-of-the-Year designation.

2015 Military. This house is called the Kathryn House but additional details are unavailable.

2037 Military. Another lovely home worth a look but for which there is, sadly, no historical information.

The Harrington Hotel at 1026 Military (just beyond the ornate Victorians). This was once the grandest hotel in Sanilac County. It is currently an assisted-living community.

Vinomondo Winery, 4505 Lakeshore Road, (810) 385-4062, *www. vinomondowinery.com*. This wine and beer making establishment is operated by Patrick and Jeanne Healy. They will be happy to explain their operation and give you a tour. Although you can buy wine and beer making supplies and become your own mini-brewery or vintner, it is easier and probably more fun to make your wine on the premises. You choose a grape product (juice) from Vinomondo's wide selection of grapes from around the world including: Australian Shiraz, Chilean Merlot, Italian Pinot Grigio, South African Pinotage, and California Stag's Leap Merlot, and many more. Making your own wine at Vinomondo is not a time consuming operation. It takes only a few minutes on the initial visit and maybe a half-hour when your product is ready for bottling about six to eight weeks later. The finished product can be labeled with your name and any kind of artwork you want. Part of the fun is having your own personal wine for special occasions like weddings and anniversaries. You can turn your wine-making experience into a festive occasion; Vinomondo welcomes small groups of up to ten people for wine tasting with light appetizers, so you can sample wines before deciding which type you wish to make. There is a charge for the wine tasting, but it can be applied to the cost of your batch. One of the benefits of making your own wine is that you will use far less sulphate than commercial vineyards. This is important to anyone who suffers sulphate headaches. If you are coming to the Thumb from a considerable distance, you will have to commit to making two trips, but that is to your advantage; it merely gives you more time to explore other Thumb attractions. Open Tues to Sat 11:00 am to 6:00 pm or by appointment for wine tasting.

Wadhams to Avoca Trail. Access the trail from I-69 Wadhams Road Exit, (Wadhams to Lapeer then left on Barlett). The trail is open year round. The Mill Creek Trestle is the showpiece of the trail. There are four overlooks that provide breathtaking views and a perfect place for picnicking. Take your camera. The trail is ten feet wide and approximately 2.75 miles of the trail (starting at Barlett Road and ending at McLain Road) are paved. It is a great place for running, cycling, and in-line skating. The remainder of the trail (non-paved portion) is about 7 miles and is surfaced with either limestone or gravel. Mileage markers are located every half-mile of the walkway.

Cruises and Ferries

Acheson Ventures Highlander Sea, (810) 966-0900, *www.achesonventures. com*. Acheson Venture's tall-ship *Highlander Sea* is a 154-foot, gaff-rigged topsail schooner. When she is in port you can view her from the deck of the Seaway Terminal. The vessel offers overnight cruises and some day cruises. Acheson Ventures is dedicated to showcasing the marine history and lore of Port Huron and the Great Lakes. They are also offering a variety of activities at the Great Lakes Maritime Center at Vantage Point. See www.*boatnerd.com* for additional details.

Huron Lady II, (810) 984-1500, *www.huronlady.com.* Just before the drawbridge in downtown Port Huron, (driving north on M-25), you will see a sign for the *Huron Lady.* Daily, seasonal, narrated, sightseeing cruises, as well as romantic sunset and moonlight cruises. You can also charter the *Huron Lady* for special events. It is wise to call for reservations.

Seaway Terminal, located on M-25 along the St. Clair River, as you enter Port Huron from the south. This is the place to pull in and collect your thoughts, as well as review your tourist information, and check out the ships offering tours. The Coast Guard Cutter Bramble Museum is docked about a half block away. There is also an activity board that will allow you to see what trips and special events are currently being offered by Acheson Ventures. Check the Web site at *www.achesonventures.com.*

Festivals

• Antique Yard Sale Trail, August. Trail from New Baltimore to Sebewaing. This is the big one if you like monster garage sales. M-25 will be crowded to capacity.

• Be a Tourist in your Town, July. Offers a tour map and lots of places to visit free.

• Blue Water Indian Celebration Pow Wow, August. Pine Grove Park.

• Carnival, July. South McMorran parking lot.

• Port Huron to Mackinac Sailboat Race, July. This is *the* big sailboat race of the season, drawing thousands of boaters and even more spectators.

• Southside Blues and Jazz Fest, July.

• Port Huron Historic Home Tour, September. Allows you to get inside some of the lovely old homes.

• Studio Tour, usually in October. This is a cooperative effort between Sarnia and Port Huron to open their studios to visitors.

Call the Blue Water Area Convention and Visitors Center for additional information and to confirm dates (800) 852-4242 .

Golf

Black River Golf Course, 3300 Country Club Drive, (810) 982-5251, *www. blackrivergolfclub.com.* Open to the public, this 18-hole, USGA nationally ranked golf course has a 300 yard driving range and short-game facility. Scenic views and a pro shop. Special golf/hotel packages available.

Fore Lakes Golf Course, 5810 Flinchbaugh Road, (eight miles or fifteen minutes from downtown Port Huron), (810) 982-3673, *www.forelakes.com.* This is a par 71 championship design with water holes. Modest prices. Public welcome.

Willow Ridge Golf Course, 3311 North River Road (one mile west of Pine Grove), (810) 982-7010. 9-hole course with Bogey's Bar and Grill and pro shop. The public is welcome.

Contacts

The Blue Water Area Convention and Visitors Bureau, (800) 852-4242, *www.bluewater.org*.

Blue Water Trolley, (810) 987-7373.

City of Port Huron Marinas, (810) 984-9745.

Greater Port Huron Chamber of Commerce, 920 Pine Grove Avenue, (810) 985-7101, or toll-free (800) 361-0526, *www.porthuron-chamber.org*, e-mail at *info@porthuron-chamber.org*.

Museum Information, (810) 982-0891, *www.phmuseum.org*.

The Port Huron Civic Theatre, (810) 984-4014.

For additional information on current activities in Port Huron, search the Web at *www.porthuron.org*.

Sarnia/Point Edward, Canada

Population: Sarnia 71,419; Point Edward 2019.

Directions:

Take the Blue Water Bridge from Port Huron across the St. Clair River.

Background and History

Sarnia is located at the north end of the St. Clair River where it connects to Lake Huron in southwestern Ontario. It is the largest Canadian city on Lake Huron. Because of the fast-flowing water leaving Lake Huron, French Explorer LaSalle originally named it "Les Rapids" or "The Rapids." LaSalle was drawn to the site by Sarnia's natural harbor that proved of great value in trade.

English settlers wanted to call Sarnia 'Buenos Ayres'. The Scottish settlers preferred the name 'New Glasgow'. The current name Sarnia comes from the Latin word for Guernsey. The city was named for the channel island of that same name. Guernsey Island is situated fourteen miles from the coast of France and is one of the smaller islands in the English Channel. It is one-hundred miles south of mainland Britain, and is famous for its production of Guernsey cattle. This particular breed is prized for its docility, hardiness and milk production. Many farms in Michigan's Thumb kept a dairy barn full of Guernsey, and you can be fairly confident they did likewise in Ontario.

Sarnia shares with Port Huron a spectacular view of the twin Blue Water Bridges. The bridges are the international gateway to Ontario from Michigan's Thumb. On a good traffic day, you can cross the bridge in minutes.

When the bridge added its second span in 1997, the Canadian land around the bridge site was carefully excavated. Many artifacts were found highlighting the Native American history of the area. Carved bird stones and ancient pottery pieces were discovered. The site is considered one of the most important archeological digs in North America.

The cities of Sarnia and Port Huron were connected by the railway tunnel even prior to the opening of the Blue Water Bridge. Sarnia is located on the Grand Trunk Railway and railway commerce is extremely important to its economic prosperity. It is also a port-of-call for freighters navigating the Great Lakes with their cargoes of ore, grain, and petroleum products. The city received a major growth spurt with the discovery of oil at nearby Petrolia.

Sarnia's beaches are major tourist stops. The two-hundred-fifty-mile Mackinac Sailboat Race starts in the waters between Port Huron and Sarnia. The race has been the highlight of the sailing season since 1925 and currently draws more than three thousand sailors a year.

James Doohan, "Scotty" on Star Trek, was born in Sarnia, as was Mike Weir, winner of the 2003 Golfing Masters. Sarnia has also been home to composers, actors, authors, film directors, and several NHL ice hockey stars.

Michael Moore shot scenes for his documentary, *Bowling for Columbine* in Sarnia, and he interviewed local residents outside the Taco Bell. Sarnia's mayor made him an honorary citizen, so it seems politicians on the Canadian side of the bridge liked the film more than some of our United States politicians did!

Two other films were shot partially in Sarnia: *Renaissance Man* with Danny Devito and *Bless the Child* starring Kim Basinger.

Until 2003, Sarnia held the honor of being the "Kissing Capital of the World," but in that year it lost the title to Santiago, Chile. So much for romance!

Point Edward is a village adjacent to and pretty much swallowed up by Sarnia, although residents fiercely protect their separateness. For reference purposes, Point Edward seems to be an extension of Sarnia, just as Fort Gratiot is often loosely referred to as Port Huron. When you cross the Blue Water Bridge to Sarnia, you are technically disembarking in Point Edward. Point Edward was founded in 1878, and named for Prince Edward.

Perhaps Point Edward's most interesting claim to fame is that it was a summer vacation spot for Al Capone, or so several local residents claimed.

You will find the Ontario Information Centre just off Highway 402 at the border (where you get off the bridge). It has a rock garden with seven sculptured Canadian geese landing into cascading water pools. It also has a terrific gift shop, Legends, worthy of a bit of your time.

You can spend several hours or several days exploring Sarnia's antiques shops, galleries, museums, and parks. You absolutely cannot miss the Stones 'N Bones Museum as it is one of the most fascinating places you will explore during your travels.

Ontario Travel Information Centre

You will find plenty of spots to grab a quick bite or enjoy a leisurely, upscale dinner. A local summer tradition is buying French fries from one of the several "chip trucks" under the Blue Water Bridge and eating them as you walk the waterfront.

It is all just a few minutes from Port Huron. **Take your passport**. In the past a driver's license has been sufficient ID for Canadian travel but that will soon change, possibly by the time this guide is published.

NOTE: For the interested traveler, there are also many enticing tourist attractions beyond Sarnia/Point Edward. There are wonderful theatres in Stratford and a smaller theatre in Petrolia. Further north along the Canadian shore, you will find Pinery Provincial Park, Grand Bend, Bayport, and miles of beaches. Those are wonderful places to visit, but this book is limited to Michigan's Thumb, and because of its proximity and accessibility for an easy day trip, the shore of Canada along the St. Clair River.

Food/Restaurants

Alternate Grounds Café, 410 Front Street, (519) 344-2228. Conveniently located across from Centennial Park. Offering meal-size salads as well as organic vegetarian soups, great wraps, and sandwiches for lunch each day. The main features, though, are the fresh roasted and organically grown teas and coffees. They sell coffee beans by the pound for home brewing. In addition to daily omelets and breakfast wraps, you can also enjoy a special Sunday brunch featuring such entrees as the Cinnamon Fruit Medley, a buttered cinnamon tortilla with fresh assorted fruit and yogurt or whipped cream. Sunday brunch from 9:00 am to 2:00 pm. Open seven days, Mon to Fri 8:00 am to 9:00 pm, Sat 8:00 am to 6:00 pm and Sun 9:00 am to 4:00 pm.

Blackwater Coffee and Tea Co, 170 Christina Street North, (519) 337-9056. You select your beans and choose your roast, and they make your cup of coffee. The coffee shop has computers available and the walls are lined with books, but the coffee aroma is the most important part of the ambiance. Enjoy your coffee with bagels, sandwiches, soups, and salads. When you are ready to leave you can purchase a pound of your favorite beans to take with you. Open Mon to Thurs 7:00 am to 8:00 pm, Fri 7:00 am to midnight, Sat 8:00 am to midnight and closed Sun.

Boathouse Restaurant and Patio at the OLG Casinos Point Edward (See below under Casinos).

Coffee Culture Café and Eatery, 130 Lochiel Street (corner of Front). A bit of explanation: this is the location of the former *New Trish In Edition*, which was in the process of moving to Christina Street when this book went to press. The Coffee Culture Café was in the process of opening up in the delightful building that formerly housed New Trish In Edition. Both are likely worth consideration but no firm details as of yet.

Degroot's Teahouse, 1840 London Road (located at DeGroots Nursery), (519) 542-7260, *www.degroots.ca*. If you are going to be in the area, this old farmhouse with four dining rooms and an outside deck is worth considering for lunch. They have daily fresh soups with hot-out-of-the-oven scones, or you might want to consider the warm Steak Salad with Snow Peas, Sautéed Mushrooms and Blue Cheese. The selection of teas, including flowering or blooming teas, is definitely worth a look. Open Mon to Sat 10:00 am to 3:00 pm.

Firenze's Pizza, 850 Colborne, (519) 337-7546. Described by local residents as the best place for pizza in Sarnia; Firenze's takes its pizza seriously.

La Dolce Vita Restaurant, 493 Christina Street North, (519) 344-3713. *La Dolce Vita* is Italian for "The Sweet Life," and according to locals who rave about the awesome pasta, the food here certainly sweetens their lives. Perhaps having a chef trained in Rome is the reason this authentic Italian cuisine is considered the best in Sarnia. You will never leave hungry and the prices are reasonable. Start with a platter of Mussels Marinara and move on to Tortellini Dolce Vita or Spaghetti Ametriciani. Most nights it is a good idea to make reservations because it is a tiny restaurant with a large following. Open Mon to Wed 4:00 pm to 10:30 pm, Thurs and Fri 11:00 am to 10:30 pm (serves both lunch and dinner), and Sat 4:00 pm to 10:30 pm.

Lola's Lounge, 100 Christina Street South, (519) 336-8088. The "IN" place to eat in Sarnia. Everyone rates this place "excellent." To really impress someone, suggest they order the rack of lamb. The menu is varied and you will likely agree, this restaurant is a cut above the average restaurant competing for your dining dollar. The ambiance is described as "funky but welcoming." It just may be worth driving over the bridge for no other reason than to eat here. Open Mon to Thurs 10:00 am to 10:00 pm, Fri and Sat 11:00 am to midnight, Sun 5:00 pm until the dinner crowd is finished.

Mama Rosa's, at Centennial Park on the waterfront. From Lola's to Mama Rosa's is a big jump. This is an absolutely no frills, inexpensive dining establishment with a view of the river. The lasagna is very good. It is not a bad place to have lunch or dinner when you are spending the day at the park.

Monet's, 751 Christina Street North, Point Edward, (located in the Village Inn), (519) 344-1157, or toll-free (800) 669-7907, *www.villageinnsarnia.com*. Creative cuisine in a pleasant, casually-classic setting. The salmon, caramelized and perfectly baked with curried cream and nestled over parmesan garlic risotto, may have your name on it. On the pricey side for what you get. Open Mon to Fri 6:30 am to 10:00 pm, Sat 8:00 am to 10:00 pm, Sun 8:00 am to 2:00 pm.

Olives Casual Cuisine, 1591 London Road, (519) 541-1333. Olive Archibald, who used to run the Garden Teahouse at DeGroots Nursery, has moved on and opened her own place. She is getting compliments from everyone who has eaten there. One customer gushed, "It's only been open for a month and I've eaten here four times already." Great salads, desserts, and specialty drinks. A variety of grilled wraps for lunch (Thai Chicken, Falafel, Canadian Clubhouse, and more) or the customer-recommended Crab Quiche or Stuffed Chicken. Dinner entrees include Seafood Paella or Atlantic Char served with a Maple Blueberry Sauce. Open lunch Mon to Fri 11:30 am to 2:00 pm and dinner Mon to Sat 5:00 pm to 11:00 pm. Closed Sun.

On The Front, 201 Front Street North, 14th floor, (519) 332-4455, *www. onthefront.com*. After you get off the elevator, you will have to turn to your right and ascend a flight of steps, which means this restaurant is not wheelchair accessible. On the Front is upscale with the best views of the water you can find anywhere. The menu is a pleasure to peruse and you should consider either the rabbit or the duck; both are excellent. On the Front serves lunch and dinner, but the luncheon menu is about half the price of the dinner menu. The entrees are not the same, but the grilled salmon and Israeli couscous with an apple pear chutney and curry butter, sounded fabulous for $12. The interior décor is simple, but it is the view that make this restaurant special.

The Open Grill, 721 Lite Street, Point Edward, (519) 336-5221. Known for their steaks and, after 4:00 pm, their tender prime rib. Salad bar, seafood, daily lunch and dinner specials. Friendly staff. Open Mon to Thurs 11:00 am to 9:00 pm, Fri 11:00 am to 10:00 pm, Sat 10:00 to 10:00 pm and Sun 10:00 am to 9:00 pm.

Paddy Flaherty's Irish Pub, 130 Seaway Road, (519) 336-1999, *www. sarnia.paddyflahertys.com*. This Irish pub's signature dish is its palate pleasing Guinness Steak and Mushroom Crock. Open Sun to Tues 11:00 am to 11:00 pm, Wed 11:00 am to midnight, Thurs to Sat 11:00 am to 2:00 am.

Salvatore's Trattoria and Ristorante, 105 Michigan Avenue, Point Edward, (519) 344-2855. This unpretentious eatery offers good, hearty, filling food at reasonable prices, and is another favorite of locals. You are advised to have reservations because customers without them often have to be turned away. The Vela Rosa; a ricotta and spinach filled pasta with cream and pomodoro sauce, is excellent. Open Mon to Sat 11:00 am to 9:30 pm.

Stoke's Bay, 485 Harbour Road, across from Centennial Park, (519) 337-8466, *www.stokesbaysarnia.com*. Casual ambiance with great baby back ribs. If you still have room after your main course, go for the deep-fried banana split. Open 11:00 am to 2:00 am daily.

Ups N' Downs, 226 Front Street North, (519) 336-0337, *www.upsndowns. net*. This bar has the feel of a local "Cheers" with good food and good friends. One customer said he always gets the fish and chips, and they are the best anywhere. Also consider the Steak and Kidney Pie. For an appetizer that is definitely large enough to share, try the Pub Combo which includes chicken wings, potato skins, onion rings, garlic cheese bread, breaded cheese and broccoli, gouda sticks, and veggies with dip. Live entertainment Fri to Sun after 9:00 pm. Open seven days 11:00 am to 2:00 am.

Waggs Steak and Seafood Restaurant, 420 Christina Street North, (519) 344-4422. Next door to the Super 8, this restaurant's house specialty is its roast prime rib of beef for which they use only Canadian Red Brand Beef. The super cut is 16 to 18 oz. They offer both a lunch and dinner menu. Open Mon to Thurs 11:00 am to 9:30 pm, Fri 11:00 am to 10:00 pm, Sat 4:00 pm to 10:00 pm and Sun 4:00 pm to 9:00 pm.

Lodging

Best Western Guildwood Inn, 1400 Venetian Boulevard, Point Edward, (519) 337-7577, or toll-free (877) 871-0423, *www.guildwoodinn.com*. Has ninety-five rooms Open year round. Extras: outdoor pool, fitness room on site, Mon to Fri continental breakfast and free newspaper, Internet, and movies. Just a short walk to the OLG Casino Point Edward.

Bluewater Motel, 1626 London Line, (519) 542-5535 or toll-free (800) 575-4682, *www.bluewatermotel.ca*, *bluewater@ebtech.net*. This is not a luxury motel and it is a bit out of the way, but if you are looking for clean and less expensive than its richer downtown cousins, you can try the Bluewater Motel. Extras: outdoor pool, free local calls, air-conditioning, and some rooms with kitchenettes.

Comfort Inn, 815 Mara Street, (519) 383-6767, or toll-free (800) 4-CHOICE, *www.choicehotels.ca/cn673*. Extras: recently renovated, free high speed wireless, fitness room, game room, 100% satisfaction guarantee, free local calls, complimentary continental breakfast, complimentary 24 hour tea and coffee.

Drawbridge Inn, 283 Christina Street North, (519) 337-7571, or toll-free (800) 663-0376. The rooms rates are less expensive than the standard rates at other major hotels and motels and seemed to be on a par with the others when comparing size and amenities. There is a heated indoor pool, and if you are seeking some extra pampering, North Shore Fitness & Day Spa is located on-site.

The Harbourfront Inn, 505 Harbour Road, (519) 337-5434, or toll-free (800) 787-5010, *www.sarnia.com/harbour*. Open all year, 102 rooms. On the waterfront and Stay and Play packages available.

Holiday Inn Sarnia/Point Edward, 1498 Venetian Boulevard, Point Edward, at the foot of the Blue Water Bridge, (519) 336-4130, or toll-free (888) 212-2252, *www.holiday-inn.com/sarniaon*. Has 217 guest rooms. Extras: high speed Internet, sauna, whirlpool, indoor and outdoor pools, fitness center, 9 hole par 3 golf course.

Super 8 Motel, 420 Christina Street North, toll-free direct (866) 337-3760 or (800) 800-8000, *manager@super8sarnia.com*. Open all year, forty rooms. Seemed a bit pricey for a Super 8 but still considered economy when compared to some of the other motels in the area. High-speed Internet, in room movies, SuperStart breakfast. According to one museum curator, the Super 8 is built on the site of the old courthouse and also the spot where the condemned were hanged.

Whether true or not, it is interesting. Regardless of the past, there are apparently no ghosts haunting the site, and you should have no fear staying there.

Village Inn, 751 Christina Street North, (519) 344-1157, or toll-free (800) 669-7907, *www.villageinnsarnia.com.* Bills itself as offering affordable elegance and that pretty much hits the mark. Open all year, forty-eight rooms. Extras: fitness center, free high speed Internet, free local calls, Jacuzzi suites available.

Museums

Sarnia Historical Museum, 137 Davis Street, (519) 336-4238, *sarhistory@ rivernet.net.* A tiny museum housing historical artifacts from the city of Sarnia. It provides an in-depth look at the Sarnia-Lambton area through its display of documents, photographs, and paintings. Open June to Labor Day Mon to Fri 9:00 am to 5:00 pm and off-season by appointment.

Stones 'N Bones Museum, 223 Christina Street North, (519) 336-2100, *www.stonesnbones.ca*, *stonesnbones@ebtech.net.* THIS IS A DO-NOT-MISS ATTRACTION, and you would never know it from the outside. Owners Jim and Allison have created a wonderful, educational and enjoyable adventure for folks of all ages. Located in the heart of the city with 10,000 square feet of Indian artifacts, stones, shells, minerals, gemstones, butterflies, and fossils, it is much larger and more fascinating that its humble exterior would suggest. The first diorama you will encounter includes a 600-pound black bear, as well as a kodiak, grizzly and even a rare blonde grizzly bear. The museum offers eleven galleries where you will view the rare and unusual: an 1891 passenger pigeon (the species is now extinct), a nest of ten hadrosaur eggs, elephant beetles big enough to eat small children, the skeletal remains of a duckbill dinosaur, teeth from a T-Rex, the jaw of a great white shark estimated from the jaw size to have been about twenty-two feet long, butterflies that have a secret, and a five-and-a-half-foot moose rack. That is just the beginning. As one astute five-year-old said, "It should be called Stones 'N Bones and everything else." You will see it all with a tour guide who is guaranteed to make the experience memorable. There is an amazing gift shop on the premises where you will be tempted by the amber and ammolite (Canada's gemstone), jewelry, fossils, butterflies, books, and nautical items. Stones 'n Bones offers this disclaimer: *"Exposure to this museum atmosphere will aggravate the self-fulfilling need to learn. When the museum is closed, temporary relief may be found at a local book store or community library."* Open March to December Thurs to Sun and holiday Mondays, 10:00 am to 5:00 pm. Open daily in July and August.

Galleries, Studios and Crafts

Ah Some Art Inc. Gallery, 112½ Michigan Avenue, Point Edward, (519) 336-6770. This fascinating gallery is neatly tucked behind the Sharkskin Shop. It is across the street and a few doors down from Salvatore's Restaurant. You need to look closely or you will go by it. The main draw is its tremendous variety and selection of artful objects. It offers creative pieces by Canadian artisans from coast to coast. Its jewelry is lovely, but it also features leather, pottery, stone, glass, metal, wood, greeting cards, funky home accents and paintings. Open Mon to Sat 10:00 am to 5:30 pm, Sun noon to 4:00 pm in the summer.

Alcove Gift and Art Gallery, 145 Christina Street South (at Wellington Street), (519) 332-8644, or toll-free (877) 332-8644, *www.alcovegallery.com*. Offers original and limited editions of a wide array of fine art and collectibles. Also has a nice selection of giftware, sculptures, blown glass, and handicrafts from various cultures. Objects of pewter, aluminum, pottery, and whimsical items round out the merchandise from around the world. The unique variety of artwork fills seven rooms. Open Mon to Fri 9:00 am to 9:30 pm, Sat 9:00 am to 5:00 pm.

Artopia Gallery, 276 Wellington Street, (519) 332-0278, *www. iknowaguycanada.com*, *artopia@ebtech.net*. The gallery displays original art work of artists from all corners of Canada including Toronto and Vancouver but also from other countries including South Africa. It has a collection of vintage photos, pottery, handmade jewelry, glasswork, and an assortment of eclectic gifts among its merchandise. The gallery is located in an architecturally interesting old house a short way from the downtown tourist area. Open Mon to Sat 10:00 am to 5:30 pm.

Bear Creek Studio, 150 Christina Street North, (Bayside Mall), (519) 337-5665, *www.bearcreekstudio.ca*. Features original oil and acrylic paintings as well as watercolors. Unique ceramics and gift items from Canada and around the world. Also offers a wide selection of art supplies, clothing, cards, and home accents. Open Mon, Tues, Wed, and Sat 9:30 am to 6:00 pm, Thurs and Fri 9:30 am to 7:00 pm, and closed Sun.

Energy Exchange, 192 Christina Street North, (519) 464-6544. Blending local art and ecology. Limited commissioned artwork displayed. Products, such as corkboards, made from reclaimed materials available as well as native teas. Open Tues to Sat noon to 5:00 pm, closed Sun and Mon.

Gallery in the Grove, 2700 Hamilton Road, Bright's Grove (a few miles beyond Sarnia, just north of Point Edward), (519) 869-4643, *www. galleryinthegrove.com*. The gallery is in the historic 1875 Faethorne House, nestled into Wildwood Park, making it a nice stop on a trip along Lake Huron. It is volunteer-operated and nonprofit. It hosts nine exhibits per year and promotes visual artists. The gallery also awards scholarships annually and offers rotating exhibits of local artists. Closed July, August, and December. Open Mon to Thurs 2:30 pm to 8:00 pm, Sat and Sun 1:00 pm to 3:00 pm.

Gallery Lambton, 150 Christina Street North (Bayside Mall), (519) 336-8127. This is Sarnia's public art gallery and it offers tours, classes, bus trips, and a gift shop, in addition to its art exhibits. It also has an outstanding collection of Canadian paintings, sculptures, and works on paper. Their permanent collection consists of more than one thousand works including about forty works from the Group of Seven. All works are relevant to Canadian cultural heritage and date from the early nineteenth century to the present. The gallery features video presentations at noon during the fall and winter. It offers many other interesting programs you can check out while you are in town. For example: "Dinner and a Movie" sounds like a pleasant way to spend an evening. Open Mon to Sat 10:00 am to 5:30 pm.

Lawrence House Center for the Arts and Sarnia-Lambton Arts Council Showcase, *www.lawrencehouse.ca* and *www.sarnia.com/groups/artscouncil*. Both the Center and Council Showcase are located at 127 South Christina Street.

The Center for the Arts, (519) 337-0507, encourages the creation and appreciation of visual, performing and literary arts. Lawrence House features public art displays, and a variety of programs to appeal to visitors of all ages. Lawrence House Centre for the Arts also offers a concert series and many other programs. The Center for the Arts is open Mon to Sat 10:00 am to 4:00 pm and may be open additional hours for specific exhibits and programs. Call for information.

The Showcase, (519) 344-2787, has a gift shop with unusual merchandise created by Sarnia-Lambton artists, painters and sculptors. You will find pottery, photographs, sculptures, fabric art, woodcarving, prints, ink drawings, birdhouses, notes and cards, and paintings. The Showcase is open Mon to Sat 10:00 am to 4:00 pm.

The building housing the Showcase and Center for the Arts is definitely worth a bit of your time. It is a lovely old Victorian House originally built by William Lawrence, but deserted in 1940. It has all of the beautiful adornments you would expect of an elegant Victorian. Apparently William's wife died, and the family abandoned the home, dishes still in the sink. Mr. and Mrs. Lawrence had three sons, and the youngest, Carrol, gave the house to the city of Sarnia. In May 1982, renovations started, but were put on hold after an arsonist tried to burn the lovely old house. Eventually, Suncor provided additional funding for renovations. The house has served as the audio visual center for the Sarnia Library, which is directly across the street. Up the elegant stairway, on the second floor, is a turret, which holds a Grand Piano that can be rented for concerts or by individuals who just want the joy of playing for an hour or two. (See Part Two of this guide for a ghost story related to this building).

Ojibwe Legends, 1455 Venetian Boulevard, Point Edward, (519) 337-7741, *www.ojibwelegends.com, jgrexton@aamjiwnaang.ca*. It is located in the new Ontario Travel and Tourism Centre, the first exit after you get off the Blue Water Bridge. Authentic Aboriginal artistic traditions of Canada's woodland peoples. This is a marvelous place filled with quality handmade items from Native American communities in the United States and Canada, with a focus on

Ojibwe arts and crafts. It is a stop you may want to make for additional tourist information, but take the time while you are there to check out this special shop. In fact, if you are looking for galleries, it is worth the stop even if you do not need any additional tourist information. Open seven days a week.

Antiques and Other Shopping

Bayside Mall, 150 Christina Street North, (519) 336-6012. This was an unusual shopping experience. If you enter through the mall doors closest to the Lambton Gallery, you will find yourself in a half-deserted building which appears to be a cross between a government complex of service agencies and a shopping mall. There is a welcome booth, a senior center, a beauty salon, United Way, some fast food restaurants, and Beanzz for coffee and light food. Down another wing there are a few retail establishments including clothing stores, a shoe store, and a couple of galleries. It generally seemed an odd assortment of establishments to be clustered together. The Gallery Lambton is described separately, but it was what made the stop worthwhile.

Blue Water Bridge Duty Free Shop, 2 Bridge Street (At the foot of the Blue Water Bridge as you prepare to drive into the United States), (800) 395-7672, *www.bridgedutyfree.com*. This is a "must stop" on the way back into the United States. If you like Swiss chocolates, any brand of alcohol that is imported into the U.S., or a special perfume, you can save up to 60%. Select and purchase gift items, leathers, and toys without the import tax. The clerks will tell you the limits on the purchase of any item. For example, you are limited to one bottle of liquor per adult in the car after a required Canadian stay, but it is a great place to purchase gin or vodka for your summer parties. There is a coffee shop on premises.

Duty-free appears to have the best exchange rate for leaving your Canadian money behind. Jot down your license plate number before you go inside because they will ask for it. Open twenty-four hours a day, seven days a week.

Feather Your Nest, 138 Front Street North, (519) 336-1617, *www. featheryournest.ca*, *info@featheryournest.ca*. The place to find lovely linens, gift baskets, gourmet foods, kitchen ware, and other self indulgent treats. Open Tues to Sat 10:00 am to 5:30 pm and the first Fri of each month open to 9:00 pm.

Grace Brothers Antiques, 156 Front Street North, (519) 332-4293, *gracebrothersantiques@ebtech.net*. An eclectic assortment of antiques and other unusual items. Recently opened an art gallery on the second floor. Open Tues to Sat 11:00 am to 5:00 pm, Sun noon to 4:00 pm.

Harbour Bay Clothing and Gifts, 214 Front Street North, (519) 344-7712. Men and women's weekend, business, and casual clothing. Jewelry and accessories, and now a wide selection of gifts and home accents. Open Mon to Fri 9:30 am to 5:30 pm, Sat 9:30 am to 5:00 pm, and Sun seasonal from mid-May through December noon to 4:00 pm.

Hutchinson's Antiques and Quality Furniture, 172 Front Street North, (519) 337-8178, *hutchinsonantiques@sympatico.ca*. One of many antiques shops along Front Street. If you are inclined to spend an afternoon antiquing, then Front Street across from Centennial Park in the Riverfront District is the place to get started. Open Mon to Fri 10:00 am to 6:00 pm, Sun 11:00 am to 6:00 pm.

Ieteke, 148 Front Street North, (519) 344-5799. Carries a selection of classic and twentieth century pieces as well as other antiques. Open Tues to Sat 10:00 am to 5:00 pm.

Lambton Mall, 1380 London Road, (519) 542-7784, *www.lambtonmall. com*. It would be hard to differentiate this mall from any of its sister malls in the United States. The anchor stores were Toys-R-Us, Sears, and Canadian Tire. Many of the smaller stores carried the same names as their counterparts in the United States and others looked vaguely familiar, but with a different name. In the parking lot of the mall was the Beer Store, which carries no hard alcohol or wine – just beer. It displays cans of the beers they carry, and you place an order. Your case is put on a conveyer in the warehouse and brought to you. They also have refillable beer bottles to help save the environment. Unless for some reason you need the mall experience, you will not likely head for the Lambton Mall.

Mandarin Arts, 150 Christina Street North (Bayside Mall), (519) 332-1322. They advertise gifts from the four corners of the world (okay, so there literally cannot be corners to a globe, but you get the picture). They carry furniture, linens, clothing, jewelry, and accents of all kinds. Open Mon to Fri 9:30 am to 6:00 pm and Sat 9:30 am to 5:00 pm, closed Sun.

Mitton Village. The Mitton Village Association is a group of business owners working together to provide support and services to the retailers in this area. Mitton Village has a Jazz Festival and other social activities, and you can check for details with the Sarnia Chamber of Commerce listed at the end of this section for additional details. Kitchen Widgits is a wonderful store and worth checking. The Mitton Village stores are listed together below:

• The Farm Market and Marketplace Restaurant just around the corner from Mitton on Ontario Boulevard. A place to buy locally grown farm products and produce. It is open Wed and Sat, but if you want good selection, be there by 6:30 or 7:00 am. By 1:00 pm they will be pretty much sold out.

• Kitchen Widgets, 129 Mitton Street South, (519) 332-0880, e-mail: *widgets@ebtech.net*. Houseware-Retailer-of-the-Year 1999. Knives by Mac, Kasumi, J.A. Henckels and Trident. Gourmet foods including the popular Wildly Delicious bread dipping oil. They also sell salmon from Alaska and an extensive collection of bar equipment. The owner described it as "a hardware store for the kitchen." Definitely an interesting shop. Open Mon to Fri 9:30 am to 5:30 pm, Sat 9:30 am to 4:00 pm. Closed Sun. Open seven days a week in December – just in case you plan to do a bit of Christmas shopping there.

• Macklin's Flowers and Anne Tiques, 108 Mitton Street South, *www. macklinsflowers.com*. In addition to being a flower shop they have a nice selection of antiques. Open Mon to Fri 9:30 am to 5:30 pm, Sat 9:00 am to 4:00 pm.

Presents Home and Garden Accents, 186 Front Street North, (519) 337-4871. This store has an interesting assortment of merchandise beyond items for your garden, making it worth a look-see while you are out strolling Front Street. Lots of custom signs. Open year round, generally 10:00 am to 5:00 pm, closed Sun.

Uptown Boutique and Sarnia's Flea Market, 100 Christina Street, (519) 339-9739. The uptown market is a group of small shops or businesses that sell antiques, new furniture, collectibles, hand crafted items, art, and retro. You will find Cowboys and Indians (Trading Post) and Needful Things (imported antiques) among your options. The Market Café offers a place to grab lunch. The Flea Market has over 50 vendors and 12,000 square feet of shopping. There is sufficient parking available. The boutiques are open seven days a week from 10:00 am to 7:00 pm. The flea market is only open on Sundays from 8:30 am to 4:30 pm.

Sunday Flea Market, 152 Front Street, (519) 336-3347. Antiques, collectibles, furniture and more. Only open Sunday as the name suggests.

Parks, Beaches and Campgrounds

Blue Water Bridge Authority, Venetian Boulevard, Point Edward, (519)

Canatara Park
Photo Courtesy of Tourism Sarnia Lambton

336-2720. A little park with picnic tables and nice views.

Canatara Park, at the end of Christina Street North, (519) 332-0330. Has nature trails and is located on Lake Huron. This park has a lifeguard-supervised beach and offers picnic tables, a playground, sports field, restrooms, and lovely scenery. Dozens of species of birds have been seen in or from this park.

Centennial Park, Front Street, (519) 862-2291. A pleasant park with a boat ramp, colorful playground, picnic tables, sports field, and restrooms. The park runs along the riverfront and is a great place to visit on a day you plan to spend meandering through the shops on Front Street. It is the site of many summer festivals and is a hub of activity.

Clearwater Community Centre, 1400 Wellington Street, (519) 332-0330. Offers a playground, sports field, and restrooms.

Country View RV Campground, 4569 London Line Road, Wyoming, (twenty minutes from Sarnia), (519) 845-3394, or toll-free (888) 610-0874, *www.sarnia. com/countryview.* If you need a place to park your RV, you may want to check this park. Open April to the last Sat in October.

Germain Park, 900 Germain Street, (519) 332-0330. A playground, restrooms, a sports field, and an outdoor pool are the amenities in this pleasant park.

McCrae Park, Point Edward, (519) 344-0908. Has a playground and picnic area.

McKenzie Seaway Centre Park, Front Street, (519) 862-2291. No services.

Point Edward Waterfront Park, Michigan Avenue, Point Edward, (519) 337-3021. Offers a playground, sports field, picnic area, and restrooms. Nice park with views of the waterfront, Blue Water Bridges, and marine activity. You would get a great view of the start for the Mackinac Sailboat Races from this vantage point.

Tecumseh Park, 334 Russell Street South, (519) 332-0330. Pool, playground, sports field, picnic area, and restrooms.

Sarnia Bay Marina
Photo Courtesy of Tourism Sarnia Lambton

Marinas

Sarnia Bay Municipal Marina, 97 Seaway Road, (519) 332-0533. *info@ sarniabaymarina.com*. Thirty beautifully landscaped acres and spectacular views of the Blue Water Bridges provide boaters a full service 'lifestyle' marina that includes over three hundred boat slips for both seasonal members and tourist (transient) boaters. For reservations call toll-free (877) 797-2233.

Other Things to See and Do

Bluewater Fun Park, 1886 London Line Road, (519) 542-1083, *www. bluewaterfunpark.com*. A recreational complex with two winding water slides and two high-speed water slides to cool you off on a hot, muggy, summer afternoon. You can also play water games or ride in the bumper boats with water cannons. Additional adventures to help create an entertaining afternoon: beach volleyball courts, pool, 18-hole mini-golf course, Caddy Shack's Par-T-Golf indoor golf, maze, roller racers and Percy's Peak, Inc. with climbing wall. Your choice for fun may be the Laser Blast, a computerized hide-and-seek game played in a multi-level arena with optical lasers. A picnic area is available and the complex has a licensed lounge and snack bar. Seasonal hours.

Bluewater Trails, *www.bluewatertrails.com*. Sarnia's linear park that can be accessed at Canatara Park and from many other points. Cycle, walk, or hike between points of interest. Map available on the Internet.

Cruises and Boat Tours

Duc D'Orleans II Cruise Ship, (519) 337-5152, or toll free at (888) 493-9941, *www.ducdorleans.com*. Departs McKenzie Park on Front Street. Capacity 194 passengers. Daily luncheon cruises as well as Sunday afternoon cruises of the St. Clair Parkway. Reservations required.

Macassa Bay Boat Tours, (519) 336-7703, or toll-free (877) 622-2282, *www. macassabay.com*. Cruises depart from Bridgeview Marina, Venetian Village, and Point Edward offering sightseeing of southern Lake Huron and the St. Clair River. Certified for 190 passengers; reservations are required.

Casino and Slots

OLG Casino Point Edward, 2000 Venetian Boulevard, Point Edward, (519) 383-7770, or toll-free (888) 394-6244, *www.olg.ca*. Overlooking the St. Clair River, at the foot of the Blue Water Bridge, OLG Casino Point Edward offers you gallons of thrills. Try your luck at 490 slot machines including: Wheel of Fortune, Blazing 7's, and the new Quarter Million $ progressive. Ante up for your favorite table games; there are thirty-two in all including Craps, Blackjack, Roulette, Caribbean Stud, and more. Or take a turn in the newly enclosed poker area, for some Hold 'em action. Enjoy a leisurely meal and spectacular riverside view at the *Boathouse Restaurant and Patio*, which is fully licensed. You must be over nineteen years old to gamble in Canada. Open Mon to Wed 9:00 am to

OLG Casino Point Edward
Photo Courtesy of Tourism Sarnia Lambton

4:00 am and 24 hours Thurs to Mon.

Slots at Hiawatha Horse Park, 1730 London Line Road, toll-free (888) 250-3309, *www.hiawathahorsepark.com*. They have slot machines, and if slots are your preferred amusement you may favor the Hiawatha Racetrack to the Casino. From April to November there is live harness racing. Open seven days a week 9:00 am to 4:00 am.

Festivals
- The Sarnia Salmon Festival, April.
- Artwalk, June.
- Kids Funfest at Centennial Park, June.
- The Sarnia to Mackinac Sail Boat Race, July.
- Rogers Sarnia Bayfest, July.
- Sarnia Lambton Arts Council Studio Tour, October.

Golf/Driving Ranges
Greystone Golf Course, 2218 Confederation Street, (519) 383-7177. A 9 hole, par 35 golf course with a pro shop.

Greenwood Golf Course, 2212 London Line, (519) 542-2212. An 18-hole, par 70 golf course with a pro shop.

Holiday Inn Golf Course, 1498 Venetian Boulevard, Point Edward, (519) 336-4111. A 9 hole, par 28 golf course with a pro shop.

Indian Hills Golf Course, 6991 Lakeshore Road, ½ mile west of Highway 21 (between Sarnia and Grand Bend), (519) 786-5505, *www.indianhillsgolf.ca*. Has an 18-hole par 72 and slope rating 133 course. This scenic championship course was designed and built by Ross Axford.

Sunset Golf, 1873 London Line, (519) 542-1779. A 9 hole par 35 golf course with a pro shop.

Theatre

Imperial Theatre, 168 Christina Street North, (519) 332-6591, *www. imperialtheatre.net*, is the place for theatre in Sarnia. It presents amateur and professional theatre year round. Box Office: (519) 344-7469, or toll-free (877) 344-7469, *boxoffice@imperialtheatre.net* for ticket information. The building housing this theatre has been beautifully restored and is a wonderful example of art-deco style. The theatre originally opened as the Capitol Theatre on New Year's Eve 1936 but closed fifty-two years later, when it was left abandoned and slated for demolition. With the help of local industry, the city, private donors, Theatre Sarnia members, and many volunteers, the theatre was saved and transformed into a live theatre venue. It has exceptional acoustical and visual characteristics. It boasts that there is not a bad seat in the house, and it can accommodate 598 people. The walls of its lobby also offer a rotating exhibit by local artists. Open Mon to Sat 11:00 am to 5:00 pm. Call for performance time and current schedule of events.

Contacts

Boating and General Information, *Coast Guard* (800) 267-6687.

Point Edward Municipal Office, 135 Kendall Street, (519) 337-3021, *www. villageofpointedward.com*.

Sarnia Lambton Tourist Information, (800) 265-0316, *www. tourismsarnialambton.com*. Information on attractions, accommodations, golf courses, theatre, marinas, parks, restaurants, and the over four hundred festivals and events held in Sarnia and Point Edward each year.

Sarnia Lambton Chamber of Commerce, 556 Christina Street, (519) 336-2400, *www.sarnialambtonchamber.com*.

Lakeport *(Also includes Burtchville Township)*

Directions:

Lakeport is about eleven miles north of Port Huron on M-25. It is sixty-eight miles north of Detroit.

Background and History

Originally, Lakeport was platted by Jonas Titus in 1837. He named the area's small stream *Milwaukie Creek* and the village *Milwaukie City*. The name came from the Pottawatomie word *"meno"* or *"mino"* meaning good and *"aki"* meaning land. The name Milwaukie City was used until 1858. Titus never recorded his platting efforts, and when the village was replatted, it was also renamed. It became Lakeport because of its proximity to Lake Huron.

Restaurants/Food

Red Pepper Mexican Restaurant, 7116 Lakeshore Road near the blinker light in Lakeport, (810) 385-7088. This restaurant has become a popular place to get Mexican food. See description of the Port Huron location; the menu is the same. Open Mon to Sat 11:00 am to 9:00 pm, Sun 2:00 pm to 8:00 pm.

Stavros Restaurant, 7870 Lakeshore Road, (810) 327-6534. The ambiance is that of a large, clean, no-frills diner. Do not mistakenly think this is a Greek Restaurant. There are a few Greek sandwiches (Greek taco, chicken gyro), and a Greek salad, but the entrees are primarily American dishes (fish, steak, chicken, pork) with a few Italian dishes thrown in. You can order breakfast anytime and the prices are reasonable. Open seven days from 7:00 am to 8:45 pm.

The Tally Ho Inn, 7933 Old Lakeshore Road, (turn from M-25 towards the lake at Pine or at the large Mobil gas station and then left onto Old Lakeshore), (810) 327-6242. Lounge with a pool table and a welcome feeling. Nice place to stop for a drink or food. The place gets high marks from steady customers and visitors alike. The perch dinner is a favorite. Kitchen open Sun to Thurs 4:00 pm to 10:00 pm, Fri and Sat 3:00 pm to 10:00 pm. Bar open until 2:00 am Fri and Sat.

Lodging

Sandy Beach Resort, 6636 Lakeshore Road, (Burtchville, just north of Lakeport on M-25), (810) 385-1600. Cottages that can be rented by the day, week or month. They appear to have been built in the '60s and are a bit more rustic than a newly constructed Holiday Inn or other major chain motel. One unit has two bedrooms, and four units can sleep up to five by utilizing the full-size bed, sleeper-sofa and rollaway. Cable TV is provided as are rowboats. You have great access to the Lake.

Shopping

Off the Beaten Path Country Store and Gift Shop, 6026 Jeddo Road, five miles west of Lakeshore, (810) 327-6488. If you have headed west from Lakeshore to visit McCallum's Orchard (see below), you might want to make a stop at this shop. It is only about three and a half miles from the orchard. From McCallum's you turn left (west), to the first road (which will be Wildcat Road), turn right, and go one mile into Jeddo Road. If you are not going from McCallum's, but rather from M-25, there will be a sign directing you to turn left onto Jeddo Road. It is literally, a little "off-the-beaten path," and you will have to decide if you want to make the detour. The Country Store carries gift and food items, potpourri, candles, rugs, and other household items. They have opened a new section with open beams and white paint giving it a beach-house feeling. It is stocked with "Life is Good" merchandise, T-shirts, mugs, totes, and much more. Open Thurs to Sat 11:00 am to 5:00 pm and Sun noon to 4:00 pm.

Parks, Beaches and Campgrounds

Burtchville Township Park, 4000 Burtch Road, north of Port Huron, (810) 385-5577. Finding this park can be a little tricky. It requires a small deviation from M-25: at Burtchville turn right from Lakeshore, which will take you past this park. The park has tennis courts, a playground, swimming beach, pavilion, and basketball nets. The park area runs parallel to a street of cottages that have the lake frontage. Therefore, the majority of the park is behind these cottages and without a view. At the north end of the park is a small, but pleasant, beach. The restrooms look ancient and you better take your hand sanitizer. All of that said, it actually is a nice little park.

Lakeport State Park, 7605 Lakeshore Road, just north of Lakeport, (810) 327-6224. This park has camping and picnicking on the lake side of M-25 and additional picnic facilities, parking, and restrooms on the west side (non lake side). A foot-bridge over the highway connects the two areas. This means that if you are picnicking on the lake side, you have to carry everything from a bit of a distance and cross the foot-bridge. The park is open from April through October and the lake side has a playground, volleyball nets, and a swimming beach. The camp has a mini-cabin available and allows pets if they are kept on a leash. The park store carries most essentials for your camping experience.

Orchard Beach, on Beach Avenue, about five miles north of Lakeport. This is a unique little beach. It is a couple of blocks off M-25, with only a small sign denoting its existence. It is about 150 feet by 200 feet of grassy, lakeside property that looks like a vacant lot missing only a *"for sale"* sign. It has a tree or two and absolutely no services, no tables, and not even a port-a-potty – nothing. The grassy area slopes down to a small sandy beach. There is a seawall on each side of the property at beach level. The sign at the park entrance indicates that you can build a bonfire on the beach (just make sure you extinguish it properly).

This is not a great family park (you would be running kids somewhere to find a bathroom every few minutes), but if you are coming on a weekend when you anticipate the parks of the area will be crowded to the max, you may find this tiny park less busy, and a nice place to spread a blanket under the tree, chill out, and read a book or just watch the water.

Other Things to See and Do

Jet Ski Rental, (at Sandy Beach Resort), 6836 Lakeshore Road, (810) 385-1600. Six machines available: one four-seater, one three-seater and four two-seaters. This past year the prices were $79 per hour, $45 per half hour and $10 per additional person during the week. Week-end rates were slightly higher. Deposit required. Call ahead if you want to be sure of getting one.

McCallum's Orchard and Cider Mill, 5697 Harris Road, Jeddo, (810) 327-6394, *www.mccallumorchard.com*. Harris Road is north of the Lakeport State Park, and there will be a sign for the orchard on Lakeshore where you turn left. It is about 4½ miles west of M-25. McCallum's produces apples, cherries, peaches, pumpkins, raspberries, grapes, and nectarines. They also sell jams, popcorn, honey, and other gift items. The cider mill offers fresh cider to go with their cinnamon donuts. In the fall they create a corn maze. If you or anyone in your family wants to experience picking your own fruit, this is your chance. Of course, you can also buy their fruit already picked. Either way, you will have fresh fruit to make a wonderful dessert and you can use one of the many recipes McCallum's has available. (Think Apple-Cherry Crumble or Apple-Praline Pie, or maybe something a bit less sweet like Apple Date Bread or Apple Cabbage Salad.) Open 8:00 am to 5:00 pm daily. Seasonal.

The slight deviation from M-25, to stop at *Off-the-Beaten-Path* and *McCallum's Orchard* may prove interesting if you have the time.

Lexington

Population: 1104.

Directions:

Twenty miles north of Port Huron on M-25.

Background and History

In 1830 Lexington became the first settlement north of Port Huron on the shores of the lake. Today, signs at each end of the village announce its stature as *The First Resort North*. Lexington Township is the oldest township in Sanilac County. The county of Sanilac was mapped by Lewis Cass in 1822 when he was governor of the Michigan Territory. Sanilac County originally included all of Tuscola and Huron Counties, except for a small area around Sebewaing. In those early days, there was nothing more than a trail through the dense pine forests connecting Lexington to Port Huron.

In 1837, John Smith brought his wife and twelve children to Lexington, where he built a log house on the hill, overlooking the lake on the south side of Huron Avenue. As beautiful as Lexington must have been in those days with its huge pine and hardwood forests, Smith felt driven to leave after a few years, because the place was simply becoming too crowded.

In 1840, Langdon Hubbard, at age twenty-four, his brother Watson, and their cousin R.B. came to Michigan from Connecticut to seek their fortunes as lumber and business men in the Thumb. The lumbering boom was well underway, and they obtained property and timberland in Lexington. Their company prospered and later they moved north into Huron County. They built a dock in Lexington to facilitate shipment of their lumber to market.

Lexington was known as Greenbush until 1846. Most of its original settlers came from Canada, and a few relocated from New England and the Middle Atlantic states. The Thumb was quite desirable with its rich forests, fertile soil, cheap land, and water access.

Three permanent boat docks were erected by 1870, initially for the shipment of lumber and later for agricultural products. Fruit grew well in the somewhat sandy soil around Lexington. Local orchards produced peaches, cherries, apples, pears, and plums; local berry patches provided raspberries, black raspberries, blackberries, gooseberries and strawberries.

The first hotel was built of logs in 1840 at the site of the current Cadillac House. It was named the Mills Hotel after its owner Clark Mills. Mills only owned the hotel for three years before trading it (some suggest as the result of a gambling debt) to his brother-in-law, for a forty-acre farm near where the current

Lakeview Hills Golf Resort is located. It is hard to say who got the better end of the deal. The Mills Hotel operated until 1859 when it was torn down and rebuilt as the Cadillac Hotel which officially opened on July 4, 1860. This second hotel was named for General DeLamotte Cadillac, who founded Fort Pontchartrain in Detroit. The Cadillac House has a local reputation of being haunted by a ghost named George. (See related story in Part Two of this guide.)

The village was named Lexington in 1846 by Reuben Diamond, whose wife was a cousin of Ethan Allen. Allen fought in the Battle of Lexington during the Revolutionary War. The village was incorporated in 1855.

The fire of 1871 spared Lexington because the townsfolk turned out to aggressively fight the flames. It helped that they had earlier carved clearings around the village. Of course, equally important was the critical and much welcomed rain that assisted their efforts. The local citizenry was instrumental in providing aid to those living further north who had been left homeless by the ravages of that horrific inferno. (For an additional account of the Great Fires, see Part Two of this guide.)

Lexington is a quaint little village with an old time feel. Its natural stone harbor is reminiscent of those along the Coast of Maine. The beautiful three-sided breakwater was built of huge stones hauled from Rodgers City. It was constructed by the United States Army Corps of Engineers. The walkway atop the breakwall is the perfect place to take a cup of coffee and greet the new day on this sunrise coast of Lake Huron. Very few experiences will leave you feeling more content and at peace with the world than watching as the sleepy harbor awakens.

Many of Lexington's historic buildings have been preserved, including the one-hundred-and-sixteen-year-old General Store that still dispenses a variety of merchandise. Lexington's population, over two thousand at one point, dwindled to 326 by 1940. Its current population is well over one thousand, thanks to its reincarnation as a resort village.

Lexington is at its best in the summer: There are free concerts in the park on Friday nights. It has a Fine Arts Fair that rivals the University of Michigan's in everything but size. Tierny Park, with its play area, beach, and picnicking, is a perfect place to spend an afternoon with the family.

The large Smackwater Development Complex takes up the second block of Huron (off Main towards the lake). In 1992, Adam Buschbacher, who had lived part of his childhood in the area, returned and bought the property. Missing the delightful old buildings that had been lost over the years, he built the current structure with 32,000 square feet of space. The development nicely complements the remaining turn-of-the-century architecture of the village, in part because Adam did not break ground until he had researched architectural styles and visited historic villages. He used only reclaimed bricks from demolished buildings in Detroit and Chicago. His attention to detail can be seen throughout in such touches as the oak floors and the cobblestone plaza in front.

The Smackwater Block now houses Aromas Coffee Shop, Smackwater Jack's Bistro, the Tasting Room Wine Bar, Vintage Fine Dining, BrewMaster's Pub, Huron Avenue Gourmet Marketplace, Gallery 7318, and a first rate theater. (See appropriate sections below for description of each business.) The courtyard has an antique fountain and benches and is often elaborately decorated appropriate to the season. Whatever else you do in the Thumb, do not miss Lexington.

Smackwater Block

Food/Restaurants

A&W, 5309 Main Street (M-25, a block and a half north of the traffic light), (810) 359-8522. Remember the old days of curb service? The A&W still has it, along with the frosty mug of root beer (made daily on the premises) to go with your order. Family owned and operated for thirty-seven years and providing many of the nostalgic menu items you thought were history such as Wisconsin white cheddar cheese curls. Open seven days in the summer, closes in November for the winter.

Aromas Coffee Shop, Huron Avenue in the Smackwater Block. A favorite with local coffee connoisseurs. Pricey, fancy coffee drinks. It is a place where you can take your coffee outside to a small café table, enjoy the local scene, and catch a glimpse of the lake. Open six days 10:00 am to 8:00 pm, closed Tues. May have reduced winter hours.

Beck's Village Café and Ice Cream, 5349 North Main Street, (810) 359-8686. Burgers, pitas, sandwiches, daily breakfast specials, splits, shakes, malts, and cones. Twenty-four flavors of soft-serve. Summer hours Mon to Thurs 8:00 am to 2:00 pm, Fri to Sun 8:00 am to 9:00 pm.

Brewmaster's Pub, Huron Avenue in the Smackwater Block. A journey back in time as you enjoy the English Architecture and the finest Ales from around the world. Eclectic pub menu and vintage cocktail selections. Open seven days 4:00 pm to midnight. May have reduced winter hours.

Bunny's Frozen Custard, 6457 Lakeshore. Many locals swear by this frozen custard and watch with eager anticipation for Bunny's sign to announce spring opening. Seasonal hours.

Bush's Family Restaurant, 6513 Lakeshore, (810) 359-5801. Inexpensive diner with a variety of menu items including steaks, chops, hot sandwiches, pitas, burgers, and salads. You can dine-in or carry-out. They serve a good breakfast all day. (Sunday breakfast ends at 1:00 pm.) Open seven days at 6:30 am. Closes Mon at noon, Tues to Thurs 8:00 pm, Fri and Sat 9:00 pm, Sun 7:00 pm, and slightly earlier in the winter.

Cadillac House, 5502 Main Street, (810) 359-7201. The house specialty is Broasted Chicken, but they also serve a variety of other chicken dishes as well as pork, pasta, and pizza. Open seven days for lunch and dinner, breakfast on weekends in the summer.

Dairy Queen, 5435 Main Street, a block north of the light, (810) 359-8068. There will be long lines on a hot summer day. Seasonal, of course.

The Flying Taco, 5520 Main Street, (810) 359-8580. The Siesta Plate has a bit of everything you could possibly want: a beef burrito, taco, tostada, tamale with chips and cheese; perhaps the name comes from the need to take a bit of a nap after eating so much food. Open Mon to Wed 11:00 am to 8:00 pm, Thurs to Sat 11:00 am to 9:00 pm (later if busy), and Sun 11:00 am to 6:00 pm.

Grama's Tacos, 5590 Main Street, (810) 359-8226. The Chicken Quesadilla is a sure winner, but the menu has many other tempting choices. Open Mon to Thurs 11:00 am to 8:00 pm, Fri and Sat 11:00 am to 9:00 pm, and Sun 11:00 am to 6:00 pm.

Lakeview Hills Golf Resort, 6560 East Peck Road, one mile west of the light in Lexington, (810) 359-7333, *www.lakeviewhills.com*. Lunch and dinner menu with interesting entrees. There is also a sports bar that often features weekend entertainment.

Newman's Pub N Grub, 7264 Lakeshore Road, (810) 359-5003 or (810) 359-8080. A no-frills bar with a taco pizza and cheeseburgers that might make the stop worthwhile. Open Mon to Wed 11:00 am to 10:00 pm, Fri and Sat 11:00 am to midnight, and Sun noon to 10:00 pm.

The Oasis Coffeehouse and Lounge, 7285 Lakeshore Road, (810) 359-5085, *www.oasiscoffee.com*. Stop and smell the coffee. Tea, beer, and wine also available. In addition to drinks you can order appetizers, salads, soups, sandwiches, desserts, ice cream, and pastries, all in a smoke-free environment. Weather permitting you can enjoy them on the patio. There is also a lot of activity at The Oasis: Scrabble Club meets there, Karaoke, Open Mic, WiFi available, and some entertainment. Open Mon and Tues 9:00 am to 9:00 pm, Wed to Fri 9:00 am to 11:00 pm, Sat 8:00 am to 11:00 pm, and Sun 8:00 am to 5:00 pm.

Patio Pastries and Organic Bakery and Spun Gallery, 7059 Lakeshore, (810) 359-5222, Great baked goods made from natural, organic ingredients like pure butter and cream. No artificial coloring or preservatives used. The cinnamon rolls are fabulous. The carrot cake is outstanding. The specialty and coffee cakes rival anything mother used to make. The art gallery is an interesting collection of pottery, beach art designs, functional metal art and glass pieces with emphasis on the process. Both businesses open Thurs to Sat 8:30 am to 5:00 pm, Sun 8:30 am to 3:00 pm.

Smackwater Jack's Bistro, 7318 Huron Avenue in the Smackwater Block, (810) 359-2791, *www.smackwaterdevelopment.com*. This is an upscale but casual dining establishment with wonderful sandwiches and homemade soups. It also has the best pizza anywhere in the Thumb. The Greek Pizza is perfect, and the Mexican Pizza is delicious, but it would be hard to convince loyal customers that there is a better pizza than the Smackwater Special with pepperoni, ham, bacon, sun-dried tomatoes, garlic, and other wonderful toppings – all piled on the most incredible crust imaginable. Definitely gourmet pizza. It is a bit pricier than your average pizza, but anytime you want to make a night special, open a bottle of wine and pick up a Smackwater Special. Open Mon 11:00 am to 3:00 pm, Wed to Sun 11:00 am to 9:00 pm and closed Tues. Reduced winter hours.

Steis's Village Inn, 5523 Main Street, (810) 359-5090. Serves soups, sandwiches, pizza (a favorite with many customers), and a fairly lengthy list of appetizers to go with a cold beer (or whatever your drinking pleasure because they have a full bar and excellent wines from around the world). Also has full entrees including charbroiled steak and ribs and nightly specials. A pool table offers a diversion. Mon to Wed 11:00 am to midnight, Thurs 11:00 am to 1:00 am, Fri and Sat 11:00 am to 2:00 am, Sun noon to 11:00 pm. (Some variation with season.)

The Tasting Room Wine Bar, Huron Avenue in the Smackwater Block, (810) 359-2791. Wine lovers and neophytes alike will enjoy tasting wines from around the world. By enjoying tasting portions you can continue sampling wines until you find the one that is most pleasing to you. It is also a place to learn more about wines and how to enjoy them. Open Wed to Sun 4:00 pm to midnight and closed Mon and Tues. May reduce winter hours.

Vintage, Huron Avenue in the Smackwater Block, (810) 359-2791. Fine inspired cuisine. Experience three private dining rooms: French Country Room, English Room, and the Mission Room. The food is inspired by regional cuisine from around the world. Open Wed to Sun, dinner 5:00 pm to 10:00 pm.

Wimpy's Place, 7270 Huron Avenue, (810) 359-5450. A hamburger joint with a loyal following for its burgers and Coney dogs. Also has a carry-out service, but you are advised to call ahead. The restaurant business is in this building's blood: Decades ago this location on Huron was the Dutch Apple Kitchen and before that there was another Wimpy's. Open for breakfast, lunch, and dinner, it is one of the few food places that remains open in the winter.

Lodging

A-1 Cottages, (810) 359-7774, *www.a1cottages.com*. Check out the Internet to see pictures of the interior and exterior of the cottages to decide if these are right for you. Three cottage rentals. Open year round. Lake views. Up to two dogs allowed.

Captain's Quarters Inn, 7277 Simons Street, (810) 359-2196, *www.cqilex. com*, *westwind@greatlakes.net*. Walking distance to the harbor, shops, Tierny Park, and restaurants. Four guest rooms each with its own private bath. Nautical motif and each room named for one of Michigan's Great Lakes. Some rooms have fireplaces to keep you warm on cool spring or fall evenings (also central air for hot, muggy days). The friendly ghost of a young woman who stayed in the room at the top of the stairs is said to haunt Captain's Quarters as does the ghost of a seafaring captain who appreciates the nautical flavor of the inn, but you can sleep easy; they mean no harm to the guests. (See Ghost Stories in Part Two of this guide.) Captain's Quarters accepts Master Card and Visa

Carroll House B&B, 7307 Simons Street, (810) 359-5702, *carrollhouse@ greatlakes.net or www.carrollhousebandb.com*. The Carroll House is close to everything that is happening in Lexington. You can walk to the summer Concerts in the Park, the harbor, shopping, restaurants, and more. Heidi Carroll will help you plan special occasions and can bring in a masseuse, manicurist, etc. The kitchen has a wonderful, warm feeling with its slab granite island and old brick wall that was originally the front of the house – before the owner made lots of money and expanded. The arched brick doorway connecting the kitchen with the living room is charming. A great place to spend a weekend.

Inn The Garden B&B, 7156 Huron Avenue, (810) 359-8966, *www.inngarden. com*. A short walk to the village shops and less than a mile to the Lakeview Hills Golf Resort. Known as the Nims-Wilcox House, this B&B was built by State Senator Reuben Nims. It was later occupied by Doc Wilcox who "doctored" nearly everyone in the area. It was built in the architectural style of an Italian country villa. The picturesque grounds are often the site of weddings and other special occasions. The hostess, Susan Lombardi, is a master gardener with her own green house and fruit trees. Her breakfasts often include produce she has grown in her lovely vegetable garden, and she offers guests a raspberry cordial made from her own raspberries. The home has beautiful woodwork, winding stairs, and antiques throughout. The parlor, with its cozy fireplace, is the perfect place to enjoy a good book on a chilly day. There are four rooms available and the inn is open year round, but if they do not have reservations booked you may not find them home.

Lakeview Hills Golf Resort, 6560 East Peck Road (a mile west of Lexington), (810) 359-7333, *www.lakeviewhills.com*. Offering twenty-nine rooms, the resort stays open year round. Most rooms have two queen beds, and some rooms on the golf course side have balconies. There are two wheelchair-accessible rooms and two rooms with a hot tub, king bed, and sitting area. There are also four efficiency apartments. The rates are reasonable, and if you are not looking for a B&B experience, this is a nice place to stay – even if you are not a golfer.

Lusky's Lakefront Cottages, 8949 Lakeshore Road, (810) 327-6889, *www. luskys.com*. Private beach, playground area, tire swing, gym sets, basketball, volleyball, ping-pong, shuffleboard, video game room, inner tubes, and paddle boats. These are clean, fully-equipped, housekeeping cottages. They have ceiling fans but not air-conditioning. You can enjoy bonfires on the beach. More rustic than the golf course or many of the B&B's, but if you have a family these might fit the bill. Guests need to bring their own linens.

Powell House B&B, 5076 Lakeshore Road (three-quarters of a mile north of traffic light), (810) 359-5533. This Victorian dates to 1852 and was originally a three-acre berry farm. It has lovely gardens and the rooms are decorated in period furniture. Four rooms, some with shared bath. Full breakfast is served in the dining room. Originally known as the Frostick House.

Primrose Manor B&B, 6740 Peck Road (M-90 one mile west of Lexington), (810) 359-2686, *www.primrosemanor.com*, *primrose58@sbcglobal.net*. This beautiful Victorian era home was built in 1854 and rests on two shady acres. It is a romantic get-away that offers three air-conditioned guest rooms with full or queen beds and private baths. The goal is to pamper guests with such extras as bathrobes and slippers, chocolates, snack baskets, and cognac in the rooms. A sit-down gourmet breakfast is served in the formal dining room each morning at 9:00 am. Coffee service is available at all times. The B&B is not suited to children.

Primrose Manor also offers a Royal Tea. If you have from eight to ten friends who would like to enjoy the ultimate in private teas, you really need to consider this as a way to relax, unwind, and enjoy a pleasurable respite from busy lives. You will be served a fruit medley, scones, tea sandwiches, savories, and dessert. The delicious meal begins and ends with champagne. Throughout, you will enjoy the signature Rose Tea. Reservations required.

Sandy Beach Cottages (See Lakeport listing).

Antiques

Gatherings Antiques, 5454 Main Street, (810) 359-5583. Gift shop on Main Street a couple of blocks past the traffic light. It is the house with the gorgeous array of flowers outside the entrance. Carries antiques, folk art, and more. Open six days in the summer 10:00 am to 6:00 pm. Closed Tues. In winter open weekends, or by chance.

Marketplace on Main *(Includes* The Victorian Emporium, the Enchanted Garden, Barn Basics and Temptations Ice Cream Parlor), 5712 Main Street,

(810) 359-7134, *www.victorianantiquesemp.com*. Specializes in quality glass and antiques, but also offers a wide selection of gift and unique garden items, Heritage Lace, a Christmas room, and Swan Creek Candles. The house is so beautiful that it is worth stopping just to see the inside. They serve Sanders' hot fudge and toppings in the ice cream parlor. The barn behind the house also has antiques. Open seven days, 10:00 am to 5:00 pm Memorial Day through Labor Day. Open weekends Labor Day until Christmas and the month of April. Closed January to April.

Village House Antiques, 5666 Main Street, (810) 359-7733. Open weekends or by chance. The owners live there, and if you ring the bell they will show you around.

Marketplace on Main including
The Victorian Emporium and Enchanted Garden

Other shopping

If you are around in the summer you can pretty much be assured most of the local shops will be open seven days a week. In the winter many reduce their hours.

Angel's Garden, 7260 Huron Avenue, (810) 359-2496 or toll-free (877) 509-5496, *www.angelsgardengifts.com*. Home and garden accessories, limited edition collectibles, hand blown glass, lamps, porcelains, original art, serigraphs, wood art and sculptures, chimes, bells, bird feeders, gazing balls, books, CD's, gifts for adults and children, angels, and cards. Occasionally has Garden Concerts (violinist, etc). Open Sun to Thurs 10:00 am to 5:00 pm and Fri and Sat 10:00 am to 7:00 pm. May reduce hours seasonally and closed January through March.

Bent on Bones, 5510 Main Street, (810) 359-8370. A place to get your pooch a free treat and check out the pet merchandise. Open Sun, Mon, and Wed 10:00 am to 5:00 pm, Thurs to Sat 10:00 am to 7:00 pm, and closed Tues.

Berry Merry on the Shore, 5512 Main Street, (810) 359-8456. Country, folk art, nautical items, lawn and garden décor, home accessories, and candles. Open Mon to Thurs 10:00 am to 5:00 pm, Fri and Sat 10:00 am to 7:00 pm and Sun 10:00 am to 4:00 pm. After the summer season, reduced hours to Christmas.

Bob Hobbs Antiques and More, 7262 Huron Avenue, (810) 359-8386. This began as an antiques store, but with quality antiques so difficult to find, it now focuses on the "more," which includes many unusual decorating items and reproductions to jazz up your home. The building housing this shop is more than 150 years old and was Graham and Company Drugs (Pharmacy) in its earlier life. Make sure you check out the original tin ceiling. Open summer Sat and Sun 10:00 am to 5:00 pm or by chance or appointment.

Crazy Joe's Surf Shop, Washington Street behind Oh! Fudge! This shop is intended to remind customers of the Florida-style surf shops with beach towels, sunglasses, beach chairs, beach toys and other paraphernalia to make your sun and sand experience more pleasurable. During the heat of the summer they are usually open 10:00 am to 8:00 pm every day.

Gallery 7318, 7318 Huron Avenue, (in the Smackwater Block), (810) 359-2791. Merchandise consists primarily of unique home furnishing items. Usually open six days 11:00 am to 6:00 pm, closed Tues.

Gazebo on Main, 5481 Main Street, (810) 359-5937. Tiny shop with a variety of signs, jewelry, candy, and accent pieces. Open during the summer Mon to Sat 10:00 am to 6:00 pm and Sun 11:00 am to 5:00 pm.

General Store, 7272 Huron Avenue, (810) 359-8900. This store really is like an old-style general store, and the staff will provide you with old-time courtesy and friendliness as well. You will find something to intrigue everyone: Penny-candy (that is just a name these days, not a price), kitchen ware, gourmet food items, calendars, souvenirs, pictures, cards, toys, books, and much more. Summer open seven days, Mon to Sat 10:00 am to 6:00 pm and Sun 11:00 am to 6:00 pm. Closes at 5:00 pm in the winter

Gifts from Michigan, 7288 Huron Avenue, (810) 359-5558, *bluewaterarea@ yahoo.com*. The food items are made in Michigan, and almost everything in the store is made in the United States. They have children's books and a delightful collection of infants' clothing as well as home accent items. Open seven days, 10:00 am to 5:00 pm (sometimes 6:00 pm). Reduced winter hours.

Huron Avenue Gourmet Marketplace, Smackwater Block. International epicurean treats, as well as a large selection of wines and ales. Guest sommeliers provide you with expert guidance in selecting the perfect food and wine pairings. Cocktail supplies, gourmet cookbooks, picnic baskets, and inspiring ideas in kitchenware and dining accessories. Open six days 10:00 am to 7:00 pm, closed Tues.

J & K 99¢ Store, 7287 Huron Avenue, (810) 359-7165, *www.jandk99centstores. com*. In a village with lots of upscale shops, this is a place to take the children or grandchildren, hand them a dollar or two and be a hero as they contemplate whether they want rattlesnake eggs or ring lights. Open Mon and Wed to Sat 10:00 am to 6:00 pm, Sun 10:00 am to 3:00 pm and closed Tues.

The Lexington Booksmith and Gallery, 5533 Main Street, (810) 359-7113. The place to get new or used books in Lexington. Explore the shelves and browse the books. Comedy, history, suspense, biographies; they have it all. If you are looking for a beach read or a book to curl up with during a quiet moment, you will enjoy this little shop. Paintings by local artists are also displayed and for sale. Open Mon 10:00 am to 5:00 pm, Thurs and Fri 1:00 pm to 7:00 pm, Sat 10:00 am to 7:00 pm and Sun noon to 5:00 pm. Closed Tues and Wed. Winter hours may vary.

Noble Lexington, 7247 Huron Avenue, (810) 359-2300, *www.noblelexington. com*. New in 2007, this store has been wowing customers since it opened its doors. The building is wonderfully restored, and your eyes simply cannot take in everything during your first visit. That is okay because you will want to come back often. The merchandise is varied and chosen with flair: kitchenware with the newest twists on classic utility, wine and treats for your summer party, or accents to enliven your garden and compliment your green thumb. From the main floor to the backyard garden, it is a special shopping delight. Open year round but hours change seasonally so refer to the Web site for times of operation, upcoming events and specials.

Oh! Fudge!, 7296 Huron Avenue, (810) 359-5908. Lots of knickknacks, T-shirts, toys, nautical and accent pieces, and a place to buy fudge and ice cream. Open April to December 10:00 am to closing which can be 7:00 pm to 9:00 pm depending upon demand.

Persuasions, 7282 Huron Avenue, (810) 359-2930, *giftshop@greatlakes. net*. Gift shop with a wide variety of merchandise and lovely home accents at affordable prices. Open seven days in the summer.

The Shop The Shop II, 5517 South Main Street, (810) 359-8100. The original shop is in Algonac. Merchandise is primarily sportswear, swimsuits, casual women's clothing, and Lexington T-shirts. Open seven days in the summer. Closed winter.

T's Shop, 7268 Huron Avenue, (810) 359-2179. Sells a large selection of T-shirts. In the early days of Lexington, the store was a tailor shop.

A Thyme to Blossom, 5612 Main Street, (810) 359-7325, *www. athymetoblossom.com*. Full-service florist, coffee, candles, and gift baskets. Open Mon to Fri 9:30 am to 5:30 pm and Sat 10:00 am to 3:00 pm. Closed Sun.

The Town Shop, 7276 Huron Avenue, (810) 359-5151. 'Unique and chic' sportswear for women and lots of accessories. Also carries china dolls. Open daily in the summer.

Weekends, 7266 Huron Avenue, (810) 359-3388. Lee and Jennifer Jones have made this a favorite shop in Lexington. They offer many special events, and customers love their fun, creative, and unusual merchandise for the home and garden or for pampering themselves. You will find lovely upscale household items, coffee beans (they will grind them for you at the shop), some clothing, garden items, and much more. It is a pleasure to meander around the counters. Step outside and enjoy their backyard garden paradise. The building, constructed more than 130 years ago, was previously Ganley's Mercantile, a dry goods store that carried hats, boots, shoes, and other such merchandise. Open seven days April through December, Mon to Sat 10:00 am to 8:00 pm, Sun 10:00 am to 5:00 pm. Closed January through March.

Parks, Beaches and Campgrounds

Lexington Park, M-25, three miles north of Lexington, (810) 359-7473. Bathhouse, showers, pavilion, beach, tennis courts, recreational field, and playground.

Tierny Park, at the harbor in Lexington. The summer Concerts in the Park and other events are held here. There is a nice beach, playground, picnic tables, barbecue grills, volleyball court, tennis courts, and public bathhouse. Great stone breakwater.

Marinas and Charters

Lexington Charter Boat, 7400 Huron Avenue, (810) 359-3000, *www.lexingtoncharterboat.com*, *info@lexingtoncharterboat.com*. A charter boat cruise of Lake Huron on the Marilou II, a forty-one-foot Carver aft cabin yacht is the perfect way of making memories to last well beyond the summer season. You can choose one of the captain's pre-charted favorites or work with him to create your special made-to-order dream cruise. You can take your own picnic lunch or order from a lunch/dinner menu. Take along sunscreen, sunglasses, a camera, jacket, and hat – the rest you can leave to the captain.

The Lexington Harbor Marina, 7411 Huron Ave, (810) 359-5600 or (810) 359-5812. Has 107 transient slips. Amenities include water, electricity, restrooms, showers, gasoline, diesel, pump-out, ice, and boat-launch. Operates from May 1 to October 1. The harbormaster is on duty May 15 to September 1 from 7:00 am to 10:00 pm.

Model T. Fishing Charters, (810) 359-8910, *westwind@greatlakes.net*. A twenty-eight-foot sport fisherman boat captained by Ron Cutler offering charters for salmon, steelhead, brown and lake trout.

Oldford's Marina, 7410 Huron Avenue (in the harbor), (810) 359-5410. Seventy-one boat slips with several that are transient. The harbor has a shower and restroom area, bagged ice, snack bar, restaurants nearby.

Stormy Chinook Charters, (810) 359-5192, *www.stormychinook.com*, or *fishing@greatlakes.net*. Although Captain Dan lives in Lexington, he prefers to

Lexington Harbor
Photo Courtesy of Joe Jurkiewicz

take his charters out of Grindstone City, where he believes the fishing is better. He primarily fishes for Great Lakes Salmon and Trout.

You can get bait at the Subway at the main intersection of Lexington.

Other things to See and Do

The Lexington Music Theatre Company, Smackwater Block, (800) 4LEXMTC, *www.lexmtc.com*, *www.smackwaterave.com*. Lexington now has its own theater. It is a beauty with rich wood paneling, cabaret seating on the main floor, and theater-style seating on the raised level and in the balcony. There is usually something scheduled every weekend during the summer and the lineup does not end in the fall. Some of the finest productions are offered in the "off-season." The entertainment is top-notch.

Water's Edge Salon & Spa, 5590 Main Street, (810) 359-5300. If boating or beach volleyball has left you in need of a massage to soothe tired muscles, give this place a call for an appointment. Also offers tanning and other spa services.

Festivals

Lexington has a festival nearly every weekend in the summer:
- Lakeside Spring Craft Show, June in Tierny Park.
- A&W Classic Car Show, June.
- Port Huron to Mackinac Sailboat Race, July.
- Concert in the Park, June to August.
- Port Huron/Lexington Sailboat Race, August.
- Antique Yard Sale Trail, August.
- Fine Arts Street Fair, August.
- Thumbfest, September.
- Bach Festival, September.

Check *www.lexingtonmichigan.org* for additional information regarding festival dates.

Golf

Lakeview Hills Golf Resort, 6560 Peck Road, (810) 359-8901, *www. lakeviewhills.com*. With two golf courses and a host of amenities, it is the only golf resort in Michigan's Thumb. Lakeview offers 36 holes of championship golf, along with practice facilities and lessons. It also has a sixteen-lane bowling alley, health club, and racquetball courts. You can purchase a daily or three-month health club membership to coincide with your time spent in Lexington. Senior golfing specials. In the winter there is cross-country skiing and you can rent equipment from the resort.

Mystic Mountain Miniature Golf, 6010 Lakeshore, (810) 359-GOLF. A great place to take the children after a day of swimming. Open Sun to Thurs 10:00 am to 8:00 pm and Fri and Sat 10:00 am to 9:00 pm, weather permitting.

Contacts

Lexington Chamber of Commerce, (810) 359-2262 or visit the Web site at *www.cros-lex-chamber.com*.

Lexington Music Theatre Company, (810) 359-2791, *www.lexmtc.com*. For current theatre information.

The Lexington Arts Council, (810) 359-8917, *www.lexarts.com*.

Resident Swans at Lexington Harbor
Photo Courtesy of Kohler Royce

Croswell

Population: 2500.

Directions:

Four miles west of the stop light in Lexington. *Note: This is a small detour from the shoreline route. You will have to decide if the following listings are worth your time.*

Background and History

By 1899 the lumber industry was in full swing in Michigan's Thumb. Lexington had been growing for about a decade, its position on the lake making it a major trade center. Ephraim Pierce decided to seek an alternate source of lumber near Lexington. He wanted his new location to offer abundant timber and the means of transporting it. He found his site, rich with forests, just five miles inland. It was also a mile west of what is currently Croswell. Pierce recognized the value of the Black River for transporting the lumber, and for generating power for the mill he set about constructing. His settlement was known simply as Black River until 1861, when it was renamed Davisville in honor of Randall Davis, who assisted Pierce in finishing the construction of the mill.

Two major players on the early Croswell scene were a land speculator named Truman Moss and his son-in-law Wildman Mills (the latter often called Wild Man Mills for his outrageous behavior). At his death Moss owned 20,000 acres of land in Sanilac County. He was believed to be a millionaire, back when being a millionaire really meant something.

Mills, like Pierce, understood the value of transportation, and was instrumental in bringing the railroad to Croswell. It had been scheduled for construction in Lexington, but Lexington already had transportation in the form of the ships traveling the lake. Croswell residents were tired of hauling their lumber and supplies over a plank road (a toll road, no less) to Lexington. The feud between the two cities vying for the railroad was bitter.

There was an additional feud brewing within Croswell between the settlers on the west and east sides of the Black River regarding which *side* of the small city got the locomotive. The west side by this time had been renamed Falcon and the east side was called Croswell, and the two sides had separate post offices for many years. Somehow, although the manner is a mystery, Croswell became one village and Falcon ceased to exist. The railroad was constructed on the east side.

Croswell was incorporated as a village in 1881 (the year of the second great fire in the Thumb), and it became a city in 1905. Many of Croswell's buildings date back to pre-Civil War times.

There is a story about the stagnant waters in the area being such a fertile breeding place for mosquitoes that people would be afflicted with a fever called the Seven Year or the Michigan Itch. And you probably believed the Seven Year Itch was something that afflicted married people who were a bit bored after a few years of wedded bliss?

After the railroad, the next major event in Croswell history was the coming of Sanilac Sugar Refinery Company in 1901. The editor of the local paper announced, "Surely prosperity and plenty in large proportions is at hand..." At one time more than a thousand people were employed in the harvesting of sugar beets. The plant was designed to slice up to 600 tons of beets per day with plans to operate it 70 to 100 days a year. In 1945, two hundred German prisoners of war were forced to help operate the plant. A sign in front of the factory today proclaims, "Adding a little local flavor for over a century."

The city is probably best known for the *Mother-in-Law Bridge*, also called the *Croswell Swinging Bridge*, which crosses the Black River at River Bend Park. This suspension footbridge was built in 1905 to provide greater access to the park, and to assist workers in getting to their designated jobs on the east side of the river. Kids and grown-ups alike, still enjoy running and shaking the bridge.

Croswell Swinging Bridge
Photo Courtesy of Susan Jurkiewicz

Restaurants/Food

Bea's Diner, 55 North Howard Avenue, (810) 679-4542. Bea's is a small diner with home-cooked food at very reasonable prices. You stop by for the food and the price, not the decor. You will find local residents reading their newspapers or chatting over their coffee. The desserts, including the pies, are homemade.

The Riverside Café, 27 North Howard Avenue, (810) 679-4771. A lot of food for little money. If you want something fancy, this is not your place but if you want a slice of Croswell, stop by and say hello.

Antiques and Other Shopping

The Ben Franklin Store, 73 North Howard Avenue, (810) 679-2470. An old-fashioned variety store that has been family owned and operated for seventy-five years. They invite you to come walk on their creaky floors and examine their variety of merchandise including thread, buttons, lace, linens, notions, Croswell sweatshirts, house wares, snacks, candy, and toys. Open Mon to Sat 9:00 am to 6:00 pm (Fri open until 7:00 pm) and closed Sun.

The Croswell Market, Black River Road off M-90 (Peck Road). The market is held on the stockyard grounds, where they still auction cattle on Monday evening. You will find a variety of produce, plants, flowers, crafts, antiques dealers, and every sort of merchandise. You can buy lovely hanging flower baskets for half the cost of regular retail establishments. One vendor sold a half bushel of tomatoes for $6. In vegetables markets in Port Huron and Lexington they were $14 and $16, respectively. The vendor actually picked out all the imperfect tomatoes and, if anything, loaded the box with more than a half bushel. This is definitely worth the trip but be advised it is only open on Monday. Hours are from whenever vendors get set up, but generally by 8:30 am, until they leave. You will want to be there early for selection.

Laura's Antiques, 133 North Howard Avenue, (810) 679-0028. Specializing in quaint or unusual Victorian merchandise. Open Fri to Mon 10:00 am to 5:00 pm, or by appointment.

Other Things to See and Do

Croswell Berry Farm, 33 North Black River Road, (810) 679-3273. Try picking your own blueberries and eating them with cream and sugar the same night.

The Croswell Fair, Croswell Fairgrounds, *www.croswellfair.com*. Since the Thumb area has no major amusement parks, many of the small towns hire carnivals and set up local fairs. A local fair is likely to have horse races, tractor pulling, cattle judging, dog shows, demo derby, rides, a game arcade, and, of course, cotton candy and hot dogs.

Croswell Swinging Bridge. Run or walk across the bridge. Bounce if you are really brave, but hang on to the railings if you do not want to lose your balance and fall. Initially, the bridge consisted simply of two cables with boards attached. (You can be assured there was no running or jumping back then.) Eventually two additional cables and fencing were added to provide handrails. Those additions helped stabilize the bridge. Obviously these "improvements" also added significantly to the safety of the bridge. You can only wonder how many people fell into the river trying to cross it before the fencing. At 139 feet, it is the longest suspension footbridge in Michigan. As you step onto the bridge you will see the sign, *"Be Good to your Mother-in-Law."* The Swinging Bridge may make the short ride to Croswell worth the effort. It is in River Bend Park, which also has a nice playground, pavilion, restrooms, and picnic tables.

Local Churches. If you are in Croswell, check out the lovely architecture of two local churches, both are located on Main Street (Howard).

Festival

- The Croswell Swinging Bridge Festival, August. Features cardboard boat races, live entertainment, fireworks and daily activities for three days.

Contacts

Cros-Lex Chamber of Commerce, (810) 359-2262, www.*cros-lex-chamber. com.*

The Cobblestone Trinity Church

First Methodist Church

℘ort Sanilac

Population: 650.

Directions:
Eleven miles north of Lexington on M-25.

Background and History

An early landmark on the Thumb landscape was Bark Shanty Point where the village of Port Sanilac now stands. Uri Raymond came to the area in 1848 and taught at the first school in Sanilac Township. He also built the first store where he sold the settlers their provisions and provided a market for the shingles, tan bark, and cedar posts that the settlers produced. Raymond's Hardware has remained at the same location longer than any other hardware store in Michigan. Raymond was also interested in preserving the history of Port Sanilac, or Bark Shanty as it was then known. He wrote the following:

> *About the year 1830, a group of lumbermen came to peel the bark from the hemlock trees to be used for tanning leather. They built a shanty to live in and covered it with bark. When leaving in the fall, they left the shanty standing and it soon became a landmark to the sailors on Lake Huron, and they called the place Bark Shanty Point.*

For a period of time, shingles were a form of currency in the area. Land was available to a homesteader for one dollar and twenty-five cents per acre with a year to pay. Eighty-acres cost one hundred dollars and the sale of shingles brought four dollars per thousand. Twenty-five thousand shingles bought an eighty-acre piece of land. A hard-working family could create a new life with nothing but the sweat of their brow. With good fortune, they could even have it paid off in a year – no thirty-year mortgage hanging over their head.

The settlement at Bark Shanty Point was organized by four men: William Thomson, Anthony Oldfield, Quentin Thomson, and Joseph Moore. They came from England to Cincinnati in 1846 and formed the partnership Oldfield and Company. These men were lumber speculators. They intended to invest in pine lands in Michigan, build a saw mill for turning the giant trees into lumber, and hopefully get rich in the process. They chartered a schooner in Toledo and arrived at Bark Shanty Point on May 10, 1850.

Between Port Austin and Lakeport, with Port Sanilac smack in the middle, there were more than thirty million board feet of lumber sawed in 1852.

Port Sanilac Town Hall

Dr. Joseph Loop, who opened a practice in 1853, was another very important Bark Shanty citizen. He remained in his practice until he died in 1904. He visited his patients by horse and buggy. The Loop Harrison House is now a wonderful museum in the village of Port Sanilac.

A post office was established at Bark Shanty Point in 1854, and the village name was then shortened to Bark Shanty. In 1857, the village was renamed Port Sanilac, honoring Sanilac County and Sanilac Township wherein it is located. One story of the derivation of the name is that it came from a Chief Sanilac, leader of a tribe of Wyandotte Native Americans. Others claim it came from the name of a Chippewa Chief. A third version of its origin says that it was named for French fur trader, John Sanilac.

One of the early aids to navigation on Lake Huron was the Port Sanilac Lighthouse which was built in 1886. (Additional lighthouse story in Part Two of this guide.)

The first of the two catastrophic forest fires to hit the Thumb dealt a major blow to the small community. (See story of the fires in Part Two.) Hit again ten years later by a second roaring inferno, Bark Shanty conceded the end of its lumbering days.

Lakeshore development began around 1915 as small summer cottages began dotting the shoreline. Many current residents only remain in Port Sanilac during fair weather – retreating to their main home in the Detroit area or spending the cruel winter months in Florida.

Today, Port Sanilac is an idyllic village with a quiet way of life set against the magnificence of Lake Huron.

Restaurants/Food

First Mate Ice Cream, Port Sanilac Marina. Features twenty-four flavors of Mooney's and Stroh's hand-dipped ice cream. You can carry a cone with you as you walk the pier or sit down and enjoy a sundae, float, or ice cream bowl. Open summers, Mon to Thurs noon to 9:00 pm, Fri and Sat noon to 10:00 pm, and Sun noon to 8:00 pm.

Huron Shores Golf Club, 1441 North Lakeshore Road, north of Port Sanilac on M-25, (810) 622-9961. Specializes in steaks and fresh fish but also has a nice Sunday brunch. Open seven days for lunch. Evening dining Mon to Sat 5:00 pm to 9:00 pm and Sunday noon to 7:00 pm.

Mary's Diner, 24 North Ridge Street, (810) 622-9377. Some local residents meet here weekly for breakfast; others show up nearly every morning to start their day. The décor is strictly small-town diner, but to some it is like mom's kitchen. Friday Cod Special. Open 7:00 am daily, closes Mon to Thurs 8:00 pm, Fri and Sat 9:00 pm, and Sun 6:00 pm.

Shady Shores Inn, 2504 Lakeshore Road, (810) 622-8172. Lots of bikers stop here. Nancy's Famous Chili is probably the most popular item on the menu but also known for its burgers. Open Mon to Sat 10:00 am to closing (whenever the crowd dies down) and Sun noon to closing.

The Stone Lodge, 156 South Ridge Street, (810) 622-6200. An interesting local bar with char-grilled salmon and walleye baskets. They have hosted wine tasting and have a Karaoke night. Call for entertainment schedule. This is a nice place to stop and have a drink after playing beach bum for an afternoon. Daily specials. Open seven days 11:00 am; closing depends on the crowd but the kitchen generally shuts down at 10:00 pm during the week and 11:00 pm on Fri and Sat, and the bar stays open later.

Uri's Landing, 7365 Cedar Street, in the Port Sanilac Marina, (810) 622-0325. Varied menu and arguably the nicest place to eat in Port Sanilac. Uri's was named after early settler, Uri Raymond, and his picture graces the wall. It has a strange elevator with two accordion-like doors, both of which need to be closed for the elevator to move. Hopefully, you will not have any trouble figuring which one has to be opened to exit. It does make the building wheelchair accessible. Since it is only one floor up, nearly everyone takes the steps. All menu items are made from scratch and the portabella fries are a good place to start. The Whitefish is excellent and the Lake Perch is always a good choice, as is the Char-Grilled Salmon with Dill Sauce. For something a little different you might try the Seafood Ravioli. Open Sun to Thurs 11:30 am to 9:00 pm and Fri and Sat 11:30 am to 10:00 pm.

Van Camp House Fine Dining and Spirits, 135 North Ridge Street, (810) 622-0558. Lovely 1870s house turned into a fine dining experience. The freshness of their ingredients is reflected in the taste of the food. The owner travels to Detroit for fish and Flint for beef the day before he needs it. They prepare a fabulous four-bone stack of lamb. Their produce comes from two local farms, one of which is organic. The fresh eggs are hand delivered from the farm. You will likely need reservations. Open Thurs to Sat 4:30 pm year round and will open for special parties.

Yianni's Restaurant & Pizza, 41 North Ridge, (810) 622-0564. Dine-in or carry-out. A place to get pizza, sub sandwiches, and casual fare including a good gyro sandwich, pasta, seafood, and calzones. Open daily 11:00 am to 9:30 pm. (Seasonal.)

Lodging

Cozy Cottage and Seldom Inn Cottage, South Ridge Street next to Sarah's Colony Antiques, (810) 622-9020. The Cozy Cottage is a one-bedroom cottage with living room, kitchen, and laundry. It accommodates three. The Seldom Inn has three bedrooms and can accommodate six or seven comfortably. Cottages can be rented by the night, week, or other.

Holland's Little House in the Country B&B, 1995 Huron View Road, (810) 622-9739. This is not your typical Victorian B&B. Instead, it is a small, Nantucket-style, country cottage located on forty acres about a mile down an unpaved side road. It is well-kept and neat, and although it is not situated on the lake, it does have a private beach with a deck about a mile away.

Lakeside Cottage, 36 Lake Street, (810) 622-8343. A two-bedroom (one with queen, one with twins, and an additional roll-away), two-bath cottage with a fireplace. Available year round, three-day minimum stay.

Raymond House Inn, 111 South Ridge Street, (810) 622-8800, toll-free (800) 622-7229, *www.bbonline.com/mi/raymond* or e-mail *hrbrlite@sbcglobal. net.* A wonderful, historic Victorian that would be my first choice of places to spend a night in Port Sanilac. There are seven rooms available, five with private

Raymond House Inn

Gallery 890

baths, two that share a bath. The house was built in 1872 for Uri Raymond, owner of the hardware. It remained in the family for 112 years. It has been completely restored and is quite lovely.

Museums and Galleries

Gallery 890, at 890 South Lakeshore, (810) 622-8343, *gallery890@yahoo. com*. This gallery, run by Katie Rafferty, is likely to be one of your area favorites. Katie has excellent taste and chooses quality pottery, glass, jewelry, sculptures, tile works, and gift items created by forty artists. Her husband Ron does wonderful mosaic mirrors. It is worth stopping, just to check out the beautiful gardens and miniature train. Open Fri to Sun 10:00 am to 5:00 pm, but you will often find it open during the week. If there is a car in the parking lot, the store is probably open. It is also open by appointment. Seasonal: opens when the daffodils come into bloom and closes the week before Christmas.

The Sanilac County Historical Society Museum and Village and Loop Harrison House, 228 South Ridge Street (810) 622-9946. Definitely a worthwhile stop during your Thumb meanderings. The grounds are the site of the Loop Mansion and a historic village including a Carriage Barn, Dairy Museum, Platt's General Store, Banner Log Cabin, Huckins Schoolhouse, and the Barn Theatre as well as the recently acquired old Forestville United Church of Christ and a hunting cabin. The museum grounds are the location of the Annual Crafters Fair, Log Cabin Heritage Days, and many other events.

The Loop Harrison Mansion was the home of Bark Shanty's first physician and the house retains many of its original furnishings as well as some of Dr. Loop's medical equipment. It also exhibits many artifacts of shipwrecks and the great fires. The home was built in 1872 and has twenty rooms. (See related ghost

The Loop Mansion

story in Part Two of this guide.) *The Carriage Barn* displays wagons and buggies, a horse-drawn hearse, and farm machinery. *The Dairy Museum* contains vintage milking machines. *Platt's General Store* allows you to browse a selection of gift items including local artwork, candy, and books on local history. *The Banner Log Cabin* is furnished with authentic pieces specific to the period. *Huckins Schoolhouse* is a furnished, 1800s-era building that is typical of many of the early country schools in the area. The *Forestville Church* traveled back roads (the last few feet through a farmer's field) on its way to the museum grounds, and its perilous journey was a source of interest to the many observers along the way. It is a beautiful addition to the growing village. The most recent acquisition is the *hunters' cabin*.

The *Barn Theatre* is rustic theater at its best. The structure is nearly 150 years old. The barn originally belonged to a local farmer who used it for storage in the winter. The barn had to be emptied every fall at the end of the theater season. All traces of the theater had to be removed as it was readied for its role of storing farm equipment during the winter. After fifteen years of such starkly contrasting summers and winters, the building was purchased by the Sanilac County Historical Society and now is used exclusively for productions.

Tours are available and museum hours are June through September, Wed to Sun 11:30 am to 4:30 pm. There are also special events during the winter.

Village Pottery Studio and Gallery, 215 South Ridge Street, (810) 622-8320. Many attractive and unusual pieces of pottery and other works of art by local artisans. Generally open weekends, call to confirm current hours.

Antiques and Other Shopping

By the Shore Flowers and More, 5 South Ridge Street, (810) 622-0071. A full-service florist with lots of gift items, candles, cards, baby items, hoodies, wall art, and garden accessories. Displays handmade items from twenty consignees. Open Mon to Fri 10:00 am to 5:00 pm (sometimes later), Sat 9:00 am to 5:00 pm, and Sun 11:00 am to 4:00 pm. Closes Sun in winter and may reduce other hours slightly. Call for appointment anytime.

The Gray Cottage Antiques, 7170 Main Street, (810) 622-8846. Furniture, decorating items, tiles, prints, and frames. Open Fri to Sun 11:00 am to 6:00 pm or by appointment.

Gull Cottage Antiques, 2096 South Lakeshore (½ mile north of Applegate Road), (810) 622-9883, *www.gullcottageantiques.com*. Among other things, Gull's carries furniture and glass lights circa 1830-1930. Open March to December, Sat and Sun 10:00 am to 5:00 pm.

Harbor Light Gift Shop, attached to Raymond House Inn, 111 South Ridge, (810) 622-8550. Features the photographic art of Gary Bobofchak and nautical items. Open summer Tues to Sat 10:00 am to 5:00 pm. Closed Sun and Mon. Open winter, weekends only or by appointment.

Karen's Creations, 15 South Ridge Street, (810) 622-8661. Sweatshirts, T-shirts, gifts, and souvenirs the children will like. Also the place to get an ice cream cone on a hot summer day. Open seven days, 9:00 am to 6:00 pm.

Memories of Ireland, 1015 North Lakeshore, (2 miles north of Port Sanilac), (810) 622-0464. Patricia Currence, the proprietor of this little shop, imports everything Irish, and you can peruse Celtic jewelry, souvenirs, sweaters, T-shirts, sweatshirts, capes, children's clothing, bags, Belleek Irish China, CDs, teas, and Irish sweets. She is licensed to do your family coat of arms. Open six days in the summer 10:00 am to 5:30 pm (closed Tues). Open weekends only in Jan, Feb and March. Since the owner lives close by you can call anytime for current hours or access to the shop.

Port Sanilac Studio B, 37 South Ridge Street, (810) 622-9000. Upscale furniture shop with lots of gift items, jewelry, accents, and home decorating pieces. Open Mon 10:00 am to 5:00 pm, Thurs to Sat 10:00 am to 5:00 pm, Sun noon to 4:00 pm. Closed Tues and Wed. May reduce hours in the winter.

Raymond's Hardware, 29 South Ridge. Unless you have the need for some hardware, you probably will not be shopping here, but the hardware is historically significant, and so it is worth mentioning. The building was constructed in 1864, originally to be used as a boat shop. Since 1888, it has operated as a hardware store, and as noted above, has been designated Michigan's oldest continuously operating hardware and a Michigan Centennial Retailer. In the early days of Bark Shanty it was the site of the local newspaper, which was merely a pad of paper left on the counter. Customers came in, read the entries, and added anything they felt was of relevance.

Sarah's Colony and Crown Antiques, 173 South Ridge Street (810) 622-9020. Authentic and unusual antique European and American furniture pieces and collectibles. Open Sat and Sun 9:00 am to 5:00 pm or by appointment

This-N-That, 19 South Ridge Street, (810) 622-9540. Antiques, collectibles and miscellaneous. Open Thurs to Sat 10:00 am to 6:00 pm and Sun 10:00 am to 5:00 pm.

Parks, Beaches and Campgrounds

Horatio Earle MDOT Roadside Park, located on M-25, (almost across from Studio 890 on the lakeshore). Although only a roadside park, it is a perfect place to pull off and enjoy a spectacular view of Lake Huron. This park has a historic plaque recounting the infamous Storm of 1913. (See The Big Blow/The Storm of 1913 in Part Two of this guide.) Restrooms and picnic tables are available.

Sanilac County Park, 2820 North Lakeshore Road (810) 622-8715. (Also called Forester Park, see listing under Forester for additional details). Four and a half miles north of Port Sanilac, this park provides camping, camp store, playground, swimming beach, pavilion, bathhouse, picnic tables, and grills.

Marinas, Diving and Water Sports

Four Fathoms Diving, Inc, 7320 Main Street, one block from the harbor, (810) 622-3483. Scuba diving, instruction, and charters. They also have equipment and supplies.

Port Sanilac Harbor Commission, 7376 Main Street, (810) 622-9610.

Port Sanilac Marina, 7365 Cedar Street, (810) 622-9651. This full-service marina has 120 permanent slips and 30 transient slips as well as electricity, water, ice, repair services, restrooms, showers, and boat towing service.

Rec and Tec Dive Charters, diving out of Port Sanilac and Harbor Beach, (586) 263-6606. Divers meet Captain Gary Venet Sr. at the boat in either city. Call to make arrangements.

Port Sanilac Marina
Photo Courtesy of Joe Jurkiewicz

Seahawk Sailing School, located in the Port Sanilac Marina, (810) 346-3443 or call the marina (810) 622-9651. Offers all levels of instruction by USCG Captains with a wide variety of experience and training.

Other Things to See and Do

The Barn Theatre, next to the Sanilac County Museum/Loop Harrison House (see Museums above). In twenty-seven years of presenting shows, the Barn has tried a little of everything and has offered something for every age and taste. Tickets are inexpensive, compared to big city productions, and the Barn offers the opportunity to try something a little different during your weekend visit. All shows start at 8:00 pm. Theatre Box Office (810) 622-9114.

The Port Sanilac Lighthouse, two blocks east of the Marina. (See Beacons Lighting the Way in Part Two of this guide.) The lighthouse is not open to the public but you can park across from it and enjoy its beauty or snap a picture.

Stillpointe Center Therapeutic Massage, 109 South Ridge Street, (810) 622-8030. Massage by appointment. Great place to keep in mind if the summer activity throws your spine out of whack.

Golf

Huron Shores Golf Club, 1441 Lakeshore, (810) 622-9961. 18-hole golf course, open to the public seven days a week. Full service lunch, dinner, and cocktails (see Restaurants above).

Festivals

• Biannual Garden Club Walk, July. Port Sanilac has an active Garden Club, and you can see the fruits (or flowers?) of their labors throughout the little village. Every other year (odd-numbered years) they host their walk with several private gardens open for your viewing pleasure. Even numbered years you can see the lovely work done by these volunteers around the village, at the marina, and the Sanilac County Historical Museum. For additional information contact April at *flowers@greatlakes.net*.

• Music in the Harbor, Free concerts on Friday nights during July and August.

• Summer Festival, Last full weekend in July. Craft show, book sale, entertainment, beer tent, harbor activities and much more.

• Antique Yard Sale Trail, August.

Contact

Port Sanilac Visitor Information Center, 11 South Ridge Street, (810) 622-0404, *www.portsanilac.net*.

Forester

Population: About a thousand in all of Forester Township.

Directions:
Five miles north of Port Sanilac on M-25. If you blink you will miss it.

Background and History
Forester's star came into existence in the mid-1800s, shone brightly for a few decades, and then was nearly extinguished by circumstances beyond her control. Like her sister cities of Port Sanilac and Lexington, Forester was heavily wooded when first settled and it was predicted to become a Thumb showplace. That expectation seemed to be fulfilling itself, as four hotels were built in the thriving little community.

Docks were built along the lake front to facilitate shipping. Then fate, and to a lesser extent man's carelessness, stepped in to frustrate Forester's future. The fires of 1871 and 1881 destroyed the great forests for which the small village was named and ended the profitable lumber industry. The fires cleared the land and the area residents turned to farming as a way of life.

The storm of 1913 destroyed the Forester docks and they were never rebuilt, so the shipping industry was also lost. The railroad was built inland and became the source of transporting goods, leaving Forester out of the shipping transportation loop.

The fishing industry brought another source of commerce, but that too was dealt a death blow. The unfortunate introduction of the lamprey eel to the lake decimated commercial fishing.

Today, downtown Forester is a mere shell of her former self. There is a unique gift shop in the building north of the local tavern, but these two businesses and the local churches are about all that have managed to survive. The last hotel to remain standing is in need of additional repair and its future is uncertain. For years it provided rooms to lumbermen passing through. In addition to a comfortable bed, it may have provided them with someone to share it with, as the persistent legend claims it was also a bordello. Now it stands empty, a nostalgic reminder of better days. The local cemetery holds the gravestone of Minnie Quay. (See related ghost story in Part Two of this guide.)

Food
Camp Fire Pizza Café. See below under campgrounds.
Forester Inn, 2422 North Lakeshore, (810) 622-8606. A local tavern - often with lots of motorcycles parked in front. No high-end or upscale cuisine, but

they do a decent steak, and the atmosphere appeals to some. As part of the décor, the bar has an overturned canoe hanging from the ceiling and a moose head on the wall. A customer, intrigued by the shaggy and somewhat mangy looking beast, commented to the waitress, "I'll bet there is a great story behind that guy." The waitress told her the owner got it at a local garage sale and thought it would provide character for the bar. Just goes to show, you can buy any kind of ambiance you want! Open Mon to Sat 11:00 am to 11:00 pm, Sun noon to 9:00 pm.

Parks and Camping

Forester County Park (Also known as Sanilac County Park), 2820 North Lakeshore Road, (810) 622-8715. This county park has 190 sites. It provides hiking trails, fishing, playground, picnic grounds, swimming beach, park store, shower, bathhouse, flush toilets, running water, electricity, group camping, RV camping, cabins, and tent camping. It also organizes lots of activities for children. During the summer months (June through August), gospel concerts are held on Saturday nights at 8:00 pm in the pavilion.

Lake Huron Campground, 2353 North Lakeshore Road, (810) 622-0110 or toll-free (866) 360-CAMP, *www.lakehuroncampground.com*. Opened in 2007 and has been bustling with activity from its first day. The campground features 426 sites for camping and RVs, and big rigs are welcome. It also has log cabins. A twenty-acre fishing lake provides the opportunity for boating: either paddle boat or rowboat. Fishing poles are available. For hikers there is a one-and-a-half-mile nature trail and a bird watching area. A small island with gazebo and flower gardens is planned. There is a playground, heated pool, clubhouse, game room, planned activities, bocce ball, bike rentals, 18-hole mini-golf, horseshoe pits, dump station, propane, tiled restrooms with showers, laundry, and a fitness center. There are day passes available if you just want to use the amenities. The camp store also has the *Campfire Pizza Café* (810) 622-0096. In addition to pizza you can get hand-dipped ice-cream cones. The store and café are open to the public.

Forestville

Population: Approximately 150.

Directions:

Sixteen miles north of Port Sanilac on M-25. (Midway between Port Sanilac and Harbor Beach.)

Background and History

Like Forester, this is a one-blink town. Keep your eyes wide open or you will miss it. To say a place is small by Thumb standards means it is really, really small. At the time it was first settled, Forestville was heavily timbered, and it was for that natural bounty that it was named. Captain E. B. Ward built the first saw mill in the area in 1854. Forestville was incorporated as a village in 1895. It is a quiet place (consider that an understatement) with a small public beach.

Food/Restaurants

Do not plan to eat in Forestville, as there are no restaurants. You can check out Marge's, if you absolutely must get something to stave off starvation.

Marge's, on M-25, is a small convenience-type store, where you can grab a sandwich and a coke if you are too hungry to make it to Harbor Beach, or if you plan to spend a while at the beach in Forestville.

Antiques and Other Shopping

Farmhouse Antiques and Collectibles, 7914 Lake Street (a block east of M-25), (989) 864-5534. Located on Lake Huron, where you can get great views while you are stopped to shop. Twenty years in business and housed in a blue and white, restored 1881 farmhouse with two rooms of antiques inside and a quaint shed outside for lots more merchandise. Fiesta, depression glass, teapots, pitchers, kitchen items from the '30s to '50s, vintage linens, and oak furniture. Memorial Day until October, Sat and Sun 11:00 am to 5:00 pm or by appointment.

Beach

Forestville Beach, off M-25. Upon entering the tiny village of Forestville from the south, you can turn to your right at the first side street and find a park with a small, sandy beach. The swimming area appears pretty rocky, and swimming may not be as much fun as it would be at the Forester County Park or Harbor Beach. On the other hand, you probably stand a chance of more privacy, and maybe even more tranquility, at this tiny beach. If you choose to stop here, you will find only an outhouse or port-a-potty, but the park has a small boat ramp.

ℋarbor ℬeach

Population: 1837.

Directions:
M-25, sixty miles north of Port Huron.

Background and History
The earliest settlers to this area arrived in 1836 and established a saw mill for processing lumber. The city was first known as Barnettsville. In 1855, as the settlement continued to grow, the town was renamed Sand Beach, for its sandy beaches which are atypical of much of the Lake Huron shoreline.

The local residents eventually decided Sand Beach lacked dignity, or was not quite impressive enough, so in 1899 they renamed their little town Harbor Beach. In 1910 it was officially incorporated as a city.

One local legend suggests that in its early years, Harbor Beach was the location of a major counterfeit operation. Leonard "Pic" Defrain tells about it in his book, *Thumb Memories.*

A Mr. Crane (probably not his real name but the one he assumed while living south of Harbor Beach), was ostensibly a hunter and fisherman. Apparently, his real skill was coining counterfeit Mexican dollars and engraving bogus Canadian bank notes. Mr. Crane did not try to pass the foreign funny-money locally, so he was mostly left alone by his neighbors. He sold his "product" in distant parts of the United States. In the forests surrounding Harbor Beach, he had several shanties for carrying out his illegal activity. Eventually, one of Mr. Crane's neighbors, Mr. Hiram Whitcomb, confronted Crane and told the counterfeiter that he (Whitcomb) was aware of Crane's real business. Further, he knew Crane was a fugitive from justice. After that, realizing his neighbors were "on" to him, Mr. Crane's activities became secretive. Although he stayed in the area for another five years, he acted like a hunted animal. Mr. Whitcomb saw Crane only once after their confrontation and that was on an occasion when Crane returned to the Harbor Beach area to recover some ingot silver used for plating German silver dollars. Crane had once been a resident of Philadelphia where he was employed by the United States Mint. In his capacity as a minter, he learned his lucrative counterfeiting skills. Mr. Crane was so skilled at his trade that even he, occasionally, became confused over what was real and what was phony. On one occasion, mistaking the counterfeit money for genuine, he put some of it into a melting pot and thus spoiled the whole batch.

While in Harbor Beach you will want to see the Harbor Beach Breakwater Lighthouse which is best viewed from the Trescott Pier. Plan to make stops at the

Frank Murphy Museum, the Grice Museum, and the world's largest man-made harbor. You may want to spend a hot summer afternoon on the beach, fish from the Trescott Pier, or make a stop at the Corner Store, where you are sure to find something you cannot resist.

Food/Restaurants

Harbor Beach does not have an upscale, fine-dining spot to recommend. It does have several places where you can get good casual food (burger, pizza, ice cream), and some family-style restaurants.

Al's Restaurant, 123 South Huron, (989) 479-9038. Family-style restaurant with great homemade soups and a bakery for pies, cookies, cakes. Open seven days, 5:30 or 6:00 am to whenever the crowd is gone.

The Crowe's Anchorage, 139 South Huron, (989) 479-9494. Family restaurant with broasted chicken, seafood, salads, sandwiches, and Coneys. Also serves breakfast and is a place to stop for ice-cream and take out. Open seven days, 9:00 am to 10:30 pm. May close slightly earlier in the winter but also may soon begin opening earlier for the breakfast crowd.

Dollar House Ice Cream Shop, 120 South Huron, (989) 479-3180. Fifty flavors of homemade ice-cream made on the premises. Sundaes, shakes, sodas, floats, or quarts and pints to take home. Open summer seven days, 10:00 am to 9:00 pm, reduced winter hours.

Ernesto's Pizzeria, 129 State Street, (989) 479-9013. Originally built in the late 1930s as Todd's Ice Cream, today you will find a menu featuring pizza, subs, nachos, lasagna, and ravioli - all at great prices. Open Mon to Thurs 4:00 pm to 9:00 pm, Fri 4:00 pm to 11:00 pm, Sat noon to 11:00 pm and Sun noon to 9:00 pm.

Hunter's Bar, 132 North Huron, (989) 479-3820. Not long on looks, but Friday night they offer a popular Lake Perch Dinner. Portions are large enough to feed a family, and the nachos come highly recommended. Open seven days 7:30 am to 2:30 am.

Lakeshore Deli, 143 State Street, (989) 479-3354. In addition to butcher meats and grocery products you can get bakery breads and an assortment of deli meats from which to create a great lunch for the beach as well as soups, sandwiches, and salads. Open Mon to Sat 9:00 am to 6:00 pm. Closed Sun. Free delivery in the Harbor Beach city limits ($10 minimum order).

Pat's Bakery, 138 State Street, (989) 479-0103. Carmel top cinnamon rolls, fritters, donuts and scrumptious cinnamon-raisin bread. Open Mon to Sat 6:00 am to 2:00 pm, Sun 7:00 am to 1:00 pm.

Randolph's Family Restaurant, 724 State Street, (989) 479-3595. Heartland foods and several Italian dishes. Basic family restaurant with emphasis on home-cooked food, not décor. Lasagna is a local favorite. Open Tues to Wed 11:00 am to 8:00 pm, Thurs to Sat 11:00 am to 9:00 pm, and Sun 9:00 am to 8:00 pm. Closed Mon.

Sarah's Hallmark and Fudge Shoppe, 109 State Street, (989) 479-6629. Besides gifts, Foundations and Willow Tree Angels, and Harbor Beach sweatshirts, the biggest reason a traveler might be interested in this shop is the delicious homemade fudge. They even make season-appropriate batches like pumpkin fudge or eggnog fudge. Open Mon to Thurs 9:30 am to 6:00 pm, Fri and Sat 9:30 am to 9:00 pm, and Sun 10:00 am to 3:00 pm. After Christmas Mon to Sat 9:30 am to 6:00 pm and closed Sun.

Smalley's, 130 South Huron, (989) 479-3477. Good place for a casual burger, fries and a brew. Most people order the Smalley Burger, but the soups are excellent and sometimes they feature prime rib. They have dartboard and games and sometimes are a bit noisy. Open 11:00 am to 2:00 am, usually seven days.

Williams Inn, 1724 South Lakeshore, (989) 479-3361. This well-known establishment is located on M-25, several miles south of Harbor Beach. It is a traditional, family-style restaurant that has been in operation since 1911. If you go during the week in the non-season, you will see the local residents hanging-out, leisurely eating breakfast over their newspaper. Other times it gets pretty busy. Historic photos line the walls. Known for its lake perch, hand-cut prime rib, and New York steaks. Open Mon to Thurs 8:00 am to 9:00 pm, Fri 8:00 am to 10:00 pm, Sat 7:00 am to 10:00 pm, and Sun 7:00 am to 9:00 pm.

Lodging

Harbor Beach B&B, 203 State Street, (989) 315-8059. Your stay includes a hearty breakfast. Three theme bedrooms: Sun, African, or Asian. Within walking distance to marina. Fireplace, cable TV, VCR/DVD, private and shared baths, air conditioning, and wireless Internet.

State Street Inn B&B, 646 State Street, (989) 479-3388. In walking distance of the shops and points of interest in Harbor Beach. Late 1800s home with your choice of three distinctly decorated rooms. Nice porch, antiques, video library, and full breakfast.

Museums

Frank Murphy Memorial Museum, 142 South Huron Ave. (989) 479-3363. A museum dedicated to Frank Murphy, Harbor Beach's favorite native son. He was born in 1890 to John T. and Mary (Brennen) Murphy. He attended the University of Michigan Law School, and after graduating he returned to the area to practice law with his father and his brother. Murphy was a politician who served as an Associate Justice of the Supreme Court. He was also the Mayor of Detroit, Governor General of the Philippines, Governor of Michigan, and U.S. Attorney General. According to the Museum, Frank Murphy held as many offices as any politician in United States history, and what he accomplished in those offices was more important than the duration of each political stint. It is wise that they offered the latter part of their assessment, or you might wonder why he could not seem to hold a job! Outside the museum is a chronology of

Frank Murphy Museum

his posts. It appears he averaged only a couple of years in each position before he moved on. He did remain several years as Justice of the Supreme Court, a job that seemed to finally take; he remained there until his career ended. The Murphy family home contains part of the museum collection. It is next door to the Museum and also serves as the Information Center. The tour includes the Victorian home, law offices of Frank Murphy, and early family living quarters. Daily tours during the summer season. Open Memorial Day to Labor Day. (See related ghost story in Part Two of this guide.)

The Grice Museum, M-25 north of Harbor Beach, (989) 479-6056, or City Hall at (989) 479-3363. There are three buildings to explore: the late 1800s farmhouse with special exhibits, a barn, and a rural school. The farmhouse was built by James G. Grice, who came to Harbor Beach in the 1860s. One hundred years later, the city of Harbor Beach purchased the property. Soon after, a group of local volunteers helped to convert the house and surrounding area into a museum. There are over 2,000 artifacts in the complex which also exhibits agricultural machinery and farm implements. Open seasonally, early June to Labor Day, Tues to Sun noon to 4:00 pm.

Antiques and Other Shopping

Brennan's Department Store, 308 State Street, (989) 479-9016. Nine thousand feet of shopping opportunities for men's, women's, and children's clothing. Custom monogramming, printing, and alterations. Men's clothing from casual to tuxedos, women's clothing from elegant evening wear to sportswear

(Woolrich, Koret, Alfred Dunner, Levi, Dockers, Southern Lady, Keren Hart, Lana Lee) with a wide selection of accessories and jewelry. Also has an Outlet Department.

The Corner Store, 108 State Street, (989) 479-3321. The store's size will surprise you. The merchandising area has been expanded over the years and includes the upstairs which was originally the family's living quarters. The shop is filled to the ceiling and wall-to-wall, as well as in every nook and cranny, with all manner of merchandise. One of the newer acquisitions is a old-fashioned candy counter, and you can get free samples. When you first enter, take note of the impressively detailed woodwork around the downstairs (main) area of the store. The building was originally constructed in 1883 for Robert Irwin. In 1892 it became Charles Pettit Drug and Optical. By the end of the century, the Allen Family bought the store and retained the drug and optical sales. They sent their daughter to pharmacy school so she could run the pharmacy. The Allen family ran the store for ninety-seven years, and during their tenure they purchased the Mahan building next door to enlarge their retail space. The Allen family lived in the roomy apartment upstairs. In 1993, Harold and Leah Smith bought the building, and today their daughter Pam Semp owns the store and continues the tradition. Ms. Semp attributes the store's longevity (more than a century) to the fact that the various owner/proprietors were willing to change their stock and merchandise to meet the current market needs. At some point, jewelry displays were added to the drug store and optical business. Currently there is also a quilting shop and a framing department. Upstairs, there is a year-round Christmas room. The original kitchen serves as the display room for household/kitchen items. The second floor has the feel of a museum, with an old time piano and other antiques

The Harbor Beach Corner Store

used to display the merchandise. Open Mon to Sat 9:00 am to 5:30 pm and Sun noon to 4:00 pm. (Closed Sundays from January to mid-April.)

Maggie's Antiques and Collectibles, 142 State Street, (989) 479-3792. The building that houses this establishment was constructed in 1886 by Captain David Dues as a two-story structure with a business on the first floor and family apartment above. Today it is filled with varied merchandise including glassware, accents, household items, and more. Open summer Memorial Day to Labor Day seven days 10:00 am to 5:00 pm and Labor Day through the end of October Thurs to Mon 11:00 am to 5:00 pm.

McNally's Antiques and Collectibles, 131 State Street, (989) 479-6788. Depression glassware, kitchen collectibles, pottery, stemware, furniture, primitives, and more. Open Mon to Sat 10:00 am to 5:00 pm and Sun noon to 5:00 pm.

The Toy Crossing, 118 State Street, (989) 479-6239. Carries toys powered only by your child's imagination (no batteries). Stock includes: blocks, wooden toys, tubs of cool action figures, Melissa and Doug wooden puzzles, stuffed animals, Groovy Girl dolls, dollhouses, kites, flying toys (like rockets), and a tree house. Your children will love this place. Open Wed to Sat 9:30 am to 5:30 pm and Sun noon to 5:00 pm. Closed Mon and Tues. Hours may be reduced from Christmas to the beginning of the summer season.

Parks, Beaches and Campgrounds

Harbor Beach Bathing Beach Park and Trescott Street Pier, located in downtown Harbor Beach. This sandy swimming beach (or Harbor of Refuge as it is called) has the 1015-foot pier that permits a great view of the lighthouse as well as the opportunity to enjoy a leisurely day of fishing. There is a nice playground area for children. The park has picnic tables, grills, restrooms, volleyball courts, and a lifeguard on duty from mid-June to Labor Day. A marker in the park describes the feat of Vicki Keith, who swam across Lake Huron from this point to Goderich, Canada, where she arrived to a cheering throng of four hundred. She accomplished the swim between July 17 and July 19, 1988. She swam 48 miles in 46 hours and 55 minutes.

North Park Waterfront Park, M-25, (one mile north of blinker light), (989) 479-9554. The park is on the waterfront with a nice playground for children. There is also a private trailer park and campground with 184 sites on the west side of the road across from the park. You will find hiking trails, fishing, picnic grounds, sanitation, volleyball, horseshoes, showers, bathhouse, flush toilets, running water, electricity, group camping, and RV camping.

Wagener County Park, Helena Road (five miles south of Harbor Beach), (989) 479-9131. This county park has ninety-six camping sites for RV and tent camping (some with views of the lake), hiking trails, a small secluded beach, fishing, picnic facilities, courtesy boat launch (boats no more than fourteen feet), sanitation and bathhouse, running water, and electricity. The playground even has a teeter-totter. Pets are allowed in the park. A pair of bald eagles have been sighted in the area.

Marinas and Diving

Harbor Beach Marina, 766 State Street, north of Harbor Beach, (989) 479-9707. Has a courtesy pier, dockside service, gas, electric, fish cleaning station, overnight docking, paved ramp, 114 boat slips, restrooms, water hookup, waste removal, and showers.

Rec and Tec Dive Charters. (See Diving under Port Sanilac listing.)

Other Things to See and Do

Fishing. If you are a salmon fisherman, this is the port or harbor for you. It offers some of the best salmon fishing in Lake Huron. Harbor Beach has both a private launch and a large public marina (see above). Besides salmon, you can try your reel at yellow perch, walleye, trout, and steel head.

Harbor Beach Breakwater Lighthouse. Constructed in 1885, this lighthouse is still active, though now automated. It was one of the more desirable lighthouses in which to work, since it was not nearly as difficult as the lighthouses further north, where keepers had to deal with dangerous shoals. The lighthouse is not currently open to tours as a result of its state of disrepair. There is a local group working to get the lighthouse renovated, and it is hoped that it will eventually be open for public tours. The best place to see the lighthouse is from the Harbor Beach Bathing Beach and Trescott Pier. It sits on a detached breakwater. (See Part Two of this guide for more lighthouse information.)

Harbor Beach Area District Library Building offers first-run movies for $4 adult and $3 students. Concessions are much less expensive than you

Harbor Beach Area District Library Building

will find in the larger mall-complex theaters. The outside of the building has interesting murals depicting scenes from the town's past, and these two-story murals are worth a couple of minutes of your time to catch a look. The building was originally built as a theater, but over the years has served as a gymnasium, courthouse, school, and even a jail. Call (989) 479-3417 to see if a movie that interests you is playing while you are in town.

Sunken Ships/Diving. The barge, *Chickamauga*, lies a half-mile off Harbor Beach at a depth of thirty feet. It sank in 1919. The Thumb Area Underwater Preserve has many sunken ships. To charter a dive see the Port Sanilac listing for Rec and Tec Dive Charters. (Also see What Lies Beneath in Part Two of this guide.)

White Rock/Tepper's Golf Course, 8773 South Lakeshore (on M-25 south of Harbor Beach), (989) 551-9153. A batting cage, sand trap, and putting and driving range. For full golf courses, see the listings under Port Austin and Caseville.

Festivals

- Lady of Lake Huron Summer Festival, July.
- Maritime Festival, July.
- Poor Man's Promotions Craft Show, July.
- Carriage House Art Fair, August.
- Antique Yard Sale Trail, August.
- Harvest Festival with Chili Cook Off, September.
- Holiday Open House, November.
- Festival of Lights, December.

Contact

Harbor Beach Chamber of Commerce, 126 South Huron, (989) 479-6477, or (800) HB-MICH5, *www.harborbeachchamber.com*.

Port Hope

Population: 300.

Directions:

Seven and a half miles north of Harbor Beach on M-25. Approximately seventy miles north of Port Huron.

Background and History

Known as the little town with the big welcome, Port Hope was founded in 1855 and incorporated as a village in 1877. It was a busy logging, milling, and shipping port. Salt production was also an important industry in Port Hope. Early resident William Stafford, a lumberman in the area, built a boarding house to accommodate those individuals working or traveling in this growing community. In 1890 Richard Herman built the Herman Hotel, a stylish brick building that offered additional accommodations. The Herman Hotel is currently known as the Port Hope Hotel, and although it no longer rents rooms, it remains in business as the local tavern, serving meals and spirits.

In its early days, the schooner *St. Andrews and the Swallow,* a propeller-driven steamer, docked at Port Hope and serviced the Detroit area as well as the upper Great Lakes. Port Hope had two long docks for deep-water sailing vessels and steamers.

After the two great fires in Michigan (1871 and 1881), the community turned to farming as its major source of support.

Food/Restaurants

Four Seasons Café, 4411 Main Street, (989) 428-3200. A little hometown café with burgers, pastas, steaks, and a Friday fish fry. Potato pancakes are among the breakfast choices. Hot apple dumpling is the favorite for dessert. Open Mon, Wed, Thurs, Sat, and Sun 8:30 am to 2:00 pm, and Fri 8:30 am to 8:00 pm. Closed Tues.

Port Hope Hotel, 4405 Main Street, (989) 428-4808. Good half-pound hamburgers (try the Leroy cheeseburger) and a friendly staff. Friday all-you-can-eat fish fry featuring pollack and lake perch. A place to get breakfast, lunch, or dinner seven days a week. Open Sun 8:00 am, Mon to Sat 7:00 am. Closing varies up to 2:30 am depending on the crowd, but the kitchen closes at 9:00 pm.

Lodging

Stafford House B&B, 4489 Main Street, (989) 428-4554, *staffordhousepthope. com.* This historic home is an example of post Civil War Eastlake, stick-style architecture and was built in 1887 as a wedding gift from W.R. Stafford to his daughter. Today it offers four rooms: Peace, Love, Joy, and the Hope Suite (three rooms including a private sitting room). Each room has a private bath. Rooms are decorated with antiques to help take you back in time to a more relaxing era. Offers candlelight dinners by request. Open year round. Provides bicycles and snowshoes. Full breakfast. Hope Chest shop behind the B&B.

Antiques and Other Shopping

Main Street Antiques, 4432 Main Street, (989) 428-1007. Originally Melligan's Store or Agricultural Hall, this is the oldest surviving commercial building in Port Hope. Today it is home to an antiques shop with glassware, jewelry, dishes, accent pieces, and an upstairs with furniture. Open Memorial Day through Labor Day, Fri to Sun 11:00 am to 5:00 pm, Labor Day through October, Sat and Sun 11:00 am to 5:00 pm.

Northern Attic Antiques, 4443 Main Street, (989) 428-3039. A nineteenth century Victorian-style building with cast iron front columns. The building was constructed in 1886 by Dr. R.C. Ogilvie as his drug store and office, and today it houses a varied assortment of antiques. Open year round Fri to Sun 11:00 am to 5:00 pm but wise to call ahead for hours.

Museum

Pointe Aux Barques Lighthouse Museum, located in Lighthouse Park (see below for additional information about Lighthouse Park). President Polk ordered the lighthouse built in 1857 to guard ships from some of the most treacherous shoals in the lake. The lighthouse was automated in 1957 and is still in service, but the keeper's residence is now a museum, and the grounds are a lovely 120-acre park with modern camping. Parking is ample and there is a museum and gift shop inside the lighthouse. Relics from shipwrecks are located in some of the rooms. You can go through the lighthouse living quarters - both upstairs and down. You are allowed part way up the lighthouse tower. (See Part Two of this guide for related stories.)

Parks, Beaches and Campgrounds

Lighthouse Park, 7320 Lighthouse Road, ten miles north of Port Hope, (989) 428-4749. This county park has 107 campsites and provides hiking trails, fishing, playground, picnic grounds, boat launch, park store, sanitation, shower, bathhouse, pit toilets, flush toilets, running water, electricity, group camping, RV spaces, and tent camping. There is not a swimming beach.

Stafford County Park, North Street, (M-25), (989) 428-4213. A county park with seventy-three campsites. The park provides hiking trails, fishing, a nice playground, picnic grounds, boat-launch, sanitation, shower, flush toilets, running water, electricity, group camping, RV parking, and tent camping. There is a reedy and rugged rocky beach and nice views.

Marina

Courtesy Pier (Downtown). Port Hope has a courtesy pier with a paved ramp and twenty-five boat slips.

Other Things to See or Do

Michigan Nature Association's Whisky Harbor Nature Sanctuary, two-and-a-half miles northwest of Port Hope, turn north from M-25 to Pochert Road, one-and-a-half miles to the dead end. This nature sanctuary includes the Kernan Memorial Nature Sanctuary and the Thelma Sonnenberg Memorial Plant Preserve. You can enjoy unique rock formations, mud-flats, native wildflowers, rare migratory birds, and artifacts washed up along the shore. The sanctuary is designed for hiking, bird watching, and photography. MNA asks that you only take out what you take in and not use motorized equipment in the sanctuary. This is NOT a park. It is a preserve area (natural state) with no restrooms, picnic tables, or other amenities. It is for those who want to blaze their own trail.

Port Hope Chimney, located in Stafford Park. The chimney was built by William Stafford. It is all that remains of the lumber mill that was established in 1858 by John Geltz. The chimney remains as a monument to the pioneers who, by their courage, developed the area. It is Michigan's only chimney standing from the lumbering era.

Port Hope Walking Tour. You can pick up a Port Hope Village Walking Tour Map at either antiques shop or restaurant on Main Street (M-25) and take

Port Hope Chimney

a leisurely stroll through the "little town with the big welcome." Some of the points of interest include The Saw Mill Chimney, the Flour Mill, the Planing Mill, Port Hope Salt Company Site, Blue Town House, the Leuty-Peterson House (excellent example of nineteenth century Carpenter Gothic architecture), Ogilvie Building (nineteenth century Victorian style), Stafford Home (current B&B) and Melligan's Store or Agricultural Hall (currently Main Street Antiques).

Festivals

• 4th of July Parade, Port Hope has an annual 4th of July parade, flea market, softball tournament, and large fireworks display.

• Antique Yard Sale Trail, August.

Contact

Harbor Beach Chamber of Commerce, (989) 479-6477. For information about local festivals and happenings. (Harbor Beach Chamber has information for Port Hope.)

ℋuron City

Directions:
Midway between Port Hope and Port Austin on M-25.

Background and History
In the late 1800s this was a city employing several hundred people and it boasted more than a hundred buildings including a blacksmith shop, general store, icehouse, roller rink, and a hotel.

The two catastrophic forest fires that raged through the Thumb in 1871 and 1881 each destroyed Huron City, causing it to lose its dream of becoming a prosperous lumber center. (See Great Fires in Part Two of this guide.) Although the city was reconstructed after these fires, the forests were gone and the local wells dried up, causing residents to abandon the city. The city no longer exists as a separate village, and the geographic area it once occupied is technically part of Port Austin. It is, however, still the site of one of the more interesting museums and historic villages in the Thumb. It is worth making time in your travels to stop here. The William Lyon Phelps Foundation operates the remaining buildings (ten open to the public) and museum as a historical site.

Museum
Huron City Museum, 7995 Pioneer Drive (Off M-25) between Port Hope and Port Austin, (989) 428-4123, *www.huroncitymuseums.com*. This museum and grounds are the legacy of Huron City and the reason it does not fade from memory. It is a restored village that offers several buildings including a log cabin, church, carriage shed, U.S. Life Saving Station (see below), barns, inn, and a general store. The information center contains a variety of artifacts. The House of Seven Gables is a restored, 1881 Victorian mansion fully-furnished with original pieces. The museum also offers Workshop Wednesdays where you can learn basket weaving, family history writing, poetry writing, stained glass, or how to use a spinning wheel. Open Memorial Day to June 30: Sat and Sun 11:00 am to 6:00 pm, July 1 to Labor Day: Thurs to Mon 10:00 am to 6:00 pm, and Labor Day to September 30: Sat and Sun 11:00 am to 6:00 pm.

Pointe Aux Barques Life Saving Station, at Huron City Museum. Completed in 1876, the life saving station was scheduled for demolition but, instead, was preserved and currently houses a remarkably complete collection of life saving equipment and artifacts. It also stages a reenactment of the training drills of the courageous surfmen. The old surfmen had a saying, "You have to go out, but you don't have to come back," illustrating the dangers involved with manning a lighthouse in these treacherous waters.

Other Things to See or Do

Just offshore there is a historical underwater site with several submerged ships. (See What Lies Beneath in Part Two of this guide.)

Contact

For additional museum information call (989) 428-4123.

Grindstone City

Population:

Grindstone city is unincorporated and is part of Port Austin Township. No separate population statistics are available, but it is a very small village. In its heyday it boasted 600 people, at one point dwindled to only ten year-round residents and more recently has seesawed up again to about sixty year rounders.

Directions:

About a mile off M-25 towards the lake just north of Huron City.

Background and History

The city was named by its founder, Captain Peer, and as the name suggests, Grindstone City was known for the grindstones it produced during the late 1800s and early 1900s. These grindstones were shipped all over the world. By 1875, the village boasted two churches and two hotels. The latter were the Huron House and the Grindstone Hotel. The major industry, and the one that employed most of its populace, was the quarry.

Today, Grindstone City appeals to fishermen from all over, and it is generally considered one of the better fishing spots in Michigan. If fishing is your vacation goal, give it a try. If you are looking for wonderful beaches, shopping, and fine dining, this will not be your ideal vacation destination.

Grindstones mark the driveways to many homes and businesses

Food/Restaurants

Captain Morgan's Grindstone Bar and Grill, 3337 Pointe Aux Barques, (on the water in Grindstone City), (989) 738-7665. A no-frills kind of place with good food. Serves perch and walleye dinners with fish often from the morning catch, broasted chicken, pizza, soups, salads, and sandwiches. Friday all-you-can-eat fish and chips, and Saturday the bar livens up with Karaoke. They will clean and cook your catch of the day. They have a special recipe for lake trout. Seasonal. Sun to Thurs 11:30 am to 9:00 pm (pizza 'til 10:00 pm), Fri and Sat 11:30 am to 10:00 pm (pizza 'til 11:00 pm).

Danny Zeb's Party Store, Bar and Restaurant, 8743 Pearson Road, (989) 738-8646. Karaoke bar. Offers primarily bar-type food (hamburgers, sandwiches, etc.) and welcomes fishermen. Open seasonally.

Grindstone General Store, 3206 Copeland Road, (989) 738-6410. Brags that it has the largest ice-cream cones in the Thumb. Also has a mini-gallery with pottery, prints, local artists' paintings, driftwood, baskets, books, and Amish preserves. Open seasonally seven days 11:00 am to 10:00 pm.

Lodging

Captain Morgan's Lodging offers four two-bedroom cabins with kitchenettes and three one-bedroom cabins. Cabins come complete with towels, dishes, coffee pot, TV, and bedding. It is located on the Grindstone Harbor next to the boats.

Whalen's Cabins and Grindstone Shores Campground, 3373 Pointe Aux Barques, (989) 738-7664. Daily or seasonal camping for RVs, pop ups and campers. Cabins and lodge rooms available. Bathhouse, washer and dryer, fire pits, gift shop, and some boat docks available. Views of Lake Huron. Open May through October.

Parks, Beaches and Campgrounds

Quarry Fields Campground, 8850 Quarry Drive. This private trailer park and campground has 107 sites and provides fishing, playground, picnic area, boat launch, park store, sanitation, shower, bathhouse, flush toilets, running water, electricity, group camping, and RV camping. No tent camping allowed.

(See ***Whalen's Cabins and Grindstone Shores Campground*** above under Lodging. Also see marinas below.)

Marina and Charters

Grindstone Harbor Marina, 3379 Pointe Aux Barques. Has a courtesy pier, dockside service, gas, fish-cleaning station, overnight docking, paved ramp, fifty-four boat slips, restrooms, and water hookup.

The Pretzel Bender, 3379 Pointe Aux Barques, (989) 738-7558. Sport fishing for salmon and lake trout on the Processer II with Captain Filion.

Stormy Chinook Charters, 4140 Lakeshore Road, *www.stormychinook. com or fishing@greatlakes.net,* (810) 359-5192. Captain Dan will take you sport fishing for Great Lakes salmon and trout. He knows where the fish are, and his long experience as a captain and his love of the sport will ensure that you have a memorable fishing experience. Captain Dan lives in Lexington, but charters out of Grindstone City because he believes the fishing is better there.

Also see Charters under Port Austin.

Other Things to See or Do

Fishing. You will find charter boat captains and serious fishermen to help you if you are looking to fish in Grindstone City. Eagle Bay is a favorite spot to try to snag the small mouth bass. You can also try your luck at catching lake and brown trout, salmon, walleye, and yellow perch. Camping and lodging are close by the fishing holes. Licenses are required and available locally.

Port Austin

Population: 737.

Directions:
Top of the Thumb on M-25. Less than three hours from Detroit. This is the other "up north."

Background and History

The history of Port Austin traces back to 1837 when Jonathon Bird became its first settler. In 1839 it was named for P.C. Austin who was part owner of a saw mill built there that year. Austin built a dock for himself and then enlarged it so others could use it as well. He put a street light on a pole for a lighthouse, and it became known as Austin's Dock, later Austin Port, and finally Port Austin.

At one time the Port Austin Harbor could accommodate steamships and sailing vessels, a fact that encouraged merchants, lumbermen, and bankers to set up business. By 1865, Port Austin was the county seat and a new courthouse was built there.

In the late 1860s, the Port Austin Hotel was built to provide lodging to stage coach passengers coming from Port Huron and Bay City.

Because of its unique location, this picturesque, lakeside community can boast both beautiful sunrises and sunsets. During the summer, the place is bustling with activity including boating, charter fishing, golfing, horseback riding, putt-putt golfing, bird-watching, canoeing, swimming, festivals, good restaurants, nearby museums, and go-carting.

Food/Restaurants

The Bank 1844 Restaurant, 8646 Lake Street, (989) 738-5353, *www. thebank1884.com*. A national historic building, The Bank prepares all entrees fresh daily. You might want to start with Escargot Stuffed Mushrooms, and then choose the Bistecca with fresh mushrooms and shallots, sun dried tomatoes, and gorgonzola cheese; or perhaps try the Chicken Milano, a chicken breast filled with sweet Italian sausage, mozzarella, and provolone, and covered with marinara sauce. The Bank was built in 1884 by Richard Winsor and Horace Snover and actually functioned as a bank. It was built after the second devastating fire swept through the Thumb and was constructed to withstand another great fire. The current owners strive to provide excellent food in rather funky surroundings. Napkin rings are made from $100 bill wrappers and mints are disguised as rolls of coins. Open seven days during the summer. Mon to Sat lunch and dinner, Sun dinner only. Open weekends in the fall (Fri to Sun) and closed Jan through March. Reservations are suggested if you are going on weekends or during peak dining hours.

Breakers on the Bay, 1404 Port Austin Road, (three-and-one-half miles west of Port Austin on M-25), (989) 738-5101, *www.breakersonthebay.com*. Lake front dining with great views of Lake Huron from every table. The tone is casual-elegance and fine-dining. The filet mignon is a mouth-watering entrée choice. Reservations suggested. Open Wed to Mon, dinner from 5:00 pm. Closed Tues. Hours reduced in the off-season. Open weekends year round.

Buccaneer Den, 1884 Port Austin Road, (989) 738-7175. Steaks and seafood. Sat prime rib; Sun fish and chips and roast chicken. Open seven days at 5:00 pm.

Corley's Thumb Restaurant, 283 West Spring Street, (989) 738-8611. Serves full breakfasts and has a supper special each night. Dessert free with dinner on weekends. Menu includes hamburgers, hot dogs, ribs, perch, and more. Open seven days, 7:30 am to 2:00 pm and then reopens from 4:00 pm to 7:00 pm.

The Farm Restaurant, 699 Port Crescent Road (eight miles from Port Austin, SR 53, south to Port Crescent Road, then two miles west), *www. thefarmrestaurant.com*, (989) 874-5700. Upscale dining in the Thumb! For many people living in little towns of the Thumb, the Farm is the number one choice for dining. Although the Farm Restaurant's food is upscale, you will feel comfortable in casual attire. The Farm Restaurant specializes in *"heartland"* cuisine, and you can start with their wonderful Three Onion Soup and then order something as hearty as a Grilled Center Cut Pork Chop or Farmer Style Swiss Steak; or try something a bit more elegant like the Pan Seared Salmon Au Poivre or Chicken and Mushroom Strudel served with spring vegetables. The house specialty is the Pan Seared Whitefish. The desserts are fabulous, so try to save room for something like the Crisp Phyllo Pastry filled with chocolate ganache served with caramelized bananas, vanilla ice cream & caramel sauce. Menu items are prepared from scratch using seasonal herbs and produce from the Farm's own garden. Prize winning recipes, homemade appetizers, soups, breads, and desserts, along with selections especially for children. The Farm also offers cooking classes. Call for reservations. Open May through October Tues to Sun for dinner 5:00 pm to 10:00 pm. Closed Mon. (See recipes for the Farm Restaurant's Three Onion Soup and Tuscany Style Tomato Soup at the end of this Port Austin section.)

The Fireside Inn, 1146 Port Austin Road, (989) 738-8232. Restaurant and bar with a family atmosphere. Pizza, antipasto, salads, fish, steaks, and a great French onion soup. The Jack Daniel's BBQ Pork Ribs are the specialty of the house. Friendly staff and good food. Open May through October Sun to Thurs noon to 9:00 pm, Fri and Sat noon to 10:00 pm. Winter open Wed to Sun 4:00 pm to 9:00 pm (possibly a bit later on Fri and Sat) and closed Mon and Tues.

The Garfield Inn, 8544 Lake Street, (989) 738-5254. Historic building housing both an inn and restaurant and offering superb cuisine and drinks in the European tradition. Features classical and traditional meals, generally priced under twenty dollars. Prime Rib has been a long-time staple on the menu and continues to be a favorite since the restaurant's recent change of management. Open Memorial Day to Labor Day, seven days for lunch and dinner and additionally opens for breakfast on weekends. Mon to Fri 11:00 am to 10:00 pm (dinner starts at 4:00 pm), Sat 8:00 am to 10:00 pm and Sun 8:00 am to 8:00 pm. The restaurant is open year round but the hours vary during the winter months, call to confirm. (Also see Garfield Inn under lodging below.)

Joe's Pizzeria & Restaurant, 8725 Lake Street (989) 738-8711. Pasta, hand-tossed pizza, subs, and sandwiches. Open Mon to Thurs 4:00 pm to midnight, Fri and Sat noon to 1:00 am, and Sun noon to midnight.

The Landing Tavern, 8724 Lake Street, (989) 738-9750. Burgers and munchies, sandwiches, and dinner baskets. Very casual and priced reasonably. Different special each day. Also has dart boards and a pool table. Carry-out. Open daily. (Kitchen stays open until midnight). Does not take credit cards.

The Lighthouse Café, 42 East Spring Street, one block west of traffic light, (989) 738-5239. Homemade soups and baked goods. Breakfast is their main draw; they make their own sausage, and they open at 5:30 am to provide a hearty morning meal to even the earliest angler. They have a lighthouse breakfast special with two eggs, two pieces of sausage, three pieces of bacon, ham, potatoes, and toast. Enough to keep a fisher-person going for quite awhile, and the price is reasonable. Serves breakfast, lunch, and dinner in a casual atmosphere. Open seven days, 5:30 am to 7:00 pm (closes Sun at 6:00 pm). Hours are seasonal.

Murphy's Bakery, 35 East Spring Street, (989) 738-7192. Cinnamon twists, many varieties of donuts, pies, cakes, and their wonderful apple strudel. No preservatives. In business for over fifty years. Open daily 5:00 am to 5:00 pm, closes after Labor day and opens at Easter.

The Oasis, 8719 Lake Street, (989) 738-SUBS. Build your own hot or cold sub. Also has breakfast sandwiches, nachos, hot dogs, Coney dogs, French fries, chili potatoes, fruit bowl, and other salads and fresh soups. Open Mon to Fri 8:00 am to 7:00 pm, Sat 7:00 am to 7:00 pm and Sun 9:00 am to 5:00 pm.

Sportsman's Inn, 8708 Lake Street, (989) 738-7520. Family dining, reasonable prices and a very casual atmosphere. Non-smoking dining room available. Full dinners, a sandwich, or pizza. The lobster chowder is a good way to start dinner or order it to accompany one of the many sandwich options. Seasonal hours. Only weekends in the winter, 5:00 pm to 10:00 pm.

The Stockpot, 8714 Lake Street, (989) 738-7111. Casual family dining featuring omelets, country biscuits and gravy, subs, burgers, salads, perch, and homemade soups. Also fresh bakery goods. Open seven days 6:00 am to 8:00 pm, after Labor Day Mon to Thurs 6:00 am to 2:00 pm and Fri to Sun 6:00 am to 8:00 pm.

Lodging

    Beachcomber, 158 West Spring Street, (989) 738-8354, *www.beachcomberpa. com*. Motel and monthly apartments on the water. Private sandy beach, in-room refrigerators, one-and-a-half blocks from fishing pier, shopping, and dining. Bird Creek Golf Course packages available. Pictures of rooms available on Web site.

    Blue Spruce, 8527 Lake Street, (989) 738-8650. New outdoor pool, clean, fully-equipped cottages, fire pit, refrigerator, and microwaves. Some two-bedroom cottages available.

    Breakers on the Bay, 1404 Port Austin Road (three-and-a-half miles west of Port Austin on M-25), *www.breakersonthebay.com*, (989) 738-5101. Open year round. Extras: spacious lake-front hotel rooms with private, white, sandy beach, and a game room. Courtesy continental breakfast.

    Captain's Inn B&B, 8586 Lake Street, (989) 738-8321 or toll-free for reservations (888) 277-6631. This colonial revival home was built in 1856 and 1857. Large library and living room with fireplace. It is available for weekends or an extended stay. Open year round. Five rooms, three with private bath. Two-and-a-half blocks from marina. Not air-conditioned. Continental breakfast.

    Garfield Inn, 8544 Lake Street, (989) 738-5254. Built in the 1830s in the French style of architecture. Rated one of the Top Five Inns in Michigan. The inn is located two blocks from Lake Huron. Six rooms; some with private and some with shared baths. Each room has a ceiling fan. The most popular room is the *Garfield* with its Queen Ann four-poster bed, sitting-area in the bay window, and two overstuffed chairs. It is on the second floor, and "yes," President Garfield did sleep there. Garfield was an intimate friend of the mistress of the house, Maria Learned. Her husband, Charles G. Learned, purchased the house in 1857. Charles was a financial genius involved in construction of the Erie Canal. He earned his first $10,000 by age eighteen. Remember, this was in the mid-1800s, and that was an astronomical amount of money. Learned set about remodeling and enlarging the house. It is said that Garfield was absolutely taken with Maria, but her husband was his best friend. Nonetheless, Maria and Garfield are rumored to have carried on an affair that lasted for many years, as evidenced by rather risqué letters exchanged between them.

    Local legend says that when Garfield was mortally wounded by an assassin's bullet in September 1881, he requested to travel to Port Austin to recover in this house because it carried so many fond memories and he felt so comfortable there. He died there instead. Maria had died of tuberculosis six months earlier. This version of the story seems to contain some dubious information. Documented historical accounts indicate Garfield lingered for eleven weeks after the shooting and he was the victim of horrible malpractice from many sources during that time. In fact, his assassin's defense at trial was that it had not been his bullet but, rather, the gross malpractice that killed the president. Obviously, that defense was not taken seriously.

The circumstances of Garfield's death are quite gruesome, and it is questionable that Port Austin had the medical staff to attend his condition. It seems more likely that he asked to go there, but his condition precluded it. Even more suspect would be the dying president's reasons for wanting to stay with the husband of his lover, since Maria was dead by then. Finally, September 1881 was the month of the second great fire in Michigan – not a time to come to Port Austin to recuperate.

In addition to President Garfield, the inn has played host to many weary travelers in its long history. It was designated a National Historic Site in May 1990. Six families have owned the inn. Because it is so steeped in history, this would be my choice of places to stay in Port Austin.

Krebs Beachside Cottages, 3478 Port Austin Road, (989) 856-2876. Resort with eight waterfront units on Saginaw Bay. Two hundred feet of sandy beach. Elevated sun deck for great views. Picnic tables, Adirondack chairs, grills, bonfire kettle. Kitchens equipped with microwaves and other appliances. One, two, three and four-bedroom cottages available. No pets during the summer. Open May to November.

Lakeside Motor Lodge, 8654 Lake Street, (989) 738-5201, or toll-free (800) 200-4208. Open year round, this motor lodge has thirty-five rooms as well as chalet apartments that can accommodate four to ten people. It also has a heated pool, volleyball court, play area, and game room.

Lake Street Manor B&B, 8569 Lake Street, (989) 738-7720. This late 1800s brick Victorian, located near downtown and the Saginaw Bay, has lovely gardens and is designated a historic B&B. Extras: video library and whirlpool. Breakfast can be ordered; served in bed. Some shared and some private baths.

Lake Vista Motel and Cottages, 168 West Spring, (989) 738-8612, *www. lakevistaresort.com*. Located on the water. The rooms are either standard or deluxe, and all offer a mini-refrigerator and microwave. Landscaped with water gardens. The largest heated swimming pool in the area. The cottages are two-bedroom or a large or extra-large efficiency, and they are rented by the week. Both the rooms and the cottages are air conditioned.

Port Austin Motel, 8761 Larned Road, (989) 738-8729, *www.portaustinmotel. com*. Water views. Rooms with a single-queen, two-queens, or two-beds with kitchenette; even a Jacuzzi room. This is an older motel, check the Internet for pictures.

Sandcastles on the Beach, 1368 Port Austin Road, (989) 738-4200. Check out the rooms at *www.sandcastlesonthebeach.com*. Located on the water, Sandcastles offers a motel and one, two, or three-bedroom, fully-equipped cottages. Older buildings; it has two hundred feet of sandy Lake Huron beach and a pool.

The Shores, 184 Farrar Street (Entrance to Port Austin Park and Beach), (989) 551-3117 or toll-free (866) 738-6202, *www.portaustinshores.com*. Fully furnished one and two-bedroom units with outdoor hot tub. Close to downtown shops and restaurants. Daily, weekly, and monthly rentals. Non-smoking.

Museums

Lighthouse Park Museum, nine miles east of Port Austin. See listing under Port Hope.

Huron City Museum, see listing under Huron City.

Antiques and Other Shopping

Port Austin has an area of unique shops and quaint boutiques:

The Haven Antiques, 31 Railroad Street, (one block east of M-53), (989) 738-8000, *www.thehavenantiques.com*. A quaint little shop with an ever-changing inventory including furniture, linens, costume jewelry, garden items, architectural pieces, and chandeliers. They also sell merchandise at the Port Austin Farmers' Market on Saturday mornings. Seasonal hour variation. Open Memorial Day through October 31, Fri and Sun 11:00 am to 5:00 pm, Sat 10:00 am to 5:00 pm. Open later during the summer.

Lake Street Emporium, 10 East Spring Street. Home accents, gifts, and antiques. Open Mon to Sat 10:00 am to 5:00 pm, Sun noon to 4:00 pm. Seasonal.

Lisa's Loft, 8735 Lake Street (above the Heins Hardware), (989) 738-7311. Lisa Heins has redone the large space above the hardware (which happens to have a spectacular view of Lake Huron) and sells greeting cards, antiques, gifts, garden items, and more. Open Mon to Sat 8:30 am to 5:30 pm and closed on Sun. Open year round.

Old Village Peddler, 124 East Spring Street, (989) 738-6445. Gift and gourmet shop. Home accents, old-fashioned candy counter, mugs, cookbooks, kitchen items, large selection of gourmet foods, and even a few antiques are displayed in a house that is 160 years young. Open seven days in July and August 10:00 am to 6:00 pm, closes at 4:00 on Sun, weekends until Christmas, other times by appointment.

Pascarella's, 8736 Lake Street, (989) 738-1187. Unique gifts, curios, a Taste of Italy, imported and hand-painted chocolates, sugar-free candies and cookies, specialty BBQ and other sauces, preserves, popcorn, great teapots, some wall art, and fudge. The only place to get Santa Maria seasonings in the state. Open seven days summer 9:00 am to 6:00 pm, weekends only after the tourist season.

Sticks and Strings, 7345 Carpenter Road. The shop is housed in a century-old granary converted into a quaint cottage and filled with hand-knit items, specialty yarns, and hand-spun wool. They also carry glass and clay buttons made by a local artist and have some knitted items for sale. A spinning wheel is available. And, as incongruous as it may seem, they sell free-range eggs. The tea kettle is always on, and there are homemade shortbread cookies for guests. Open Tues to

Sun 10:00 am to 6:00 pm. Closes an hour earlier in the winter. Closed Mon.

Timeless Treasures, 8637 Lake Street, (989) 738-3131. A shop filled with antiques and collectibles including vintage jewelry, kitchen items and glassware, and videotapes of the local area. Summer open Mon to Sat 10:00 am to 5:00 pm, Sun 11:00 am to 3:00 pm. Winter hours are reduced.

Towne and Country Casuals, 110 East Spring Street, (989) 738-7778. Ladies' casuals: sportswear, sweaters, jewelry, purses, and accessories. "You won't see yourself coming and going," is how the owner describes her fashions. She does not want to order the same fashions you will find at the mall and she purchases only a couple of any given style. Open Memorial Day to Labor Day Mon to Sat 9:00 am to 6:00 pm. Open Labor Day to Jan Thurs to Mon 9:00 am to 5:00 pm, and open April to Memorial Day Thurs to Mon 9:00 am to 5:00 pm.

Up the Grove Gifts and Antiques, 8673 Lake Street, (989) 738-7427. An eclectic mix of merchandise including antiques, crystal, interesting pieces of furniture and fine gifts, and collectibles. Summer hours 10:00 am to 9:00 pm seven days; winter 10:00 am to 5:00 pm.

Parks, Beaches and Campgrounds

Bird Creek County Park, M-25 in the heart of Port Austin (day-use only), (989) 269-6404. This county park has fishing, playground, pavilion, picnic tables, large sandy swimming beach, bathhouse, pit toilets, flush toilets, running water, and electricity. No camping.

Duggan's Family Campground, 2941 Port Austin Road, (989) 738-5160. Eight miles west of Port Austin. Playground, laundromat, pool, showers, store, dumping station, activity center, and rustic and improved sites. Daily, weekly, and seasonal rates. Winter storage available.

Gallup Park, M-25 in Port Austin (day-use only). This county park provides hiking trails, tennis, fishing, playground, and picnic area. No camping.

Huron County Nature Center Wilderness Arboretum, nine miles east of Caseville or nine miles west of Port Austin, just off M-25, turn south on Oak Beach Road to Loosemore Road, then east to the Nature Center Entrance. This 280-acre nature center was founded in 1990 on property that had been owned by the county since 1941. There is a 120-acre wilderness arboretum, accessible trails, a beautiful pavilion, restrooms, and many walking trails which run through the wilderness. You can expect to see red pine, white pine, white oak, and birch trees in the wooded areas. You may also spot pink lady's slipper, white trillium, gaywings (fringed polygala), clintonia (corn-lily), and a variety of other species in season. Bird-watchers should be able to sight the eastern bluebird, wood thrush, great-crested flycatcher, American redstart, scarlet tanager, and rose-breasted grosbeak. There are a variety of educational programs offered.

Jenks Park (day-use only), M-25, four miles south of Port Austin. This lovely little park is a state rest area. It provides fishing, playground, picnic grounds, trails for hiking, swimming beach, pit toilets, and running water. No camping.

McGraw County Park, M-25 between Port Austin and Caseville (day-use only). County park with hiking trails, fishing, playground, picnic grounds, swimming beach, bathhouse, flush toilets, and running water. Also lovely view of the water.

Oak Beach County Park, M-25, eight miles north of Caseville, (989) 856-2344. This county park has fifty-five sites, fishing, playground, picnic grounds, boat launch, swimming beach, park store, sanitation, shower, bathhouse, pit toilets, running water, electricity, group camping, RV camping, and tent camping.

Port Crescent State Park, located on M-25 near the tip of the Thumb, (989) 738-8663. Port Crescent has nearly three miles of white, sandy beach, making it a favorite summer stop. At one time, Port Crescent was a little town in the Thumb. Now it is primarily a lovely park and recreation area. In earlier days, the sand of this area was "mined" for manufacturing uses, but that practice stopped when it became cost prohibitive. Three hundred thirty-five acres were acquired from Sand Products Corporation of Detroit in 1975 and are now the day park. The total park size is nearly six hundred acres of varied terrain and woods of jack pine and oak. It is a great place to spot deer and explore hidden ponds. Facilities include a modern beach house with change courts, restrooms, picnic pavilion, and arguably the best swimming beach in the Thumb – complete with small sand dunes. The park has playground areas, horseshoe courts, and hiking trails. There are paved roads, parking lots, stoves, and water supply. A canoe slide is located in the first parking area. Small car-top boats can also be launched. There is a bird-watching platform available. This park is the site of the Annual Hawk Watch which takes place the fourth weekend in April. Many trails are groomed for cross-country skiing in the winter. There are some campsites available along the beach and old river channel. Each site has an electric outlet, fire circle, and picnic table. Campers, motor homes, and trailers may use the sanitation station to take on water and dump sewage. Plant life is abundant in the park and you can find berries and wild flowers in the spring and summer. Birds and other wildlife are frequently seen in their natural habitat. Fishing is allowed in the park waters. (You must possess a valid Michigan fishing license.) Legal hunting and trapping is allowed from September 15 through March 31.

Thompson Scenic Turnout, between Port Austin and Caseville, is worth a stop. Michigan's Thumb has numerous turnouts that provide the driver with a break and a lovely view.

Waterfront Park, Spring Street a block west of the stop light. Pier, sandy beach, tables, playground.

Marinas, Water Sports, Boat Rentals, Diving and Fishing

Chuck's Marine (diving and cruises), 119 East Spring Street, (989)

738-2628. Offering dockside service, electricity, paved ramp, twenty-six boat slips, restrooms, and water hookup. You can also arrange dive and snorkel trips here. The marine provides boat cruises for up to five people. Times are flexible. During the cruise you will see the Port Austin Lighthouse and Turnip Rock.

Eagle Bay, two miles east of Port Austin on M-25. Allows car-top boats only. Seven boat slips and water hookup.

Port Austin Area Charter Service, (517) 230-4326 or (989) 738-3474, *www. fishportaustin.com*. Providing Lake Huron fishing charters with Captain John Atwell aboard the Osprey (a Marinette Sportsman with a fly bridge that is 31' LOA by 11½' wide) docked in downtown Port Austin. Rated number one for most trout and salmon caught per charter trip.

Port Austin Kayak and Bicycle Rental, Spring Street downtown, (989) 550-6651, *www.thumbkayak.com*. The place to rent kayaks, bikes, or water trampolines. Delivery and shuttle. Also arranges river trips and guided tours. Open seven days, 10:00 am summer only.

Port Austin State Dock, north of light in Port Austin. Has a courtesy pier, dockside service, gas, electric, fish-cleaning station, overnight docking, paved ramp, forty-nine boat slips, restrooms, water hookup, waste removal, and showers.

Pro's Line Charters, Brown's Marina, (989) 670-5613, *jsstro@aol.com*. Charter fishing aboard the Fish-On with full time Charter Captain Harold. Guaranteed fish. Lake trout, salmon, steelhead, or walleye.

Shores Cottages and Marina, 184 Farrer, (989) 738-6202. Has electricity, overnight docking, ten boat slips, and water hookup.

Tip of the Thumb Canoe Rental, 2471 Port Austin Road (M-25 at the Pinnebog River Bridge), (989) 738-7656. Day trips to the beautiful Port Crescent Park and the sandy shores of Lake Huron.

Other Things to See or Do

Family Go-Karts, a quarter mile south of Port Austin on M-53, (989) 738-5130. Go-Karts for ages three and up, paint-ball, bumper-cars, trampoline-bungee-cords, Hoops basketball, Aerotrim, and free Kiddyland. Open seasonally, Memorial Day through Labor Day, 10:00 am to 10:00 pm.

Farmers' Market, Waterfront Park, Spring Street. Over a hundred vendors selling produce, flowers, baked goods, jewelry, antiques, arts, and crafts. Also entertainment. A definite place to go on Saturday morning. Open 9:00 am to 1:00 pm in season.

Fishing. See above under Marinas.

Indoor Ice Arena, (800) 35-THUMB. Open to the public from November through March. Open skating Sat and Sun. Call for details.

Knoblock Riding Stable, 1001 Hunter Road, just east of M-53, (989) 738-7228. Approximately seventy horses. Open summer seven days 10:00 am to

6:00 pm, weekends in September and closes for season in October.

Port Austin Community Players, 35 Railroad Street, (989) 738-5217. Year round theatre. Call for details.

Port Austin Reef Lighthouse, Two-and-a-half miles north of Port Austin in Lake Huron. The lighthouse was constructed in 1878 and then abandoned in 1953, when it was left to deteriorate. (See additional story about this lighthouse in Part Two of this guide.) It is currently being restored.

Golf

Bird Creek Golf Course, 7850 North Van Dyke (M-53, 1½ miles south of Port Austin), (989) 738-4653, *www.birdcreekgolf.com*. An 18-hole golf course, par 72 slope 126 with cart rental, club rental, snack bar, range, and pro shop.

Port Austin Putt Putt Golf, 8660 North Street (Corner of Railroad), (989) 738-5120. Open Memorial Day to Labor Day, seven days, opening at 10:00 am.

Sandy Dunes Adventure Golf, 2755 Port Austin Road (M-25, located between Port Austin and Caseville), (989) 738-6066. An 18-hole course and a game room. It also has an ice cream bar with hand dipped and soft serve frozen treats.

Festivals

• Winter Chill Thrill, January. (Bonfire, hayrides, broomball tournament, polar bear dip, live music, kids' games, and more.)
• Easter Egg Hunt, April.
• Lady's Slipper Festival, May.
• Fishing Tournaments, June.
• Bocce Ball Tournament, June.
• Thumb Arts Guild Art at the Garfield, June.
• 4th of July Parade, July. (Parade and fireworks.)
• Huron County Nature Center's Annual Auction and Craft Sale.
• Sawmill Days, August.
• Antique Yard Sale Trail, August.
• Art in the Park, September.

Contacts

The Greater Port Austin Area Chamber of Commerce, 2 West Spring Street, P.O. Box 274, Port Austin, MI 48467, (989) 738-7600, *www.portaustinarea. com*.

The Huron County Visitors' Bureau, (800) 35-THUMB.

Port Austin Community Players, 35 Railroad Street, (989) 738-5217 for theatre schedule.

The Farm Restaurant's Three Onion Soup Recipe

Ingredients:

1 Quart	Red Onions, sliced
1 Quart	White Onions, sliced
2 Cups	Leeks, sliced
1 Tablespoon	Garlic, minced
3 Cups	Brown Veal Stock
2 Cups	Chicken Stock
1 Cup	Beer
2 Tablespoons	Flour
4 Tablespoons	Clarified Butter
	One Standard Sachet**

Seasoning Salt, Pepper, pinch of Cayenne, Sugar, few drops Balsamic Vinegar.

Method:

1. Heat a large skillet with the butter and sauté the red and white onions until caramelized.

2. Add the leeks and garlic and continue to sauté until soft.

3. Stir in the flour.

4. Deglaze with the beer and add the stocks. Whisk.

5. Add the sachet and simmer 20 minutes.

6. Remove the sachet and add and adjust the seasoning (last line of ingredients).

7. Garnish with a crouton and top with parmesan or mozzarella cheese.

**A standard sachet is a "sack of spices" or a little pouch of cheese cloth or a coffee filter filled with bay leaves, a sprig of thyme, a few peppercorns and parsley stems.

The Farm Restaurant's Tuscany Style Tomato Soup Recipe

Ingredients:

1 Pound	Italian Sausage Meat (Sweet)
¼ Cup	Olive Oil
2 Cups	Onions, diced
2 Teas	Garlic, minced
3 Cups	Ground Tomatoes
1 Quart	Chicken Stock

Garnish

1 Cup	Fresh Basil Leaves, stems removed
1 Cup	Zucchini, diced
2 Cups	Baby Spinach Leaves
As needed	Pesto
As needed	Grated Parmesan

Method:

1. Heat a soup pot with the olive oil and brown the sausage meat and break it up.
2. Add the onions and garlic, sauté until transparent.
3. Add the tomatoes and the stock, bring to simmer.
4. Simmer for 10 minutes.
5. Add the zucchini and simmer for 2 minutes.
6. Turn off the heat and wilt in the basil and spinach leaves.
7. Season with salt and pepper.
8. Top with pesto.

Caseville

Population: 888 (over 2,000 within the township boundaries).

Directions:
M-25, eighteen miles beyond Port Austin.

Background and History

Caseville was originally known as Port Elizabeth and was settled in 1836 by Ruben Dodge. The first sawmill was constructed in 1852 to further the important lumbering industry. Ship building and salt manufacturing also played key roles in the economy of Caseville. Today tourism seems to be this tiny village's economic mainstay. If you visit during the summer, Caseville is lively and well-populated. When the summer ends, the village transforms into a tiny, quiet hamlet. The view remains equally spectacular in all seasons, and sunsets here are unparalleled.

Caseville has one of the most popular beaches in the Thumb, giving the town a beach-party flavor all summer. The drive to Caseville, along M-25, is filled with lovely views of the Saginaw Bay: its islands and several parks and turnouts.

The Cheeseburger Festival is probably the rowdiest, craziest, and longest festival in the Thumb. It runs more than a week and has a Margaritaville flavor - literally and figuratively. By the time it is over, the townspeople are happy to reclaim their small village, but it sure is fun while it lasts!

Food/Restaurants

Bay Café, 6750 Main Street, (989) 856-2676. A casual family-type restaurant with a menu that includes hamburgers, seafood, steaks, and pasta. Pies are homemade, and there are daily specials like homemade apple cobbler. The Big Buoy Burrito and the Turkey Reuben were both excellent. The reuben had none of the thin, watery turkey that is so often a mainstay in sandwiches; this seemed like real, thick-sliced, turkey roast. The Big Buoy Burrito was huge and every bit as delicious as it looked. The décor is rather stark, but not unpleasant. The most notable attempt at ambiance is a palm tree with little white lights, and a parrot – everyone gets into the spirit of the Cheeseburger Festival though it had ended months ago. Open for breakfast, lunch, and dinner daily. Closed Sun in the winter.

Baywatch on the Beach, 6626 Beachway, (989) 856-4764. Delightful views of the Saginaw Bay. You have to try their Corned Beef Sandwich. Seasonal. Open mid-May to mid-September, seven days 11:00 am to 8:00 pm (last grill order at 7:30 pm and closes at 6:00 pm on Sun).

The Depot Restaurant and Bakery, 7063 Main Street, (989) 856-8900. Casual food where one favorite is the Country Fried Steak. Also has pies, muffins, sugar free desserts, and cookies. Open Sun to Thurs 7:00 am to 8:00 pm, Fri and Sat 7:00 am to 9:00 pm.

Duffy's Blue Water Inn, 6584 Main Street, (989) 856-3663. Dark and smoky bar with wide-screen TV (think sports events), pool table, darts, and a two-story deck overlooking the harbor. Thursdays all-you-can-eat spaghetti, and Friday is fish-fry night. Open seven days, 8:00 am to 2:30 am. Closes slightly earlier in the winter.

Elizabeth's Favorite Things Coffee Shop, (See below under Shopping.)

Giuseppe's Pizzeria, 6562 Main Street, (989) 856-2035, or (989) 856-4233. Besides pizza, Giuseppe's serves BBQ ribs, lasagna, ravioli, tortellini, and spaghetti. If you are not into Italian food, you can order their lake perch or chicken.

Hersel's on the Bay, 6024 Port Austin Road, (989) 856-2500. Enjoy postcard-perfect sunsets while you eat. Full dinners including blackened salmon, Mexican entrees, sandwiches, salads, soups, and pizzas. Some entertainment: DJ, dancing, comedy shows. Open seven days.

Lefty's Diner and Drive In, 6937 Main Street, (989) 856-8899. Not bad for fast food, this classic 1950s-style diner serves burgers, hot dogs, foot-longs, French fries, fried mushrooms, homemade onion rings, and milk shakes. The outside is painted a bit garishly, but you cannot judge the food by its exterior. Open 8:00 am to 9:00 pm, seven days a week. Closes earlier in the winter.

Lemon Tree Coffee Shop (See below under Shopping).

Mitch's at Hidden Harbour Golf Course, 7521 Port Austin Road, (989) 856-4747. This fine-dining restaurant has a lovely ambiance and good food. Open Mon to Thurs 11:00 am to 8:00 pm, Fri to Sun 11:00 am to 9:00 pm. Seasonal.

Port Elizabeth Grill, 6567 Main Street, 989-856-9210. Gets rave reviews. Boaters can walk from the harbor to the Port Elizabeth Grill. Nice menu featuring prime rib, seafood, and pasta dishes. You can sit on the deck in the summertime, sip margaritas, and try the cheeseburgers they created in honor of the Cheeseburger Festival. Open Tues to Thurs 4:00 pm to 8:30 pm, Fri and Sat 4:00 pm to 10:00 pm. Closed Sun.

The Riverside Roadhouse, 6540 Main Street, (989) 856-8606. According to loyal patrons, the best pizza in town. Another favorite is the Chicken Club Salad, or you can opt for sandwiches, burgers, or the house special, Bourbon White Fish Dinner. Open summer seven days, 11:00 am to 2:00 am, (Sun opens at noon). Off-season hours reduced.

Shakers Ice Cream Parlor, 6685 Main Street, (989) 856-2663. Excellent ice cream. Also serves burgers and sandwiches in an informal setting. Sun to Thurs 8:00 am to 8:00 pm, Fri and Sat 8:00 am to 10:00 pm.

Walt's Restaurant, 6618 Main Street, (989) 856-4020. Local down-home flavor to this restaurant. It has a loyal following in Caseville. This is the place for a really early breakfast if you are headed out fishing for the day. You can get enough food to keep your stomach from growling for hours, and the prices are reasonable. Open seven days 4:30 am to 5:00 pm.

Lodging

Bella Vista Inn and Sunset Bay Resort, 6024 Port Austin Road, (989) 856-2650, *www.bella-caseville.com*. Offers a wide variety of accommodations, from single motel rooms to cabins, efficiencies, cottages, and suites. The penthouse in Bella Vista sleeps eight and has a Jacuzzi tub, full kitchen, sunroom, central air, and a large outdoor deck with a gas grill. The most important feature is its seven hundred feet of private, sandy beach. It also has two heated outdoor swimming pools. Check Web site for pictures of rooms.

The Cabins, 5949 and 5953 Port Austin Road, (989) 561-2347, *www. snlprop.com*. Log cabins situated in a wooded setting. The master bedroom has an attached bath, and there is a second bedroom with a second full bath. Separate dining room and fully-supplied kitchen. The Cabins are air-conditioned, have free cable and local phone calls, and can accommodate up to six people. They can be rented by the week or month. There is also a special rate for a three-night stay. There is an extra charge if you do not supply your own linens. Walking distance to the lake. Clean, nice place to stay.

Charter House Inn, 6519 Riverside Drive, (989) 856-2323. In the heart of everything. Located on the river in town and boat accessible. Air conditioning, pool, coffee.

Crews Lakeside Resort, 4750 Port Austin Road (several miles east of Caseville), (989) 856-2786. Located on the water, these condos have 1400 to 1600 square feet of space with two fireplaces, two bedrooms, and two full baths per unit. The condos are fully furnished and equipped but bring your own linens.

Dale's Lakefront Cottages, 4744 Port Austin Road, (989) 874-5181 or (989) 550-0911. For rental of cottages, condos, and homes in Caseville.

Farmstead Inn B&B, 5048 Conkey Road (half a mile from Sleeper State Park), (989) 856-3110. A country farmhouse overlooking forty acres of woods, meadows, and fields. Walking trails through the property afford opportunities to observe birds and other wildlife. Hot tub available for guests.

Port Elizabeth B&B, 6729 Ash Street, (989) 856-4431. The three bedrooms upstairs share a common bathroom. There is an additional bathroom downstairs for the fourth bedroom located on that floor, and it is open to any guest who wishes to use it. If you are not willing to share a bathroom with strangers, this may not work for you. Continental breakfast served the week of the Cheeseburger Festival as the host is busy with festival activities. The dining room has interesting antiques and dishes.

The Lodge at Oak Pointe, 5857 Port Austin Road, (989) 856-3055, *www. oakpointelodge.com*. The lodge features suites with two-person whirlpool tubs, queen canopy beds, screened porch, and gas fireplaces. A private cottage-suite is also available. Private and secluded with thirty acres of nature trails where you are likely to encounter deer and other wildlife. The inn has a library and a great room for your activities. Light breakfast with fresh fruit, homemade muffins, bagels, juice, and coffee.

Museum

Caseville Maccabee Hall Historical Museum, currently at the Independent Bank Building, 6727 Main Street but will be moving to Maccabee Hall, a historical landmark at 6733 Prospect, (989) 856-9090. History of Caseville and Huron County with over three hundred history books, military and nautical artifacts, tools, and other interesting exhibits. Open seasonally, Wed to Fri 11:30 am to 4:30 pm.

Shopping

Caseville is not an upscale shopping hot spot, but then neither is any other small town in the Thumb. It is a tourist town to be enjoyed for its wonderful beaches and water activities. However, as you wander down Main Street you will have the opportunity to peruse many little knickknack shops where you may just find that perfect something.

The Briar Patch, 6832 Main Street, (989) 856-3144. Candles, cards, gifts, Jim Shore and other collectibles, T-shirts, Christmas decorations, picture frames and books including Johnathan Rand's American and Michigan Chillers series. Open Wed to Sat 10:30 am to 5:00 pm, Sun 11:00 am to 3:00 pm. Closed Mon and Tues. Usually closes January to April.

Cottage Outfitters, 6815 Main Street, (989) 856-4291. Casual décor, gifts, cards, candles, and gourmet pastries. Also consignment from twenty local artists. Open seven days 10:00 am to 5:00 pm in the summer.

Elizabeth's Favorite Things, 6815 Michigan, (at Main), (989) 856-8979. This is one of the newer stores in the community. It combines a retail store, Internet café, and coffee shop. Outdoor patio available. Features delectable pastries, and you can bring your own laptop or they have two for customer use. Merchandise includes: Life is Good clothing, household items, sweatshirts, T-shirts, jewelry, Fossil watches, Botanika make-up, soaps, and more. Open Tues to Sat 9:00 am to 7:00 pm, Sun 10:00 am to 2:00 pm, and closed Mon. May have longer hours during summer festivals.

Harts Floral, 6003 Main Street, (989) 856-3567. Gifts and home décor in addition to floral. Open Mon to Sat 10:00 am to 5:00 pm, Sun 11:00 am to 3:00 pm.

Helping Hands Thrift Store, 6495 Main Street, across from the Methodist Church, (989) 856-2439. Thrift shops are not generally included in this guide, but Caseville's volunteer operated thrift shop has a vintage section which may be worth a look. It seems everyone in Caseville likes to stop here to see what is new. Open Mon to Sat 10:00 am to 5:00 pm.

Ibiza, 6556 Main Street, (989) 856-9464. Cute, two-piece swimming suits, bikinis, cover-ups, beach bags, sarongs, sunglasses, and accessories. Open Tues to Sat 11:00 am to 5:00 pm, Sun noon to 4:00 pm, and closed Mon. Seasonal.

Jac's by the River, 6576 Main Street. A house with each room filled with unique merchandise: collectibles, children's gifts, nautical, wood carvings, Christmas, jewelry, stuffed animals, toys, bowls, and kitchenware. Open seven days 10:00 am to 6:00 pm. Seasonal.

Keepsakes Gifts, 6576 Main Street, (989) 856-3006. Largest gift shop in the area. Cards, tea cups, jewelry, and miscellaneous items. Open daily 10:00 am to 5:00 pm, July and August extended hours of 9:00 am to 9:00 pm. May have even longer hours during the Cheeseburger Festival.

Key North Surf & Beach Shop, 6508 Main Street (989) 856-7266. Florida style beach shop with swimsuits, clothing, beach chairs, and other summertime needs. Seasonal, generally closed after Labor Day.

Le Blanc's Store, 6611 Main Street, (989) 856-2799. Le Blanc's General Store was built by John McKinney. In 1892 he added a second building to the north side of the store. In 1917 Alice and Fred LeBlanc left their jobs as buyer and bookkeeper for a large department store in Alpena to move to Caseville and pursue their dream of owning and operating their own little store in this beach town. The store retains an old-fashioned feeling with its wood floors and merchandise including dry goods, posters, geodes, souvenirs, toys, clothing, and a little bit of everything else. Open seven days.

Lemon Tree Marketplace, 6604 Main Street, (989) 856-8733, *www. lemontreemarketplace.com*. This shop is a coffee shop (specialty coffee drinks including latte, mocha, espresso, and cappuccino, as well as smoothies, Chai tea, and other drinks), antiques shop, and gift shop. You can peruse gifts, cards, vintage looking candy, gourmet packaged foods, T-shirts, flip-flops, hats, home décor, accessories, books, games, puzzles, beach wear, jewelry, garden items, and fun stuff for all ages on the main floor. The Tree House (upstairs) displays shabby chic, cottage style furnishings, antiques, painted furniture, glassware, and collectibles. The building was originally a bank. Open summer Memorial Day to Labor Day, Mon to Sat 7:30 am to 6:00 pm, Sun 7:30 am to 4:00 pm. Closed off-season.

Linda's Basket Case/At the Beach, 6900 Main Street, (989) 856-2277. Beachwear, sandals, accessories, cards, food products, cheeseburger memorabilia, wall art, Life is Good clothing, and chimes. Open seven days 10:00 am to 5:00 pm in the summer, weekends after Labor Day and closes November to April.

The Official Cheeseburger Store, 6912 Main Street, (989) 856-3818.

Primarily Cheeseburger in Caseville paraphernalia. Seasonal.

The Screamin' Monkeys, 6906 Main Street, (989) 856-4800. Definitely kid-oriented with gifts and toys to catch the attention of the younger set. Carries stuffed animals, Eeboo, Mud Puppy, HABA, Rich Frog, and other lines. Also carries Japanese Stationary items. Tries to carry something for all ages from rattles for babies to school bags for teens. Great selection of children's books. Open seven days during peak tourist season, follows the crowd to determine hours.

Shore Winds Gifts, 6682 Main Street, (989) 856-2300. Gift items, jewelry, garden accents, and more.

Two Blondes and a Business, 6600 Main Street, (989) 856-7050. Resort wear, half price paperbacks (good selection), cards, souvenirs, accents, and fudge. Summer open Mon to Thurs 10:00 am to 7:00 pm, Fri and Sat 10:00 am to 9:00 pm, and Sun 10:00 am to 5:00 pm. Off-season open Fri to Sun.

Water's Edge Gifts and T-Shirts, 6616 Main Street. The building was originally a grocery store started in 1852. It is now the outlet to LeBlanc's (see above). This could be your place to get that Cheeseburger Festival T-shirt. Open seven days.

Parks, Beaches and Campgrounds

Caseville County Park, M-25, at the northern limits of Caseville, (989) 856-2080. This county park has 214 sites and offers fishing, playground, picnic tables, swimming beach, sanitation, shower, bathhouse, flush toilets, running water, electricity, group camping, RV camping, and tent camping. It is located on the lake and provides picturesque views.

Philp's County Park, M-25, six miles north of Caseville (day-use only). This county park has a picnic ground and swimming beach.

Rush Lake State Game Area, two miles north of Caseville near Sleeper State Park. Two thousand acres for hunting. You will have the best success hunting waterfowl, but there is also some deer hunting.

Albert E. Sleeper State Park, 6573 State Park Road, (989) 856-4411 or toll-free (800) 447-2757, *www.michigan.gov/dnr*. Located on the shores of Lake Huron with more than seven hundred acres of forest, wetlands, sandy beach and dunes, hiking trails, and a secluded campground. Spectacular sunrises and sunsets. The four miles of hiking trails are groomed in the winter for cross-country skiing (assuming sufficient snowfall). Hikers also have access to more than two thousand acres of adjacent Rush Lake State Game Area, an area of forests and wetlands populated by many types of wildlife. Many rustic and primitive trails wind through the game area presenting a challenge for the more adventurous hiker. The park hosts many special events such as the Harvest Festival in the fall and a Civil War Re-enactment during the summer. The campground has two modern toilet/shower facilities, both of which are wheelchair accessible.

Campsites are available from mid-April through late October. Sanitation stations and a fish cleaning station are available. A mini-cabin that sleeps up to four is located in the campground and may be rented throughout the year. It is furnished with a heater, lights, electrical outlets, and outside fire circle. The day-use visitor will find beautiful sandy beaches, a public restroom (accessible), picnic tables and grills. There is a pavilion for rent. This state park has 226 sites and allows both RV and tent camping.

Also see the Port Elizabeth Marine and Yacht Club below.

Water Sports, Marinas, Boat and Jet Ski Rentals

Bayshore Marina, ten miles south of Caseville, (989) 656-7191. Has a courtesy pier, dockside service, gas, electric, overnight docking, paved ramp, seventy-four boat slips, restrooms, water hookup, waste removal, and showers.

Beadle Bay Marina, off Sand Point, (989) 856-4911. Has a courtesy pier, gas, electric, fish cleaning station, overnight docking, paved ramp, forty-eight boat slips, restrooms, water hookup, waste removal, and showers.

Bella Vista Water Sport Rentals, 6024 Port Austin Road, (989) 856-2500. Jet ski, jet boat, pontoon, and water sport rentals. Also sunset cruises. (See Bella Vista above under lodging.)

Caseville Municipal Harbor, 6632 Main Street, Downtown Caseville, (989) 856-3632. Has a courtesy pier, dockside service, gas, electric, overnight docking, paved ramp, fifteen boat slips, restrooms, water hookup, and waste removal. Fishing is allowed off the breakwater with appropriate license.

Hoy's Saginaw Bay Marina, northeast side of the river, (989) 856-4475. Has a courtesy pier, dockside service, gas, electric, overnight docking, paved ramp, 110 boat slips, restrooms, water hookup, waste removal, and showers. This marina is wheelchair accessible.

Port Elizabeth Marina and Yacht Club, 6635 River Street, (989) 856-8077. Full service marina with a courtesy pier, dockside service, fish cleaning station, paved ramp, overnight docking, forty-eight boat slips, electric, restrooms, water hookup, and showers. Also has campsites. Open May to October each year.

Other Things to See or Do

Caseville Amusement Center, 7079 Main Street, (989) 856-3478. Giant dry slide, go-cart track, game room, batting cages, and bumper-boats.

The Caseville United Methodist Church, 6495 Main Street. Snap a picture of the oldest and most photographed historic church in Michigan. It is an example of Gothic architecture.

Charity Island Lighthouse. Get there by boat, a short cruise from Caseville to Big Charity Island. The island was named by the lake mariners for its location "through the charity of God" midway between the city of Au Gres and the Thumb at the entrance to the Saginaw Bay. (See additional story about this lighthouse in

Part Two of this guide.)

Civil War Monument, downtown Caseville. A tribute to those who served their country in time of war.

The Crawford House, 6249 Main Street. This mansion was built in the 1860s by Francis Crawford on the Pigeon River bank. It has heavy, walnut front doors with frosted glass from France. There is a square belvedere on top of the house. The home was moved from its original site to its current place on Main Street where it serves as the Champagne Funeral Home. It is worth looking at as you go by.

Fishing. Caseville is nicknamed the *Perch Capital of Michigan*, and not without reason. It has three hundred thousand shallow, sandy acres of water which are favored by lake perch. Farther from shore, the water depths can reach nearly one hundred feet and offer great opportunities to snag walleye, lake trout, and salmon. The Charity Islands have a reputation for providing fishermen with

Parade of Fools
Photo Courtesy of Joe Jurkiewicz

the place to catch their limit.

Golf

Caseville Golf Course and Driving Range, 5848 Griggs Road, (989) 856-2613. A 9-hole golf course with carts and club rental. Also has a snack bar, driving range, and pro shop.

Hidden Harbor Golf Course, 7521 Port Austin Road, (989) 856-3991. A 9-hole golf course with clubs and cart rental. Has a lounge, snack bar, driving range, and pro shop.

Putt-Putt Golf and Games, 7057 Main Street, (989) 856-2170.

Festivals
- Trash and Treasure Day, May.
- Swing into Summer Classic Car Show, June.
- Island Hopper Concert, July.
- Fireworks Display, July.
- Walleye Tournament, July.
- Antique Car Show on the Beach. (Dates to be announced.)
- Antique Yard Sale Trail, August.
- Founders Day Dinner, October.
- Hollyberry Festival, November.
- Noel Night, November.
- Spirit of Christmas Night, December.

and

The Annual Cheeseburger in Caseville Festival, August. *www. casevillechamber.com*. This one is the biggest and craziest of all small-town festivals. It lasts more than a week as Caseville transforms into Key North. The celebration includes a two-hour-long parade, aptly named the Parade of Fools. It seems every organization and business from all the villages within a fifty-mile radius decorate a pick-up, flatbed truck, wagon, bus, scooter, car, or golf cart and enter the parade. Lacking a motorized vehicle, many walk the parade route, and everyone throws candy and bead necklaces to children along the sidelines.

One memorable float had a giant crane on the back of the flatbed (in its real life it probably moved drywall or other heavy construction materials). The crane was completely disguised as a flamingo and from its bill dangled a live man in scuba diving gear. Parade watchers did a double take and wondered if the diver got a touch of motion sickness after the first hour. The parade is estimated to draw up to fifty thousand onlookers.

The Farm Restaurant, generally known for it is high-end, upscale dishes, set up a tent and served - what else? Cheeseburgers! You can grab elephant ears, cotton candy, kettle corn, funnel cakes, or the soon-to-be-famous cheese dogs from local vendors. Margaritas are the drink of choice, Jimmy Buffet music fills the air, and you can catch a great concert in the park. Wander the crowded street for a peek at the most outrageous costumes you will see in the Thumb.

Contact

Caseville Chamber of Commerce, 6632 Main Street, P.O. Box 122, (989) 856-3818, or toll-free (800) 606-1347, *www.casevillechamber.com*.

After Caseville

Getting home — or where to go from here.

You have made it to Caseville. You admired the lake as it peeked through trees along your way to this destination. You savored beautiful sunrises on the east shore, and spectacular sunsets in Port Austin and Caseville. Hopefully, you have been swimming and boating, eating and playing, and shopping and exploring to your heart's content. The journey "home," wherever that may be, requires a decision. The next section of the guide offers you a few places to stop along the way - whichever route you take. You have three primary options:

1. Continue down the west coast of the Thumb to Sebewaing.
2. Travel the center of the state through Kinde and Bad Axe.
3. Retrace your steps, and enjoy for a second time the coastal spots you have encountered along your way. Maybe stop at a few of the places you missed the first time.

Option One:
From Caseville to Sebewaing and beyond, along the west coast of the Thumb, offers a different type of beach. The little towns will have a different flavor too. You will find marshy waters along the lake shore. You will not find as many shops geared to tourist interests. You will not find as many charming or upscale restaurants.

Along the western shore of the Thumb beyond Caseville, it is more difficult to find great, or even decent, places to eat and stay. One rather questionable looking establishment sported a sign in front advertising food and rooms for rent. I hoped it would be much nicer inside than it looked from the curb.

The interior was dark and smoky, and several local customers were eating a late lunch and sipping beer. I stood at the counter wondering what possibly had induced me to enter this place alone, but I was there, and I at least wanted to check a menu and hopefully see a room.

A sullen looking waitress finally walked over to me, after begrudgingly halting her animated conversation with a fellow at the bar. She had given me plenty of time to leave, but I stubbornly continued to stand there, shuffling brochures and fliers, and she simply could ignore me no longer.

I briefly told her about the travel guide. She responded with an icy glare, as she handed me a menu and stood silently - probably waiting for me to order. I glanced at the food selections (nothing terribly impressive there), and then said, "You also have rooms?" "Yeah. We got rooms."

Trying to engage her to more stimulating dialogue, I continued, "How much?"

She replied, "$15 a night and the bathroom's down the hall." She did not offer to let me see a room and I figured it was just as well. I knew this was not a place I was ever – under any circumstances - going to stay. Nor was I going to recommend it to anyone else – not even as an alternative lodging spot to consider when everyplace else is full. I am also very aware, however, that someone just wanting a bed to drop on, before or after a day spent fishing, might be looking for exactly that type of accommodation. Every traveler has a different agenda and different taste. That is why this guide has all levels of accommodations and restaurants. Sorry, though, this one simply did not make it!

Not to be discouraged, I tried another place for lodging on the west shore. It looked rather nice, but there were three cats on the paint-chipped front porch and a bunch of dogs howling behind (only one dog came to greet me, and fortunately he was not hungry). I love cats but it was not the kind of place most tourists would find charming.

With all of this said, the west side of the Thumb certainly has its appeal. Its marshy wetlands are full of wildlife. Sebewaing is a great place for fishing. Bay Port has a Fish Festival and refers to itself as "the place where the fish caught the man," meaning that you will love it so much you will be caught. If your vacation plans include fishing, watching wildlife, and exploring natural areas or wetlands and if you are not adverse to slightly less than par accommodations, then by all means continue down the west coast of the Thumb. The west shore is an amazing place for certain types of recreational pursuits; just do not go this route expecting lovely sandy beaches. They pretty much end at Caseville. Quaint and lovely B&Bs, shops, and restaurants are not plentiful either.

If a trip to Bay Port and Sebewaing does not sound like what you signed up for, you have additional options.

Option Two

You can try a route through the middle of the state on M-53. You can forge your way through Kinde, Bad Axe, and Gagetown. You will get a second chance to visit the Farm Restaurant. Your children may enjoy the Petting Farm and the Octagonal Barn. You can certainly divert their attention by pointing out the buffalo along the roadside, and they may be ready for the biggest waterslide in five counties.

Bad Axe has a couple of museums, decent restaurants, and antiques stores to occupy a bit of time. You will pass the Petroglyphs, the Mennonite Store (not a big place but some interesting food/baking items), and you may want to indulge in what could be the biggest ice cream cones I found anywhere in the Thumb. The Grindstone General Store makes that claim but it must be a toss-up. The route through the center of the state will take you to M-46, and from there you can head west to I-75.

Your trip along the Lake Huron Coast provided a great opportunity to enjoy the natural beauty of that massive, "freshwater sea" that is so dearly loved by everyone who lives near it. This short trip inland will show you how Michigan's Thumb residents have supported themselves for decades. You can observe first hand the farms, the fields, and the barns of this agricultural area.

Option Three

The final option is the obvious one; simply backtrack around the east coast of the Thumb, and enjoy for a second time the great beaches of Caseville, Port Austin, Harbor Beach, and Lexington. Stop at a different restaurant this time, and maybe catch a store or two that you missed on the way up the Thumb.

So, the choice is yours: (1) On to Bayport and Sebewaing (2) A trip through the heart of the Thumb, or (3) Retracing the shoreline.

Bay Port *(Continuing Down the West Coast)*

Population:
Bay Port is an unincorporated village. The township population is approximately 1300.

Directions:
Nine miles south of Caseville on M-25.

Background and History
The first state maps referenced this area as Geneva. The little town was also known as Wild Fowl Bay before it became Bay Port.

It is probably best known for its fishing. The Bay Port Fish Company is located here and runs a year-round fishing operation. The factory is open to visitors. Children and adults alike will enjoy the tour. Commercial fishing was first established off Bay Port Island in 1868 by R. J. Gillingham, who expanded it that same year to mainland Bay Port. W. J. Orr and W. H. Wallace established the Bay Port Fish Company in 1895.

In early years, fisherman used sailboats to make their runs, placing and tending their nets. In the winter they chopped holes through the ice so they could continue fishing. Much of the catch would be salted and packed in kegs for preservation.

At the peak of the fishing industry, in the 1920s and 1930s, refrigerated rail cars carried tons of fresh herring, perch, walleye, and whitefish to Chicago and New York.

There is a historical marker at the foot of Promenade Street near the entrance to the Harbor. It notes the significance of Bay Port's contribution to the commercial fishing industry.

In its infancy, Bay Port was home to a luxury hotel; wealthy families from the city would swarm to its restful and inviting rooms to enjoy a welcome respite at this lake-side retreat. The Bay Port Hotel is gone; its location is marked by a plaque in remembrance of its early glory days.

According to local village lore, the German settlers who came here were part of the religious village of Ora Labore in Germany. Additional research failed to reveal a village in Germany by that name, but the history of one village may shed light on the connection. Hirsau, Germany was known mainly for its Benedictine Monastery. More than three hundred years ago the motto at the Abbey was "Ora et Labore," which translates to "pray and work." One thing is clear, the German settlers who came to this area were hard working, industrious folks with a deep attachment to their church.

The local quarry, the Wallace Stone Plant, is still operating in Bay Port. At one time it was the "company store," and a mainstay of the local economy. It provided jobs and homes for hundreds of people.

The public access to the bay offers an entry spot for fishing. There are opportunities for sailing, water skiing, and other water sports. Winter does not close down activity in Bay Port. Hunters of small game and the whitetail deer find this a perfect area to track their quarry. Winter also brings the opportunity for cross-country skiing and ice fishing.

Food/Restaurants

Bay Port Inn, 827 Promenade Street, (989) 656-9911. Smoky old saloon with a down-home appearance, but locals enjoy the Friday night fish fry and Saturday specials. Open year round.

Lefty's Drive In, 9505 Port Austin Road, (989) 656-9950. This fast food place has two locations, Bay Port and Caseville. Bay Port has car-hop service (no inside dining room). In spite of the colorful buildings, the hamburgers are decent. Open seven days, 11:00 am to 8:00 pm. (Seasonal only.)

Scenic Golf and Country Club Restaurant, 8364 Filion Road, 4.79 miles northeast from Bay Port, (989) 453-2233. This restaurant offers a fish fry on Friday nights from 5:00 pm to 10:00 pm. It also has a Sunday buffet brunch. It is seasonal from May 1 to September 30.

Sweets by the Bay, (989) 656-0375, *www.geocities.com/sweetsbythebay/home3.html*, *homecooking@midmich.net*. Homemade foods reasonably priced. This is primarily a catering service but Sweets also does great "picnics to go."

Lodging

Brushes, one mile south of Bay Port on M-25, (989) 656-9989. Rustic camping and twenty-five sites with electric and water hookup. Anticipates having boat slips in the future.

Sweet Dreams Inn Victorian B&B, 9695 Cedar Street, (989) 656-9952. Historic 1890s mansion with nine rooms, five with private baths. Each room has a theme, and one of the more popular is the Sarah Rose Room with a queen canopy bed and private bath. There is also a two-bedroom suite with a mini refrigerator and microwave. The house originally was owned by William Wallace, a prominent citizen of Huron County. It is situated on four acres with views of Lake Huron's Wildfowl Bay. The home has an interesting architectural style including a wrap-around front porch. Home cooked breakfast served in the dining room. For additional information go to *www.iloveinns.com*.

Boat Access, Marina and Courtesy Pier

Bay Port Boat Access, downtown Bayport. Has a courtesy pier, paved ramp, thirty-five boat slips, and restrooms.

Bayshore Marina, 2612 Wallace Cut, (989) 656-7191. A marina with 102 boat slips, dock, electric, water, showers, and gas.

Other Things to See or Do

Bay Port Fish Company, on the dock in Bay Port, (989) 656-2131. "Flopping Fresh Fish Caught by Our Own Boats Daily." That is how they advertise this commercial fishery, and they invite you to bring your children for the unique experience of seeing the live fish and a functioning fishery. (Call first because they have "live" fish only at certain times.) Bay Port's history and livelihood is steeped in fishing, and if you travel to Bay Port, you should consider this stop. It is a great place to buy fresh fish to cook up for a very special dinner.

Fishing. Everything you have read so far should tell you that Bay Port, with its protected harbor, is all about fishing. Sand Point stretches several miles into the Saginaw Bay to North Island off the mainland. The reefs of the local islands offer excellent walleye fishing. The islands are revered for their excellent bass fishing. The shallow areas along the shoreline provide a perfect place to haul in perch. There is a public access that provides the way to the deeper waters.

Birdwatching. Fish Point Wildlife Area, seventeen miles from Bay Port is a premier place to bird watch. (See listing under Sebewaing.)

Golf

Scenic Golf and Country Club, 8364 Filion Road (about four-and-a-half miles from Bay Port), Filion Road is slightly northeast of Bay Port, (989) 453-3350. This is an 18-hole, par 71 golf course with carts, club rental, showers, lockers, a lounge, snack bar, driving range, and pro shop. Scenic Golf and Country Club is a parkland design golf course founded in 1945. It is semi-private, but the public is welcome.

Festivals

• Bay Port Fish Sandwich Festival, first full weekend in August. This three-day festival includes raffles, helicopter rides, bake sales, fireworks, arts and crafts, a Rising Star Talent Contest, parade, and live entertainment. You cannot leave without trying the famous fish sandwich and fries. The festival is a tradition started one summer when Mr. Henry Englehard and his wife decided they needed a way to help raise money for their three daughters' college expenses. They came up with the unusual idea of selling fish sandwiches from a stand in their front yard. They had a secret recipe from their friend, a local restaurant owner, and their ingenious idea caught on. The fish sandwich requires two hands to eat. More than twelve thousand are sold at the festival. It is about the only thing on the menu.

• Antique Yard Sale Trail, August.

Contact

Bay Port Chamber of Commerce, (989) 551-9929. *www.bayportchamber. com*. The Web site will direct you to what is currently happening in Bay Port: fishing recreation, hunting, snowmobiling, and more.

Sebewaing

Population: 2000.

Directions:
Eleven miles south of Bay Port on M-25.

Background and History
Sebewaing is located on the Saginaw Bay at the mouth of the Sebewaing River. It was originally named Auchville, in honor of the Lutheran Missionary who brought settlers with him to this area during the first half of the nineteenth century. Later it was renamed Sebewaing which means "crooked river" in the Chippewa language. The Chippewa were the early inhabitants along the Sebewaing River that meanders through the city.

The city's industries include fishing and farming. Sugar beets are a notable local crop, and they provide the basis for the annual Sugar Festival.

Food/Restaurants
Lamplighter Restaurant, 8850 Unionville Road, (989) 883-9224. Daily specials for each meal. Friday night all-you-can-eat fish fry. Sunday breakfast bar. Open seven days, Mon to Thurs and Sat 6:00 am to 8:00 pm, Fri 6:00 am to 9:00 pm and Sun 7:00 am to 7:00 pm.

Peking City, 747 North Beck Street, (989) 883-3106. Daily specials. The menu includes Chinese and American entrees, and they serve breakfast. Open year round, Sat to Thurs 7:00 am to 8:00 pm, Fri 7:00 am to 9:00 pm.

Village Pizzeria, 638 North Center Street, (989) 883-2091. To belabor the obvious, this place is a pizza joint, but they also offer subs, salads, and breadsticks. Open Mon to Thurs 11:00 am to 10:00 pm, Fri and Sat 11:00 am to 11:00 pm, Sun 12:30 pm to 10:00 pm.

Lodging
(See Fish Point Lodge below under Other Things to See and Do.)

Museums and Galleries
Burns Gallery (Previously the Heidelberg Center Gallery), 27 Center Street. Features community art and offers free shows. Open Sat and Sun 1:00 pm to 4:00 pm.

Charles W. Liken House Museum, 325 Center Street, (989) 883-2341. In 1865 John Liken came to Sebewaing where he opened a cooper business and several other commercial enterprises. Liken shipped large quantities of white oak staves to Germany. He built two saw mills and four stave mills which employed more than two-hundred workers. Six years after he arrived in Sebewaing, he built a brick building where residents could buy anything from dry goods, to household items and drugs. He had branch stores in Bay Port, Kilmanagh and Unionville. He owned fifteen hundred acres of land in Huron and Tuscola counties and died a wealthy man in 1920.

The museum is the former home of Charles W. Liken, John's son. John built a total of five wonderful homes in Sebewaing, one for each of his children (Charles and three daughters) as well as one for himself. Three of these homes remain in existence. One is on the historical register and is now a private residence still occupied by the descendents of John Liken. It is not open to the public.

The museum has wonderful architecture and the interior is enhanced by beautiful wood floors including the original parquet floor in the dining room. An original chandelier and lighted china cabinet with leaded glass further enhance the dining room. Various collections and Victorian furniture have been donated to the museum. Dedicated historical society members are doing much of the restoration and the museum is a work in progress. Open to public June through beginning of November Sat. 1:00 pm to 4:00 pm or by appointment.

Luckhard Museum and Indian Mission, (989) 883-2539. In the mid-1800s, this was a Native American mission building. The museum displays original furniture, dishes, and Native American artifacts. Open first Sunday of June, July, August, and September from 2:00 pm to 4:00 pm. Guide available. Also open during various festivals.

Sebewaing Township Hall, located in downtown Sebewaing, (989) 883-9113 or (989) 883-2391 (Carol) or (989) 883-2341 (Janet). In November 1998, this hall was designated a historical site. The museum contains local memorabilia. Call for information.

Park

Sebewaing County Park, 759 Union Street, (989) 883-2033. This county park has sixty-four sites and provides hiking trails, fishing, sanitation, shower, flush toilets, running water, electricity, RV camping, and tent camping.

Marina

Sebewaing Harbor Marina, downtown Sebawaing. (989) 883-9558. Courtesy pier, dockside service, gas, electric, overnight docking, paved ramp, 104 boat slips, restrooms, water hookup, waste removal, and showers.

Other Things to See or Do

Fishing. Sebewaing is known for its excellent walleye fishing in the bay's weed beds. The Sebewaing River offers a great place to catch perch and bass.

Fish Point Lodge, 4130 Miller Avenue, Unionville (about ten miles from Sebewaing, south on M-25, left on Gotham/Bach Road, right on Miller), (989) 674-2630, *www.fishpointlodge.com*. Turn of the century, rustic hunting lodge with friendly staff and a slow pace. They put out the welcome mat for your dog and the seasoned guides take care of your needs from sunrise until the day's shooting is over. During the pre-hunt breakfast, they will prepare you for what lies ahead, whether it is the type of clothing best suited for the morning, or how the decoys will be set. It is a place to hunt waterfowl or, in the winter, to do some ice fishing.

Fish Point Wildlife Area (Bird Watching), 7750 Ringle Road, (M-25 South to Gotham to north on Ringle Road) about seven miles from Sebewaing, (989) 764-2511. Fish Point is the most popular spot in the Saginaw Bay for observing the thousands of tundra swans and Canadian geese that stage here each spring. According to area birders, there is no one spot that guarantees sightings because the food supply in the various fields changes from year to year. It is suggested that you keep an eye for the large flocks that will be feeding in the corn stubble that remains from the previous year. Another suggestion is to check the observation tower at the intersection of Ringle Road and Seagull Lane near Fish Point. The tower will give you a good overview of the area. You can hope to see yellow-headed blackbirds, snow geese, raptors, red-tailed and red-shouldered hawks, northern strike, snowy owl, fox sparrow, Forster's gull, bald eagle, wood duck and hooded merganser, pied-billed grebes, mallards, willow flycatchers, American and least bitterns, northern shoveler, cattle egret, little blue heron, and American white pelican. All have been sighted in the area.

Festivals

• Sebewaing Sugar Festival, June. This is Sebewaing's big festival, and it runs from Wednesday to Sunday. A midway opens the first day and other events include town-wide garage sale, petting zoo, children's games, bingo, crowning of the Sugar Queen, chicken BBQ, car show, tractor pull, band concert, and entertainment.

• Walleye Tournament.

• Antique Yard Sale Trail, August. This is the last stop on the trail.

Contact

Sebewaing Chamber of Commerce, 108 West Main Street, (989) 883-2150. Obtain more Sebewaing information at *www.sebewaing.org* and *whatsup@ sebewaing.org*.

From Sebewaing you can follow M-25 (West Bay City-Forester Road) to 1-75 in Bay City to continue on your route home.

$\mathcal{K}inde$ (Traveling the Center of the Thumb)

Population: 500 (maybe!).

Directions:
From Caseville take West Kinde Road east to Kinde or drive south seven-and-a-half miles from Port Austin on M-53.

Background and History
Kinde was originally known as Dwight Crossing, but in 1883 it was renamed for John Kinde, a local merchant who operated a general store, lumber yard, and elevator at that site. John Kinde also became the tiny village's first postmaster. In 1884, a railway station of the Port Huron & Northwestern Railroad located there.

Kinde once had the distinction of being the "Bean Capital of the World." The title was based upon the percentage of acreage allocated to the production of navy beans (those little, white beans that are so great in bean soup). In more recent years, however, the agricultural economy in the area has shifted. Corn is being produced in greater quantity both for alternative fuel and to feed local livestock. Alfalfa is also produced to meet livestock needs. Sugar beets are a bigger cash crop today than they were in the past. Actually, nearby Pigeon now produces more beans than Kinde.

Kinde is another *do-not-blink,* kind of village. However, if you have chosen to go down the center of the Thumb on your return home, you will find little treasures to enjoy in Kinde.

Restaurants/Food
Biff's Bowling Bar, 4680 North Van Dyke Road (M53), (989) 874-6423. You can eat as well as bowl at Biff's. The full menu includes chicken, fish, burgers, appetizers, and cocktails. (Alliteration aside, this is probably the only Biff you will find in the Thumb.) Open seven days.

Country Parlor Ice Cream and Arcade, next door to the Pasta House and run by the same owners. Sixteen hand-dipped flavors, shakes, sundaes, banana splits, or just a cone. L-shaped pool table, pinball machines, air hockey, and homemade crafts. Seasonal only.

The Farm Restaurant (see listing under Port Austin). You are just a short drive away.

The Pasta House, 337 Main Street, (989) 874-4070. Serves great hand-tossed pizza and unique pasta specialties. This family-owned-and-operated business has been written up in many local papers. At first you will wonder how it could stay in business since Kinde's population is, at most, five hundred. The owner explained: it is pretty centrally located and can draw from Port Austin, Caseville, and Bad Axe. Good food probably has something to do with it. The building was constructed in 1930 as a bank, and after it outgrew its usefulness in that function, it was slated for demolition. Instead of perishing under the blows of a wrecking ball, however, the building was rescued and turned into the Pasta House. The owner attempted to retain much of the architectural integrity. By noon on Sunday, people line up outside waiting for the restaurant to open. The signature dish is chicken alfredo, but they also serve barbecue ribs, and on Saturday night, prime rib. Lunch and dinner specials daily and hand-tossed pizza. Open seven days a week, Mon to Thurs 11:00 am to 8:00 pm, Fri and Sat 11:00 am to 9:00 pm, Sun 9:00 am to noon for breakfast, and noon to 8:00 pm for lunch and dinner.

Things to See and Do

Campbell Bison Ranch, 1205 Kinde Road (drive M-53 to Kinde Road and then one-and-three-quarter miles west, or catch it on your way into Kinde from Caseville on Hwy 5), (989) 874-4213. Sells buffalo meat, mounts, and souvenirs. Open by appointment only, but the buffalo are fenced on the side of the road, and they are fully visible and interesting to watch as you are driving by. If your children have not seen buffalo recently, they may think this is pretty neat. Actually, I have not been a kid in many years, and I thought it was way cool.

Eddie's John Deer Museum, M-53 to Kinde, six miles east on Kinde Road, and a quarter mile north on Verona Road, (989) 874-6225. The grounds house several farm buildings: one filled with toys and another with a tractor and farm implements as well as dairy equipment. The owner has also assembled Sebewaing Brewery and railroad collectibles as well as memorabilia accumulated over fifty-six years. The exhibits are a rather eclectic but interesting assortment. You need to call to let the owner know you are coming because it is only open by chance or appointment.

Campbell Buffalo Ranch

Eddie's John Deer Museum

Maplewood Farm Petting Zoo and General Store, 5790 North Van Dyke (M-53), one-and-a-half miles north of Kinde, (989) 874-6177. Sheep, goats, donkeys, pigs, chickens, and miniature horses (pony rides available) to see and pet. You will also get to see peacocks and a llama. Many unique hand-made items available in the General Store. They offer wagon rides after 6:00 pm Wed to Sat and all day Sun or by appointment. Open June, July, and August, Wed to Sun 1:00 pm to 8:00 pm, weather permitting.

Miniature Golf and Wiley Coyote Water Slide, 311 Main Street next to the Pasta House and Ice Cream Parlor in Kinde, (989) 874-4070. A charming 18-hole miniature golf course in a small park-like setting. There are bumper cars and rock climbing, but the big new attraction is the heated, jet-stream Wiley Coyote Water Slide which is the largest in five counties at 360 feet long and 4½ stories high. Great way to let the little ones cool off. There is a changing area and picnic facilities along with concessions. Mon to Fri specials. Open daily at 11:00 am during the summer.

Festival

Kinde Polka Fest, September. A relatively new festival celebrating the Polish heritage in the area. Continuous polka music by some of the country's top polka bands and a sixty-foot stage on which to display your dancing finesse. For additional information go to *www.polkamusicsound.com*. Lots of food and drink.

Bad Axe

Population: 3462.

Directions:
M-53 and M-142 in the center of the upper Thumb.

Background and History

Bad Axe was named by Captain Rudolph Papst. He was the leader of a group of men surveying the trail from Harbor Beach to Sebewaing in 1861. In their camp they found an axe left by earlier hunters who perhaps used it for dehorning elk. On their surveying map they noted the spot where they found this axe as "Bad Axe Camp." The name later became Bad Axe Corners, and finally just Bad Axe. It was incorporated as a village in 1885, and grew up to be a city in 1905.

Captain Pabst had come to Michigan in 1858 from Goderich, Ontario and settled in Lexington. The citizenry of Bad Axe made two attempts to change the name Bad Axe to Huron. Each time, Captain Papst made the journey from his home in Lexington to Bad Axe to insist the name not be changed. Papst was a decorated hero of twenty-two major battles in the Civil War, and his opinion carried a lot of weight. Out of respect for his service to his country the name Bad Axe was retained.

The original *bad axe*, supposedly the one that gave the city its name, is housed in the Bad Axe District Library. When a road was built through Bad Axe, at the intersection of what are now Huron and Port Crescent streets, an axe was found. Mr. Crawford, from nearby Gagetown, was the builder of the road. During construction, he cut down a huge pine tree and saved a burl containing the axe. In 1884 Crawford gave the axe to his brother-in-law, M. Lyman, an early physician in the Thumb. Dr. Lyman died in 1946 and left the axe to Mrs. William Goldman, his office nurse, who also happened to be his sister-in-law. After her death in 1967, the axe went to her son, Robert Golding, who subsequently presented it to the library in 1972.

Although historians agree on the origin of the name Bad Axe, there is disagreement over whether the axe Crawford found was *the* axe. Some argue it does not match the original description given by Rudolf Pabst of the broken axe he found in 1861.

In 1891 eighteen families of Russian Jews settled in Huron county about three miles from the town of Bad Axe. They called their settlement Palestine. In 1897 there were thirteen men, eleven women and thirty-nine children in their colony, but it failed to become self sufficient. Even with tools and food provided by the Beth-El Hebrew Relief Society of Detroit, these farmers did not become successful. Instead they assimilated into the town or moved away.

As you drive into town and come to the "Main Four Corners" (Port Crescent and Huron where the axe was found), you can drive to the west on a street that is Norman Rockwellian in appearance – pure Americana with well-kept houses, perfectly manicured lawns, and a variety of architectural styles – all fronted by tall hardwood trees. If you drive along the side streets of the village, you will see that churches dominate the architectural landscape.

Bad Axe, centrally located in Huron County, is the county seat, and a little known fact is that on the steps of the Huron County Building, Richard M. Nixon gave his last campaign appearance as president on April 10, 1974.

Food/Restaurants

China King, 162 Huron Avenue, downtown Bad Axe, (989) 269-2900. Family dining: lunch, dinner, and Sunday buffets. Carry-Out. Open Tues to Sat 11:00 am to 1:30 pm and 4:00 pm to 8:00 pm. Sun noon to 3:00 pm and 4:00 pm to 8:00 pm. Closed Mon.

The Coffee Cup Plus, 171 Huron Avenue, (989) 269-6808. Breakfast served anytime. Their most popular breakfast special is an egg with choice of meat, onions, green peppers, mushrooms, and American cheese on grilled ciabatta bread for only $2.25. Original Detroit Sanders cakes and Sanders candies and toppings, sandwiches, wraps, hot dogs, specialty coffees, and chillers. Open Mon to Fri 8:00 am to 4:00 pm, Sat 8:00 am to 1:00 pm, and closed Sun.

Cousins Food and Spirits, 113 South Port Crescent, (989) 269-2236. Ribs are the specialty, and they make great homemade deep-fried mushrooms and onion rings (not frozen) and deep-fried baked potatoes. Of course you can get a plain old hamburger and you can shoot a game of pool while you are there. Open seven days 10:00 am to 2:00 am (kitchen closes earlier).

The Franklin Inn, 1070 East Huron Avenue, (989) 269-9951. Varied menu offering pork chops, barbecue ribs, chicken, pasta, salads, seafood, steaks, and sandwiches. The Franklin Inn specializes in buffets with one every night. Popular Sunday brunch spot 9:00 am to 2:00 pm. Friday night seafood buffet 5:00 pm to 9:30 pm. Saturday night prime rib buffet 5:00 pm to 9:30 pm.

Huron's Finest Meat Market, 1520 North Van Dyke, (989) 269-7200. Locals come with freezer chests to fill up with shrimp, lobster, tilapia, orange roughy, New York strip sirloins, and other meats. Also a farm market with Michigan grown honey rocks, sweet corn, and other produce in season. Open Mon to Sat 8:00 am to 8:00 pm and Sun 10:00 am to 6:00 pm.

Mancino's Italian Eatery, 610 North Port Crescent Road, (989) 269-4040. Specializing in Italian dishes including a variety of pastas, meatballs, and oven-baked grinders. Also salads and pizza and pasta bar. Open Mon to Thurs 11:00 am to 9:00 pm, Fri and Sat 11:00 am to 10:00 pm, and Sun noon to 8:00 pm.

Murphy's Bakery, 110 West Huron Avenue, (989) 269-8291. Great baklava and pastries. Also has pies, donuts, and bagels (fresh bagels are hard to find in the Thumb), and a full line of baked goods. Has a coffee shop overlooking the main street. Closed Sun.

Peppermill Restaurant, 685 North Port Crescent Street, (989) 269-9347. Family-style restaurant. Simple décor and hearty, well-priced meals. Homemade breads. Sandwiches, chicken, pasta, Mexican dishes, and breakfasts. Mon to Sat 6:00 am to 9:00 pm, Sun 7:00 am to 9:00 pm.

Tuscany Breeze, 898 North Van Dyke (M-53), inside the Econo Lodge, (989) 269-2800. Italian and Greek dishes including pizzas, antipasto, calzones, soups, salads, steaks, burgers, sandwiches, Italian specialties, ribs, and seafood. Outside patio, weather permitting. Open Mon to Sat 11:00 am to 11:00 pm and Sun 11:00 am to 10:00 pm. (Kitchen closes at 10:00 pm daily, 9:00 pm Sun.)

Bad Axe also has more than its fair share of fast food places, so if you cannot make it another day without a McDonald, BK, Subway, DQ, Wendy's, KFC, Taco Bell, or other fast food fix, you will have no trouble satiating that craving.

Lodging

Econo Lodge Inns and Suites, 898 North Van Dyke, (989) 269-3200. Newer Econo Lodge, some rooms with whirlpools. Exercise room. Weekly rates available.

The Franklin Inn, 1070 East Huron Avenue, (989) 269-9951, or toll-free (800) 645-0211. This motor lodge has been owned by the same family for over thirty years, and the rooms are clean and spacious. There is a restaurant on the premises and a lounge with a fireplace (see restaurant listing above).

Holiday Inn Express Hotel and Suites, 55 Rapson Lane, one mile north of the junction of SR 142 and M-53 (Van Dyke), (989) 269-5293. Extras: heated indoor pool, whirlpool, and exercise room. This is a new Holiday Inn located close to many fast food restaurants.

Museums

The Allen House Museum, 303 North Port Crescent Street, (989) 269-7674. This 1902 Dutch Colonial home was built by Wallace Allen, the longest serving mayor of Bad Axe. Many of the home's features are original, and it is furnished with antiques throughout. There is a 1950s room with memorabilia from that era. Open by appointment.

Bad Axe Museum of Local History, 110 South Hanselman Street (one block east and one block south of the main corner), (989) 269-7674. Area artifacts dating from the mid-to-late nineteenth century including clothing displayed on manikins, old jewelry, doctors' implements, dolls, replicas of several local buildings, quilts, rugs, a display of old hats, wedding dresses, furniture, organ, and WWI artifacts. The museum occupies the second floor of the Old City Hall building. Currently the museum is open by appointment only.

Pioneer Log Village, located in Bad Axe City Park, along Hanselman Street

Back Side of Old City Hall with Hose Tower
Currently the Bad Axe Museum of Local History

(one block east and one block south of the main corner), (989) 269-7674. The village includes a blacksmith shop, general store, country school, chapel, family home, and a barn. All are restored pioneer log buildings with period furnishings from the late 1800s. Open Sun 2:00 pm to 5:00 pm, Memorial Day to Labor Day. There is also a Log Cabin Days Festival in June.

Antiques and Other Shopping

Amish Country Crafters, across from Mancino's on Port Crescent Road (about four blocks north of the main four corners). Rockers, baby clothes, doll clothes, benches, tables, chairs, quilts, and special orders. Open Mon to Thurs 8:00 am to 5:30 pm, Fri 10:00 am to 6:00 pm, Sat 8:00 am to 1:00 pm, and closed Sun.

The Candlestick Maker, 126 East Huron Avenue, (989) 269-2281. A little shop offering candles, collectibles, and unique gifts. Tues to Fri 10:00 am to 6:00 pm, Sat 10:00 am to 3:00 pm, closed Sun and Mon.

The Clothes Closet Resale, 104 West Huron Street, (989) 269-8181. If resale interests you, you might want to make a stop here. Open Mon to Sat 9:00 am to 5:30 pm (Sat to 4:00 pm).

The Country Village Antiques, 2787 North Van Dyke (M-53 north of Bad Axe), (989) 269-2113. An old-fashioned village of several buildings where you will find a few surprises. A sampling of the varied, merchandise includes coffee grinders, dried flower arrangements, oil lamps, and interesting antique pieces. If you like antiques stores, this place is worth a stop. Open Tues to Sat 10:00 am to 6:00 pm, Sun noon to 5:00 pm, and closed Mon.

Main Street Mercantile, 163 East Huron, (989) 269-5070. Twenty-two

Bad Axe Pioneer Log Village

venders under one roof. Antiques, glassware, vintage linens, old chests, jewelry, collectibles, crafts, and gift items. Also custom embroidery. Make sure you check out the downstairs. Open Mon to Thurs 9:00 am to 5:30 pm, Fri 9:00 am to 6:00 pm, Sat 9:00 am to 5:00 pm, and closed Sun.

Parks

Bad Axe City Park, Hanselman Street. Offers a pavilion, play area, and picnic tables and would be a good place to spend an hour or so letting children rid themselves of excess energy.

Wilcox Park, 650 Whitelam Street. Playground, grills, sand volleyball, and picnic tables.

Other Things to See and Do

Bad Axe Farmer's Market, Downtown Bad Axe on Heisterman Street. Baked goods, produce, collectibles, and live entertainment. Fri 4:00 pm to 8:00 pm, Memorial Day weekend through second week in September.

Bad Axe Hot Air Balloon Adventure, (989) 269-8001, *www.badaxeballoon. com badaxeballoon@yahoo.com*. Hot air balloon flights for any occasion, a special romantic summer evening, or a treat for the family. Beautiful sunrise or sunset flights.

Bad Axe Theatre, 309 East Huron, (989) 269-7911 (twenty-four-hour movie information). Old-fashioned, small-town theater with three shows daily, popcorn refills 25 cents. Thumb's only Dolby Digital Surround Sound Cinema.

Heleski Elk Ranch, 1908 Atwater Road, (989) 658-2804, *heleskielkranch@ hotmail.com*. Tours are available, corn maze, pumpkin patch, and wagon rides.

Verona State Game Area, six miles east of Bad Axe, (989) 872-5300, *www.*

michigan.gov/dnr. You may have difficulty locating this property because it is not well-marked, but the Internet site has maps. This is a state owned piece of land, open to the public for hunting and other recreational pursuits. You must abide by the hunting regulations (season/license). You can watch birds, pick berries, and hike. No motorized vehicles allowed.

Festivals
- Car Show and Cruise Night, June.
- Log Cabin Days, June.
- Bad Axe Hatchet Festival, June.
- Can-It Basketball Tournament
- Huron Community Fair
- Santa's House
- Christmas Parade

Golf

Verona Hills Golf Club, six miles east of Bad Axe on M-142, (989) 269-8132, *www.veronahillsgolf.com*. This semi-private golf club is an 18-hole, par 71, slope 126 course. It has a full-service clubhouse and bar and a complete pro shop.

Contact

Bad Axe Chamber of Commerce, (989) 269-6936, or toll-free (888) 369-6936, *www.badaxemich.com,* or e-mail *badaxemich@yahoo.com*.

Gagetown

Population: 300.

Directions to Octagonal Barn:
M-53 south from Bad Axe (10 miles) turn right on Forester/Bay City Road (6 miles), to Richie Road, turn right and proceed less than a mile to the barn.

Gagetown is included because the Octagonal Barn is a tourist stop worth considering.

From Gagetown you can return to M-53 (turn right) and continue to M-46 (turn right) to I-75 as you leave the Thumb. Or, you can take a short side trip to the Petroglyphs.

The Octagonal Barn, (989) 665-0081, *www.thumboctagonbarn.org*. The barn was built for James Purdy in 1923 and 1924 and was modeled after a barn Mr. Purdy had admired during his travels. It is seventy feet tall and has 8,600 feet of space. Special events are scheduled throughout the summer season, call for details. The barn offers the opportunity to take a peek at early nineteenth century farming with guided tours of both the barn and the farm. You will also find an ice house, wood/coal shed, chicken coop, and corn crib. Open seasonally from Memorial Day to Labor Day during daylight hours.

Gagetown State Game Area, (989) 872-5300. This state-owned piece of land is open to the public for hunting and other recreational pursuits. You must abide by the hunting regulations (season/license). You can watch birds, pick berries, and hike. No motorized vehicles allowed. Check the Web site for maps and further information at *www.michigan.gov/dnr*.

The Octagonal Barn

Petroglyphs Of Sanilac County

Directions:
Ten miles south of Bad Axe on M-53 turn left onto Bay City - Forestville Road (4 miles), to right on Germania Road, and the park will be about half a mile on the right. (Or if you are coming back from the Octagonal Barn, continue east, past M-53 on Bay City - Forestville Road (4 miles), to right on Germania to the park (half a mile on right), (989) 856-4411.

Petroglyphs
This Historic Sanilac County Site is a 240 acre park open for hiking. The actual Petroglyphs are early Native American Rock Drawings that are, unfortunately, being eroded by weather and other forces.

The drawings are etched in sandstone and represent mythical water panthers, deer, and a Native American archer. Carved by unknown prehistoric artists, the rocks were first discovered among the ashes of the massive forest fire that swept the Thumb area in 1881. The estimated age of the drawings is from between three hundred to one thousand years. (Additional history provided in Part Two of this guide). A pavilion was raised over the rock drawings to help keep out the weather elements, and a sign was erected requesting visitors refrain from climbing on the rocks or otherwise touching the drawings. Today a chain fence surrounds the petroglyphs and you are only admitted when park staff is there to oversee.

There is a pleasant hiking trail and in the stillness, surrounded by trees, you can almost imagine a time, several hundred years ago, when Native Americans walked this land and made their drawings.

Staff is available to allow visitors inside the fence protecting the drawings from Memorial Day to Labor Day, Wed to Sun 10:00 am to 5:00 pm. If you are traveling from a great distance and the petroglyphs are the major reason for your trip, you are advised to call first, (989) 856-4411.

After Visiting the Petroglyphs, turn right and continue on Germania Road to M-46 and then right to I-75. You may wish to stop at the Country View Bulk Food Store on the way.

Country View Bulk Food Store, 4635 Richards (fifteen miles south of the petroglyphs, and right on Richards). This store is operated by individuals of the Mennonite faith, and you are requested to dress modestly if you are entering. They offer large chunks of cheese that are considerably less expensive than at the local grocery. They also have a stock of interesting baking items (such as caramel chips) sold in bulk.

About a mile past Richards, Germania road will cross M-46. Turn right to get to I-75. There is one additional places to consider as you wind your way home.

Scott's Quick Stop, at the Corner of M-53 and M-46. This is not a place you might normally think of stopping for ice cream, but they have the largest cones imaginable. A baby cone can last for twenty miles of your journey. There is no sign indicating ice cream is a big deal there, it just looks like a mini-mart and gas station.

I hope you had a great time visiting the places listed in Part One, and I hope you come back to visit often.

Part Two

A bit of History and a Bit of Fun

Introduction to Part Two

The next several chapters are included to give the traveler a historical overview of the Thumb area. Certain events were so critical that they literally changed the face of the Thumb. For example, the *Fires of 1871 and 1881*, as well as the *Great Storm of 1913*, were so catastrophic that they changed the area's economy and resources forever.

Some chapters, like *Walking the Beach* and *Ghost Stories for Around the Campfire*, are included just for fun.

I am not a historian, and I did no original research. I say that by way of disclaimer, and to simply let you know that I believe the information contained in the following chapters is true and accurate; I have researched it to the best of my time constraints and abilities. The material was collected from a variety of sources including local libraries, conversations with residents of various Thumb cities and villages, musty books more than a half century old that my father left me, newspapers, various booklets, encyclopedias, Internet searches, discussions with many Chambers of Commerce, and anything else I could get my hands on.

Hopefully, you will find some of this information interesting or entertaining, and, hopefully, it will enrich your Thumb experience and pique your curiosity.

Lake Huron
Photo Courtesy of Susan Jurkiewicz

About Lake Huron

"Moody and withdrawn, the lake unites
a haunting loveliness to a raw desolation."
-Dale Morgan

My Love Affair with the Great Lake

She is simply my lake. I was born one block from her shores and have loved her since I first set eyes on her beautiful, rolling, azure waves.

Imagine Henry Wadsworth Longfellow sitting along the shoreline at Sault Ste. Marie where Lake Huron reaches out and touches Lake Superior. Captivated by the splendor of "The Big Sea Shining Water" he found his inspiration for *Hiawatha*. His descriptions of the shores of Gitche Gumee refer to Lake Superior, but they just as aptly describe the majesty of Lake Huron. Personally, I think his creative juices flowed in response to both.

Samuel De Champlain called her "La Mer Douce" or "The Great Freshwater Sea." Champlain meant the name for her alone because he was unaware of her sister lakes.

French Cartographer, Nicholas Sanson, on his misshapen, but somewhat accurate, 1696 Map of the Great Lakes designated her *Karegondi* which in the language of the Petan Native Americans simply meant "Lake." (Sanson labeled Lake Michigan "Lac De Puans" or "Lake of the Stinking Things.")

The name that has endured, Lake Huron, comes from "Lac De Hurons" which was the other name by which she was often designated on early maps. The Hurons were the Native Americans living in the area during the time of the French exploration. By whatever name, she remains as majestic and mysterious, as alluring and as awesome. Our words mean nothing to her.

Man's love affair with the Great Lake doubtless began when the first human walked through a dense forest that opened to reveal her immense and dazzling splendor.

She has offered us a watery highway for travel. She provides sustenance in the form of her whitefish and salmon, her walleye and perch. She provides recreation and a means to cool off on those hot, muggy, ninety-degree, Michigan summer days. These gifts she offered to the first people reaching her shores, and she continues to graciously extend them to everyone visiting her today.

But Lake Huron demands respect. The fury of storm-driven, thirty-foot waves have terrorized many a hapless sailor. Thousands of sunken ships pay a silent, ghostly testament to her raging power. We recognize her unpredictability and watch safely from a distance when her mercurial temper flares, her white caps warning of her anger. Even then we are transfixed by her dark mood.

We always forgive her, unable to hate something so noble and glorious. When she turns a cold shoulder, and a gloomy sky melts into her murky gray waters, we stay inside and watch her sullen movements. In her more melancholy moods, the rhythmic pounding of her waters lulls us to sleep.

She helps us keep things in perspective. She existed so many millions of years before us and will go on that many years after. She makes any minor crisis seem irrelevant, for it too shall pass and she will go on.

We are awed by her almost unfathomable size. She may not be an ocean, but standing on her banks, unable to see anything on the other side, we must concede she is a mighty body of water. When the *other side* is not in sight, the degree of "big" becomes insignificant.

She makes us laugh: watching children belly-flop against her surface or watching water skiers take an ungainly tumble. One recent spring morning after several unseasonably, warm days, Michigan threw one last winter hurrah. From my window I spotted a body flailing about in the lake's waves, but before I could dial 911, the Yeti-like figure exited the water and stood upright on the beach – surfboard in hand. And then a snow-covered friend joined him. For a couple of hours these two characters surfed in the middle of this snowstorm, their wetsuits the only things keeping them from freezing. It still makes me smile thinking about the incongruity of the situation: surfing in a winter blizzard.

Lake Huron
Photo Courtesy of Susan Jurkiewicz

More smiles were engendered by a couple of young men who pulled their pickup truck next to the small hill beside our condominiums. They began shoveling out the snow with which they had filled the truck-bed. They labored for the longest time creating a mini-mountain suitable for snowboarding. Once that was accomplished they had a great old time. Luck was with them and their snow did not melt for several days, so every afternoon they returned to hone their skills.

I am willing to share my lake, but she will be my "Big Sea Shining Water" until the day she goes on without me. And, I will love her every day until then.

Three billion years ago the underlying structure for the Great Lakes Basin was created during the Precambrian Era. That era represents over eighty percent of all geological time and was marked by great volcanic activity and glaciers. The volcanoes formed great mountains and the melting of the glaciers formed huge glacial lakes. The original lakes, left behind by these retreating glaciers, were much larger than the Great Lakes as we know them today. Evidence of their original size can be seen in the beach ridges and eroded bluffs hundreds of feet above and beyond the current shore.

Lake Huron reaches depths of 750 feet and has a water surface of 23,000 square miles. Her shoreline stretches more than 3,800 miles, if you include her 30,000 islands. She has a length of 206 miles and a breadth of 183 miles. Her average depth is 195 feet. She is either the fourth or fifth largest lake in the world, depending upon whether you include the Caspian Sea, which is salt water. She is the second largest of the Great Lakes. The Great Lakes are estimated to hold *6 quadrillion gallons* of fresh water. If that is anywhere near true, then Lake Huron must hold well over a quadrillion all by herself. That is a number that simply boggles the human mind and is impossible to grasp.

Unfortunately, other than what the geologist tells us about her creation, the lake has no recorded history until humans came into contact with her. The history we have of her earliest people comes less from them than from the explorers and settlers and traders who arrived later on the lake's shores and offered their own European view of the Native Americans. That perspective must be considered incomplete, clouded by the customs and beliefs of the newcomers, and therefore somewhat suspect.

It is a curious fact that Huron was the first Great Lake discovered. Of the chain of five, she sits smack in the middle. It seems logical that early explorers would first have stumbled upon Lake Ontario. The Great Lakes are part of the St. Lawrence Seaway, the largest fresh waterway in the world. A direct path from the Atlantic Ocean would have led an early explorer to Lake Ontario. However, the fear of the Iroquois inhabiting the region of Lake Erie and Ontario kept European explorers away from those lakes, despite their closer geographic proximity to the American east coast.

The first Europeans, or non-native people, to explore Lake Huron were the French in the early sixteenth century. Jacques Cartier began exploring Canada in 1535 and gave the French their first claim in "New France." He entered through the St. Lawrence Gulf and traveled a short distance inland on the St. Lawrence River, oblivious to the vast chain of lakes that remained ahead of him.

The first French settlement was at the Island of Sainte Croix on the Sainte Croix River. New France is primarily thought of in terms of Quebec, Three Rivers, and Montreal.

Champlain, who named our Lake Huron, La Mer Douce, explored the Great Lakes Region from 1609 to 1615 and during that time entered the tip of Lake Huron at the Georgian Bay. Like Cartier, he was unaware of the great waterway passage from the Atlantic to Lake Superior and Michigan via the St. Lawrence Seaway.

In 1669 Louis Jolliet was sent by Champlain on a mission to take supplies to Father Jacques Marquette, a Jesuit priest, who had established a mission at Sault Ste. Marie. Jolliet was unable to carry out his assignment because of threatened tribal wars on Lake Superior. While at the Sault, he rescued an Iroquois prisoner who was about to be killed at the stake. Jolliet decided to take his new charge back to Quebec, and the prisoner suggested they follow a route directly south from the St. Mary's River.

It was the first time Europeans had descended Lake Huron to the St. Clair River. Jolliet continued through Lake St. Clair and the Detroit River coming eventually upon Lake Erie. With continued good luck, Jolliet might have discovered the whole water system from the Sault to the Niagara River. However, growing fearful of a band of Andaste Native Americans, he landed about half way through the length of Lake Erie, hid his canoe, and proceeded eastward by an overland route.

René-Robert Cavelier, Sieur de La Salle began a journey in 1679 that took him through Lakes Ontario, Erie, Huron, and Michigan. Eventually La Salle traveled down the Mississippi and arrived at the Gulf of Mexico in 1682. He had constructed his vessel, the *Griffon*, just above the Niagara Falls and sailed via the lakes to Green Bay, Wisconsin. He was the first person in recorded history to traverse the entire Great Lakes waterway. On the return trip the *Griffon* became the first major vessel to vanish in Lake Huron. There is more than one story about where her bones rest.

The above chronology gives credit where history has decided it is due. There is, however, every likelihood that Étienne Brûlé was the first European to actually travel extensively in the Great Lakes region and it is he, perhaps, who first saw much of the lake now known as Lake Huron. Unfortunately for Brûlé, he could neither read nor write, so kept no written journals of his travels. As is almost always the case, the glory for discovery went to the explorer or explorers who kept a recorded version of their exploits.

Champlain had sent Brûlé, then a very young man, on a mission that undoubtedly took him into the far reaches of the Great Lakes. Brûlé adopted the dress of the Native Americans and could speak the Algonquin tongue. He would have been a great asset to the French in these regions, except for his disloyalty. He sold his services to the English in their ongoing bickering with the French over control of the area. Brûlé was considered a traitor by Champlain. He was eventually killed in a drunken brawl and some historians say his body was cannibalized by one of the local tribes.

The early explorers were pushing to find the Northwest Passage which they believed would open up trade with China. So intensely did they believe in their quest of reaching China that French explorer Jean Nicolet met the Winnebago Indians, in what is now Wisconsin, dressed in Oriental silks with patterns of flowers and birds. The Native Americans probably dismissed his costume as no stranger than those of the Jesuits, who came to Christianize them wearing long black robes, completely unsuited to the densely forested and primitive land. History reflects Nicolet died without achieving his goal of finding a shortcut to China.

The French policy in the New World was three-fold: find better trade routes to the East, exploit the natural resources of the new land including her fur-bearing animals, and missionize the native people. They were not terribly successful, however well-intentioned, in either the first or last of these goals although they did manage to exploit the fur trade for many years.

Native American In The Thumb

"Treat the Earth well.
It was not given to you by your parents;
It was loaned to you by your children."
-Native American Proverb

They were the first to glimpse her beauty

This is a fascinating yet perplexing story. Due to the lack of complete historical records, telling it can be likened to trying to unravel a ball of yarn after a cat has been playing with it - and all you get are loose ends.

Native Americans kept oral histories passed down over hundreds of years and many generations. These oral accounts include a chronicle of their traditions, teachings, and beliefs. Some of these oral histories are very detailed and describe migrations that may have occurred thousands of years ago. Others are more metaphoric and tend to be harder for the Euro-American culture to grasp.

Without a written account to translate, Europeans wrote their own versions of Native American life as they observed it. At best, the early European accounts are a partial view that distorted the true picture. Always the story was told through the experience, culture, and moral compass of the story teller, no matter how assiduously he or she tried to be fair and accurate.

Some histories of the Native Americans attempt to classify the tribes according to similar language models, others by cultural similarities, and still others categorized by the seasonal migratory patterns of the tribes. Most serious historians tried to consider all factors, including not only those three, but also anthropology, genetics, mythology, and several other perspectives. As a result some research suggests there were three major tribes residing in the Thumb area, some that there were five major tribes, and yet others concluded there were even more.

Accuracy is important, but true accuracy may be unobtainable. In spite of that frustration, the Thumb cannot come alive for you without at least reflecting on our best guesses regarding the first people.

As you travel along M-25, consider that it originated as a Native American trail around the Thumb. As you gaze out on the ships and boats in various harbors, let your mind's eye imagine a time when canoes traveled close to shore and there were no freighters. Picture woods and forests where trees occupied every space where a building now stands.

This chapter on the Native Americans in Michigan's Thumb will not attempt to sort out various tribes and clans, nor piece together a complete history. Instead, it will merely identify some of the names you will undoubtedly encounter during your Thumb meanderings. It will offer a bit of general information regarding interactions between Native Americans and the Europeans that began arriving in the area in the sixteenth and seventeenth centuries. Mainly, let it remind those who travel the Thumb not to forget the critical role the Native Americans played in the Thumb's history

Earliest Man.

It is believed that during the Ice Age, or the Pleistocene Epoch, so much of the earth's water was in the form of glaciers that the height of the oceans actually dropped by nearly four hundred feet, enough to dry up the narrow area of sea separating Siberia and Alaska, forming a temporary land bridge to the North American continent from Asia.

By best estimates, prehistoric man began to populate the Thumb at least 12,000 years ago. The end of the Ice Age paved the way for the first humans to begin a slow migration into the Great Lakes Region. For the first time the area became habitable – not hospitable, but habitable. Scientists establish this time frame from carbon dating trees and shells that they know appeared in the area that long ago indicating life in the previously barren ice fields.

The Ice Age was followed by the Archaic Period which, in the Great Lakes Basin, covered a span from roughly 3,000 to 8,500 years ago. During this age hunting and gathering cultures arrived.

A tool that dates back 10,000 years establishes the presence of humans in North America at least that long ago. Other scientific research claims evidence of people reaching South America by 12,500 years ago, long before the land bridge would have been available. Does this mean humans arrived on the American continents by other means, specifically boats, even earlier than they are believed to have crossed the Siberian-Alaskan land bridge?

Such debate is left to scientists capable of wrestling with it. For our purposes, a few thousand years one way or the other is irrelevant. Using the lesser period of 10,000 years, we are still dealing with approximately five hundred generations of aboriginal people in a location where, by contrast, European settlers have been approximately fifteen generations.

Tribes of Native Americans in the Thumb at the time of the European Exploration and Settlement:

The Chippewa or Ojibwe

In 1622 the Chippewa were the first Native Americans along the Great Lakes shores to come in contact with Europeans. They fished along the St. Mary's River. The Chippewa are also called the Ojibwe.

After the establishment of a French post at Detroit in 1701, the Chippewa were reported in the Lower Peninsula as far down as the head of the St. Clair River where they may have been enticed by the opportunity to trade. The Chippewa were primarily seasonal hunters. Agriculture did not appear to be as important a factor in their economy as it was to their brother tribe, the Ottawa. The Chippewa may have moved about in response to their seasonal needs. In the spring they might join with other families at various locations to take part in activities such as making maple sugar, a staple in their diet.

During hot summer months they chose areas where the streams and lake offered an abundance of fish. Their favorite, the whitefish, was caught in nets, and sturgeon were speared along the islands in the Saginaw Bay.

During other seasons the northern forests provided a rich resource for the game they sought. They may have traded furs and meat to the neighboring Ottawa tribe for corn. They hunted wild turkey and passenger pigeons. The former were so numerous that catching them was hardly sport, and the latter came in such flocks that they darkened the sky. Extended family groups of Chippewa broke from the main group for specialized hunting.

Native American agent Henry R. Schoolcraft writes that "[v]iewed as a distinct and leading branch of the Algonquin, the Chippewa are preeminently expert and brave warriors and woodsmen and foresters, delighting in seclusion, forests and mysticism, but placing their main stake in life on the chase." Respect came to a Chippewa for hunting and fighting well. Schoolcraft married a Chippewa woman.

American Poet William Cullen Bryant in *Letters of a Traveler* wrote in 1850 the following description of a Chippewa village he found on the St. Clair River:

> *Log houses, at the distance of about a quarter of a mile from each other, stood in a long row beside the river, with scattered trees about them, the largest of the forest, some girdled and leafless, some untouched and green, the smallest trees between them having been cut away. Here and there an Indian woman, in a blue dress and bare-headed, was walking along the road. Two females came down the bank with paddles, and put off into the river in a birch-bark canoe, the ends of which were carved in the peculiar Indian fashion. A little beyond stood a group of boys and girls on the water's edge. The boys in shirts and leggings, silently watching the stream as it shot by them. Still farther on a group of children of both sexes, seven in number, came running with shrill cries down the bank. The boys in an instant threw off their shirts and leggings and plunged into the water with shouts, but the girls were in before them for they wore only a kind of petticoat which they did not take off, but cast themselves into the water at once and slid through the clear water like seals. The Indian Settlement on the edge of the*

forest extended for several miles along the river, where its banks are highest and best adapted for the purpose of settlement. It ends at last just below the village which bears the name Port Saranac.

The name Chippewa is a common one in the Thumb area. You will see it on streets, businesses, and sport teams. The Chippewa are part of the history you will encounter along the way.

The Ottawa or Odawa

Champlain contacted the Ottawa on the upper Ottawa River east of Lake Nipissing. The term Ottawa means "traders," and early accounts describe them as traveling about encumbered by goods. They also produced much of the corn relied upon by neighboring tribes and used it as part of their trade merchandise.

During the first half of the seventeenth century, Ottawa groups were reported along the Ottawa River and in the eastern Lake Huron area, including Manitoulin Island. During the last half of the seventeenth century, the majority of the Ottawa groups settled at the Straits of Mackinac although many continued hunting to the south in the Thumb of Michigan. The Ottawa or Odawa were critical to the fur-trade, which is often called the "soft gold" of Michigan.

The Pottawatomie or Bodéwadmi

The name Pottawatomie was given to the tribe by their "brother tribe" the Chippewa. It is believed to mean, "people of the place of fire." The Pottawatomie carried out both winter and summer hunts, and their ancient home was in the lower peninsula of Michigan. They lived primarily in southwestern Michigan in the St. Joseph area, but there were also groups near Detroit. The Pottawatomie were part of a long-term alliance with the Chippewa and Ottawa, collectively known as the Council of Three Fires. In the Council of Three Fires, Pottawatomie were considered the "youngest brother."

According to oral traditions, these three tribes (Ottawa, Chippewa, and Pottawatomie) are part of an immense group that traveled down the eastern shores of North America as a single people. Often these tribes are spoken of collectively as Algonquin speaking people because of the similarities of their customs and language. After their migration into Canada, Michigan, and Wisconsin, the "three brothers" split at the Georgian Bay, Ontario, Canada, each to a different area. As with many Native American tribes or clans, it is difficult to pin down geographically exactly where each was at any given time. The city of Algonac took its name from the Algonquin living there. The Algonquin people supported themselves in part by their agriculture: raising beans, peas, squash, melons, corn, and whatever else was suited to their land.

The Sauk and the Fox

Both the Sauk and the Fox lived at one time in the Thumb area of Michigan, and both tribes were also part of the Algonquin-speaking people. The Sauk lived along the banks of the Black River in what is now Port Huron. (See related story of Sauk warriors in Part Two of this guide.)

The Huron

It is perhaps the Huron whose name is most prevalent in the Thumb. Port Huron, Huron City, Lake Huron, many Huron Streets, and dozens of businesses with Huron in the name attest to their early presence. Cartier came in contact with the Huron at the Georgian Bay and Champlain later visited Huron villages just south of that site. Many priests and explorers lived with these groups, leaving detailed accounts of their experience. The Huron warred with the neighboring Iroquois, particularly with the Seneca, and by the middle of the seventeenth century, the Iroquois acquired guns and destroyed many Huron villages. In 1701, surviving Huron groups moved to Fort Pontchartrain (Detroit), first to the west side and then to the east.

The Huron played a strong role as traders. There are accounts of their stockaded villages with as many as two hundred long houses, each containing many families. The Huron raised corn, beans, squash, and sunflowers. Corn was a staple in their diet. They augmented their diet with wild cranberries, plums, grapes, and acorns. They sun-dried fish or smoked them to be used later. They hunted deer and bear.

The Huron division of labor and specialization may have unwittingly contributed to their destruction by the Seneca. The Huron sent groups out to perform specific functions, such as hunt. When the group was broken into these smaller units the Seneca could attack and destroy a village. When the absent Huron returned to a destroyed village they had no option but to join other groups, since the crops on which they were dependent, would also have been destroyed. The Huron were known as Wyandotte in the Detroit area, where that name is almost as prevalent as Huron is in the Thumb.

Mrs. Anna Jameson came to America in 1836 for the purpose of writing a book about our young country. She traveled around the north shore of Lake Erie and up Lake Huron during the summer of 1837. After her trip she wrote a letter to her dear friend Mrs. Schoolcraft, wife of Native American agent Henry Rowe Schoolcraft. Mrs. Schoolcraft was the granddaughter of a great Chippewa chief and warrior. Mrs. Jameson describes how she enjoyed her experience and then concluded her letter, "the propinquity of the white man is destructive to the red man; and the further the Indians are removed from us the better for them. In their own woods they are a noble race; brought near to us, a degraded race.

We are destroying them off the face of the earth." The fallacy of her thinking is not Jameson's conclusion that the Europeans had a negative impact on the Native Americans but rather her conclusion that the Great Lakes Indians should be removed from their own land instead of the Europeans discontinuing their encroachment.

The Petroglyphs of Sanilac County

No summary of Native Americans in the Thumb, no matter how abbreviated, can end without mentioning the petroglyphs. The word "petroglyph" comes from the Greek *petro* meaning "stone" and *glyphein* meaning "to carve."

The circumstances of the Sanilac County Petroglyphs and who carved them remain shrouded in mystery. They are roughly at the corner of Bay City-Forester Road and Germania Road. They are marked by a sign denoting them as Sanilac Petroglyphs State Historic Park.

Estimates of the age of the petroglyphs range from more than 1,000 years to a mere 300 years. Stanley Cain of the Cranbrook Institute of Science reviewed the rocks in 1946 and offered his conclusion that they were probably carved during the early historical or very late prehistoric period.

The most interesting glyph may be the "Manitou," or god, named Gitche-a-nah-mi-e-be-zhew which translated loosely means "the great underground wildcat." The Chippewa believed this creature guarded the native copper deposits. The Manitou looks like a cat or dog with a tail encircling its entire body.

The Chippewa also believed in the spirit of Michibissy, a fearsome sea monster, as well as a great water panther whose switching tail caused high winds and tempests. Perhaps these legendary creatures are the basis for some of the drawings.

There are also drawings of a human figure with bow and arrow, game animals, animal tracks, and a few abstract and unidentifiable forms. The carving of the bowman or archer is nearly a foot high.

We know that many Native Americans traveled through this part of the Thumb during their hunts. Some camped in the area, but who drew these figures and when they did it cannot be conclusively determined.

The drawings were unearthed by a local farmer on whose land they were situated. They are carved on an outcropping of Marshall Sandstone. This soft rock leaves them susceptible to weathering by the elements, and therefore a protective roof was erected over them, and eventually the actual carvings were closed to the public unless a park ranger is present.

Additional information on the petroglyphs as well as specific directions are included at the end of Part One of this guide.

What Lies Beneath?

"So much that I should see
And yet so little time
There is silence all around
And the only sound for miles
Is the sound of my breathing
I am scuba diving."
Gina Durst

An Underwater Preserve, a Drowned Forest, and Maybe Even a Few Monsters

Overwhelmingly beautiful as we view her from above, Lake Huron is a virtual museum below. She reveals her treasures to adventurous divers willing to brave her depths.

Underwater Preserve

Lake Huron is a greedy lake with a voracious appetite. In the final accounting she is believed to have devoured forty percent of the Great Lake shipwrecks.

In 1980 the Michigan legislature enacted a law to preserve Michigan's endangered underwater resources. That law designated underwater preserves for abandoned property on the bottomlands of the Great Lakes. It allows for the issuance of salvage permits in appropriate situations. Divers must comply with the requirements of this law prohibiting them (unless they have a special permit) from removing any abandoned property from the Great Lakes bottomlands.

From the Harbors of Lexington, Port Sanilac, Harbor Beach, and Port Hope, you can dive and explore shipwrecks claimed by the lake in her moments of fury. The following list identifies nearly four dozen ships in or near the waters of Huron's harbors. Those marked with ** are especially popular dive sites.

The sunken ships are identified in approximate order from Lexington to Port Hope:

1. *The City of Port Huron*, a steamer, foundered off Lexington in 1876.

2. *The Eliza Strong* burned and went down in 1904. She lies 0.9 miles from the Lexington Harbor on a heading of 121 degrees in 28 feet of water. She lies upright on the bottom with her keel and some decking intact. She is a good dive for beginners. **

3. *The Sport* lies three miles from Lexington Harbor on a heading of 98 degrees in 49 feet of water. She was a tug that sunk upright listing to her starboard side. Her cabin is missing. She was discovered by another tug boat and became a very popular dive site because she lies at a perfect depth for beginning divers. She sank in 1920. **

Map of Lake Huron Shipwrecks

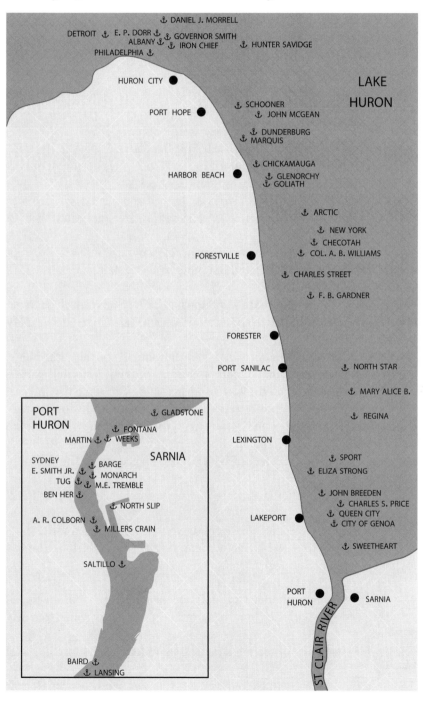

DANIEL J. MORRELL

DETROIT   E. P. DORR   GOVERNOR SMITH
ALBANY   IRON CHIEF   HUNTER SAVIDGE
PHILADELPHIA

LAKE
HURON

HURON CITY

PORT HOPE   SCHOONER
JOHN MCGEAN

DUNDERBURG
MARQUIS

CHICKAMAUGA
HARBOR BEACH   GLENORCHY
GOLIATH

ARCTIC

NEW YORK
CHECOTAH
COL. A. B. WILLIAMS

FORESTVILLE

CHARLES STREET

F. B. GARDNER

FORESTER

PORT SANILAC   NORTH STAR

MARY ALICE B.

REGINA

PORT
HURON   GLADSTONE

FONTANA
MARTIN   WEEKS   LEXINGTON

SARNIA

SYDNEY   BARGE   SPORT
E. SMITH JR.   MONARCH   ELIZA STRONG
TUG   M.E. TREMBLE
BEN HER

JOHN BREEDEN
CHARLES S. PRICE
NORTH SLIP   QUEEN CITY
A. R. COLBORN   LAKEPORT   CITY OF GENOA
MILLERS CRAIN

SWEETHEART

SALTILLO

PORT
HURON   SARNIA

BAIRD
LANSING

ST CLAIR RIVER

4. *The Regina* was a victim of the storm of 1913. (See related story in Part Two of this guide.) Built in 1907, the *Regina* lies 6.4 miles from Lexington Harbor on a heading of 45 degrees. She came to rest upside down with her bow facing north. She is considered a premier dive site in the Great Lakes. Her captain stayed with his ship. Nine months later his body washed ashore in Port Sanilac. The *Regina's* final resting place was not discovered until 1986. **

5. *The Mary Alice B* is a new wreck found in the preserve and one of the more popular dive sites. She rests upright and totally intact in about 54 feet of water. **

6. *The Forester,* a schooner, was lost near Port Sanilac in 1898.

7. *The North Star* sank in a collision near Port Sanilac in 1908.**

8. *The F. B. Gardner* sank on September 15, 1904, 6.5 miles northeast of Port Sanilac. Equipment is scattered widely around the wreck site.**

9. *The Charles A Street,* a 165-foot steamer, burned and went down in 1908. She lies 11.5 miles north of Port Sanilac. It is a shallow dive, not more than 15 feet deep at the maximum.**

10. *The Colonel A. B. Williams* was lost in an 1864 storm. This 110-foot schooner is missing her masts and cabin but otherwise is in fair shape. She lies 12.5 miles northeast of Port Sanilac.**

11. *The New York* is a steamer that went down in 1876. She rests close to the *Checotah* in about 120 feet of water and is recommended as a dive site for only more experienced divers.**

12. *The Checotah* is a schooner that lies upright on the bottom and is located 12.2 miles from Port Sanilac Harbor. Her rear cabin, deck, and part of the starboard gunwale have pulled away from the ship. The winch, windlass, capstan port anchor, and stem boiler remain on the bow. This historic wreck is surrounded by several pulleys and other small artifacts. At the stern are the ship's wheel, steering gear, and rudder. She went down on October 30, 1906. The *Checotah* rests in about 120 feet of water and is considered a site for more advanced divers.**

13. *The Arctic* is a propeller steamship that went down near Wagener Park/Harbor Beach in 1893.

14. *The Glenorchy* is a steamer that went down in a collision ten miles east-southeast of Harbor Beach in 1924. She was carrying a cargo of grain. She lies upside down at a depth of 356 feet.**

15. *The George H. Wand* is a sailing vessel stranded off Harbor Beach.

16. *The Dunderberg* is a schooner that collided six miles from Harbor Beach in 1868. She went down with her load of corn and passengers. She rests at a depth of 155 feet.**

17. *The Peshtigo* is a wood steamer stranded 1,240 feet off the lighthouse at Harbor Beach.

18. *The St. Clair* is a barge that foundered 1.33 miles southeast off Harbor

Beach in 1888. Five lives were lost.

19. *The Chickamauga,* a double-deck schooner, foundered one mile north of Harbor Beach and was removed to one mile outside of the harbor at a depth of 35 feet. She went down in 1919.**

20. *The Colonel Brackett,* a sailing steamer, was stranded one mile northeast of Harbor Beach alongside the breakwater in 1890.

21. *The H. A. Emery,* a sailing vessel, was stranded in 1899, slightly more than one mile north-northeast of Harbor Beach while attempting to enter the harbor.

22. *The Minnedosa,* a cannon four-mast sail vessel, foundered eight miles northeast of Harbor Beach while being towed by the steamer *Westmount* in 1905. All nine sailors aboard were lost.

23. *The R. G. Coburn,* was a passenger propeller that foundered 6.5 miles off Harbor Beach. Thirty-two lives were lost when she went down in 1871. She lies intact in 21 fathoms of water.

24. *The E. Cohen,* a schooner-barge, was stranded 8.25 miles, 158 degrees off Pte. Aux Barques Lighthouse on Port Hope Reef. She went down in 1890 and was a total loss.

25. *The Hunter Savidge,* a sailing vessel, capsized near Pte. Aux Barques Lighthouse ten miles and 45 degrees off Port Hope. She sank in 1899 with five lives lost. (See related story in the Ghost Stories chapter of this guide.)

26. *The Marquis*, a schooner, was lost north of Harbor Beach in 1892. She was carrying black stone and currently rests at a depth of 10 feet.**

27. *The John A. McGean,* was lost in the storm of 1913. Her entire crew of twenty-eight perished. (See related story in The Big Blow / The Storm of 1913 in Part Two of this guide.)

28. and 29. *The Philadelphia,* a steel propeller collided with the propeller *Albany* and took the *Albany* in tow. They both foundered trying to make shore. The *Philadelphia* lies upright and intact in 124 feet of water, 5.5 miles northeast of Pte. Aux Barques Lighthouse. These ships went down in 1893 with the loss of twenty-four lives. The *Philadelphia* was loaded with iron stoves and packaged freight, and the *Albany* was carrying grain. **

30. *The Seaton,* a sailing vessel, went down in 1892, 1.5 miles north-northwest of Pte. Aux Barques Station.

31. *The S. H. Kimball,* a sailing vessel collided with the towing steamer *George Stone* and foundered 3.8 miles northwest of Pte. Aux Barques. She went down in 1895 but the crew was saved.

32. *The Keystone State,* a side-wheel passenger steamer, was bound for Milwaukee from Detroit. She was last seen three miles northeast off Port Austin. Wreckage foundered off Pte. Aux Barques. She sank in 1861 with thirty-three lives lost.

33. *The Iron Chief,* a steamer, foundered off Pte. Aux Barques in 1904 loaded with coal. She rests at a depth of 135 feet. **

34. *The Berlin,* a sailing vessel, struck Burned Cabin Reef one mile north of Grindstone City. She sank in 1877 with four lives lost. She was carrying a load of lumber and limestone. She rests in 10 feet of water.**

35. *The Maggie Ashton,* a steamer, was stranded 3.5 miles and 80 degrees off Grindstone City. She went down in 1899.

36. *The Albion,* a sailing barge, was stranded 1.25 miles 56 degrees from Grindstone City. It sunk in 1887.

34. *The E. P. Dorr*, a tug, went down in Saginaw Bay in 1856 and rests at a depth of 180 feet.**

35. *The Governor Smith*, a steamer, sank in a collision in Saginaw Bay in 1906.

36. *The Frederick Lee*, a tug, foundered northeast of Pte. Aux Barques in 1936 with five lives lost.

37. *The Osceola,* a steamer, foundered in 1888, 1.5 miles, 35 degrees off Port Austin.

38. *The Santiag*o, a schooner, was lost near Port Hope in 1918.

39. *The Troy*, a steamer, foundered in the Saginaw Bay in 1860 with twenty-three lives lost.

40. *The City of Detroit*, a propeller steamship, sank in the Saginaw Bay in 1863 with all on board lost.

41. *The Jacob Bertschy,* a steamer, sank in 1879 when it wrecked on the Port Austin Reef.

42. *The Eugene,* a sailing vessel, was stranded on the south side of Port Austin during a storm in 1867.

The Daniel Morrell

A 43rd ship also rests on the bottom of Lake Huron in the Thumb, but for several reasons, she deserves more than a sentence or two.

The Daniel Morrell went down in 1966 near the shores of Harbor Beach where today each of her halves sits upright in about two hundred feet of water. She stands as testament that not all of the great ships that sank in Huron's November wraths did so in the late 1800s or during the first half of the twentieth century. Even today, a great ship cannot always beat Lake Huron.

On Monday, November 28, 1966, the town of Harbor Beach was shrouded in snow from one of those blinding, wind-driven storms that comes to warn Michiganders that winter is crushing down upon them.

The Daniel Morrell, a 356 foot iron-ore carrier, was headed for her last run of the season when she began battling the storm. As midnight ushered out Monday, Tuesday arrived with the tempest growing yet angrier. The early morning hours were enough to terrify even the bravest of seamen. At approximately 2:00 am the ship was torn in two and all aboard thrown into Lake Huron's frigid waters. The temperature dropped to 20 degrees.

Deck watchman Dennis Hale was fortunate enough to find himself in a lifeboat with three of his crewmen. Within six hours, two of his comrades lost their battle with the bitter elements. Several hours later the third of his buddies died, leaving Hale, the lone survivor, wondering how long before he too would lose the struggle. (See related story in the Ghost Stories chapter of this guide.)

The storm continued spitting its snow and ice with gale force as it tortured the near dead sailor. On December first, the body of another *Morrell* Crewman was spotted by the vessel *G.G. Post*. Soon after, Hale was rescued by a Coast Guard helicopter. He was the only survivor of the wreck of the *Daniel Morrell*.

Divers might also be interested in the caves located near the edge of the reef near Port Austin Lighthouse. The caves were created by eroding limestone. Near Grindstone City divers will find submerged grindstones and near Lexington there is a Drowned Forest.

The Drowned Forest

In 1988 scuba divers made a startling find. For years, people had been discovering ships that had gone down as a result of Huron's November gales. No one, however, could have possibly expected to find an ancient, underwater forest that Huron had lovingly preserved for more than seven thousand years! This forest is located just a few miles off the harbor in Lexington under a mere 40 feet of water.

The prehistoric forest is the result of Ice Age glaciers that advanced and receded repeatedly on the North American Continent. At various times in the past eleven thousand years, the Great Lakes had been much higher than they are today, but at other times the water was three hundred feet lower. Much of the Thumb area that now touches the Lake Huron shoreline had no lake at all, and there was no St. Clair River.

Back then, there was dry land with forests of spruce, hemlock, white pine, cedar, and ash. Scientists have measured some of the stumps in the drowned forest and have found trees five feet in diameter. It has also been determined by tree-ring dating that one spruce stump was 157 years old when it died, and one hemlock was 112.

The prehistoric forest has scattered tree remains over approximately a seven-acre area of the lake bottom. Carbon dating of samples also indicates the trees (or at least the samples) sprouted from 7,409 years ago to 7,936 years ago, the latter the age of one granddaddy white pine.

The remains of the drowned forest owe their preservation to the fact that the lake level rose very rapidly from the massive glacial melt water release. An important factor in their preservation was their burial in sediment around the time of the flooding. The sediment has kept them from deteriorating.

A Few Monsters to Stir Your Imagination

Every lake must have its monsters, and Huron is no exception. There are always a few stories about the Nessie-like shadows seen underwater or a huge fish-like monster that is far beyond ordinary. While none of those can be documented, Lake Huron has its freshwater version of a killer shark. Hiding away and lurking beneath her waters are the northern pike, the musky (muskellunge), and their hybrid, the tiger musky. All have been accused of eating small dogs. They have mouths lined with razor-sharp teeth.

The occasional report of a huge water snake may actually be a sighting of mutated pike that have grown larger than average.

These are no small fish. The northern pike can attain a weight of fifty pounds and grow to nearly four feet in length. It is a long, jut-jawed fish prized as a worthy game fish. Some merely see it as a "slimy snake" that preys on other smaller fish. It is a voracious predator, and it enjoys a good meal of golden shiners, yellow perch, bluegill, or suckers. The pike's diet will even include frogs, small mammals (like muskrats), and birds. Occasionally, it will bite a fishing rod in two, mistaking it for some freshwater delicacy. Northern pike inhabit protected, weedy bays. After the spring ice melts, they move farther into the shallows and marshes to spawn. They retreat to deep, cool waters in the summer.

Muskellunge or musky are another predator of Lake Huron's deep. They have been known on rare occasion to reach a weight of seventy pounds (actually 69 pounds and 11 ounces, caught in Wisconsin), and a length of over five feet. Like the northern pike, with whom they are often confused, they have razor-sharp teeth. To catch a legal-sized musky may take 20 to 80 hours. A musky can live to be thirty years old and haunt his/her section of the lake for decades. They usually lurk near drop-offs from rock or sand bars in the middle of Lake Huron. They are sometimes found close to shores fringed with overhanging trees. The stealthy musky hunts by waiting motionless and then striking, impaling its prey on its large canine teeth, rotating it and swallowing it headfirst. It is a fish that uses ambush as a means of attack. Like the pike, these voracious predators have been known to devour muskrats, ducks, shrews, mice, and frogs. Their aggressive nature has even led to reports that they have attacked boat motors. Some suggest that such rogue attacks demonstrate the nasty disposition of this sea monster. The truth is probably that the fish has mistaken the motor for more edible prey. There are isolated reports of musky attacks on humans. It may not make you feel any better, but you are not in any real danger – the musky cannot eat anything larger than what it can swallow whole. If it attacks a human hand or foot (you are many times more likely to be struck by lightning), it has probably mistaken the appendage for a duck or other small animal. In spite of its frightening teeth and the fact that it makes puncture wounds, it does not rip or do much serious damage. It would likely be attracted by the color or motion of a toe or finger on the water's surface. However, once it chomped on your pinkie it would realize that your hand is not worth eating, and, thoughtfully, it would let you go.

The tiger musky is a hybrid of the pike and the musky. It does not spawn or produce young, but it can grow to forty inches long and is known to grow to thirty-five pounds (1990 in New York). Of course, there may be larger tiger musky still hiding in Huron's deep waters. To this fish, everything is edible, and it has those same rows of clamping and goring teeth that both the musky and pike contribute to its gene pool. It is an extremely aggressive fish that would choose to seek and destroy all that swims or comes into its waters. There is a reported instance of a man actually catching one of these predators with his foot. The fish grabbed on and was pulled into the boat – still attached to the foot. The Department of Natural Resources was notified and confiscated the rogue tiger musky because it was undersized, regardless of the bait used!

The sea lamprey is a slimy creature that invaded Lake Huron in the early 1930s and left fishing communities and fisheries decimated. This predator probably entered the Great Lakes via the Hudson River.

Adult lamprey are shaped like eels and feed by attaching their hideous sucking mouths to other fish and extracting blood and other body fluids from the host.

The next time you stick your toes in the water or wade in for a refreshing swim, do you need to worry about one of these monsters of the deep attacking? The answer is a resounding "no." As shark-like as some of these predators appear, they never intentionally attack a human and when they do, no long-term damage is done. The risk of an attack is miniscule. There has never been a serious injury to a swimmer. So, swim away.

Walking The Beach

> *"To myself I am only a child*
> *playing on the beach,*
> *while vast oceans of truth*
> *lie undiscovered before me."*
> Isaac Newton

How Better to Greet the Morning?

There cannot be a person alive, at least not in Michigan, who has not enjoyed the simple, relaxing pleasure of walking a beach. It frees us to indulge that primordial urge to shed sandals and feel the sand massage our toes or shallow water cool our bare feet. Michiganders are blessed with over three thousand miles of shoreline, compared to Florida's approximate two thousand and California's meager one thousand.

Your right to walk the beach

There has been an ongoing debate in Michigan over what exactly are your rights to walk the beach. Property owners on occasion post signs declaring the beach in front of their cottages "Private," or warn you to "Keep Out." Beach walkers have worried that they have no right to walk along the shore. Sometimes, seduced by the great lake's majesty, they ignored their guilt and simply did it anyway. There was always the fear that someone would come out and yell at them or shoo them away.

In 2005 the Michigan Supreme Court heard the issue of who owns the beaches, or at least that narrow strip at the water's edge. One side argued that citizens did not have a right to walk on land they did not own. The other side retorted that the beach at the water's edge is owned by the public and everyone can walk it and enjoy it.

The Supreme Court's ruling, although not providing complete clarification, declared that the land up to the "ordinary high water mark" is not owned by individual land owners, and anyone can walk on it. Of course, the question begging additional elucidation was how you can determine the "ordinary high water mark." It is not always as easily distinguished as the high court would seem to suggest. Regardless, you are probably safe walking the water's edge without fear of being chastised (at least not legally) by anyone.

Searching for Treasure along the Shore

Every child, or the child in every one of us, thrills not just to walking the beach, but to finding new treasures in the midst of such splendor.

It is easy to spot limestone, shale, slate, granite, and quartzite along Huron's shores. You will also find Petoskey stones, Pudding stones, driftwood and sea glass, so take along something for carrying your finds.

Petoskey Stones

The most easily identifiable rock for collecting purposes is the Petoskey stone. Petoskey stones were formed about 350,000,000 years ago. What is now Michigan was near the equator, and a warm, shallow sea covered the state. In this sea habitat there developed trilobites, fish, and many other forms of life, including the coral that is now fossilized as our Petoskey stone. The soft, living tissue of the coral was called a polyp and at its center was a "mouth," used by the coral for food intake. During the petrification process, this "center" filled with silt, giving it the dark spots of the stone. Surrounding the center you can see the tentacles that the coral used to gather plankton into its mouth.

A Petoskey stone is a colony coral. Each separate chamber of the fossil was a member of the colony.

The derivation of the name Petoskey (the stone is named for the city because so many are found in the area) is the subject of local lore in the Petoskey area. It goes something like this:

Antoine Carre, a descendant of French nobility, visited the Petoskey area in the late 1780s. He became a fur trader with the John Jacob Astor Fur Company and eventually married an Ottawa Indian princess. Carre assimilated into the tribe and eventually became chief. He was given the Native American name of Neaatooshing.

In the spring of 1787, after spending the winter near what is now Chicago, Neaatooshing and his family began their trek back to northwest Michigan. One night during this journey they camped on the banks of the Kalamazoo River. Before daybreak a son was born to the chief. As the sun rose in the sky, its rays fell on the newborn's face. Seeing the sunshine on his child's face, the chief

Petoskey Stones

proclaimed, "His name shall be Petosegay and he shall become an important person." The translation of the name is *"rising sun," "rays of dawn,"* or *"sunbeams of promise."*

In the summer of 1873, just a few years before the death of Petosegay, a city was founded along the bay at Bear Creek. The site had a few nondescript buildings and a field overgrown with June grass. The population was no more than fifty or sixty. The city was named Petoskey, an English adaptation of Petosegay, in honor of the chief who gave his land, his name, and the heritage of *"sunbeams of promise."*

The Petoskey fossil is found in rock strata called the Gravel Point Formation located in the Traverse City and Petoskey area. However, these interesting stones are found on Lake Huron's shores as surely as they are found on the northern coast of Lake Michigan.

Polishing Petoskey Stones

Often these stones are fairly well-polished by the natural action of the wind, waves, and sand. Petoskey stones found inland lack the definition of their beach cousins. Even those along the shore appear more defined with a bit of polishing. If the stones you find are not polished to your satisfaction, a bit of sandpaper, a piece of corduroy and polishing powder can enhance the finish.

The sanding process should involve three grits of sandpaper: 220, 400, and 600. With the 220 you can remove any scratch marks. The 400 grit should remove any coarse spots. The 600 grit will make the stone smooth. You start with the coarsest grit and the trick is to sand longer than you think the stone needs it. Sprinkle the polishing powder (available at hobby stores) on the corduroy fabric and begin polishing the stone. Rinse and you should see a new luster. If you are unhappy with the finish you can sand some more and repeat.

Pudding Stones

A pudding stone is a conglomerate rock and that description helps you identify it. You are looking for a rock that appears to have smaller rocks (usually black or red, although sometimes brown or pink or even purple) embedded in it.

These stones were formed a billion years ago. They are sedimentary and metamorphic. A sedimentary rock is made from layers of sediment. Little bits of earth, broken down and worn away by wind and water, are washed downstream where they settle to the bottom of lakes, rivers, and oceans in layers. One layer of earth is piled atop the next and pressed down until the bottom layers slowly turn into rock.

The metamorphic aspect of the rock references the fact that it was changed, or metamorphosed, by great heat or pressure. When the sedimentary rocks were

Pudding Stones

buried deep beneath the earth's surface, the millions of years of heat and pressure changed them into a different form. Both igneous and sedimentary rocks are subject to the metamorphic process. As examples, limestone can turn into marble, sandstone can become quartzite and shale can be turned into slate.

The white or gray in the pudding stone is quartz sand which has cemented itself together over millions of years. Mixed with it is a combination of other pebbles and stones of various sizes, shapes and colors. Some may even contain fossils. Pudding stones are also referred to as quartz conglomerates, meaning they are sedimentary rocks composed of quartz and various other minerals. If you have a keen eye, you will find these unusual stones along the Thumb shores.

Shale, Slate, and Skipping Stones

Shale is a sedimentary rock formed by deposits of successive layers of clay or volcanic ash. Slate is a fine-grained, homogeneous, sedimentary rock which has been metamorphosed from shale to the harder and more permanent slate. Neither is very pretty and both are common along Huron's shores. Shale appears to crumble in layers. The beauty of this stone is its value as a great skipping stone.

Skipping stones is an ancient amusement, quite possibly as old as the relationship between man and lakes. Different countries call it by different names, but everywhere there is a lake, there is the pastime of skipping stones over its surface. The British call it stone skimming. The Irish reference it as stone skiffing. To the Danes it is smutting and to the French it is ricochet. Guinness listed 38 jumps, or skips, as a record.

If you can throw a stone at (not into) the water so it hits at the right angle to make it touch the water and jump up from the water at least once, you have skipped a stone. The point, of course, is to make it skip as many times as possible.

Driftwood

Pieces of wood that have fallen into the lake and been subjected to long periods of tossing and tumbling in the waves and sand become driftwood. Pieces often look contorted in shape. Because the wood is also deadwood, once dried it is very light. Large pieces are interesting adornments to gardens and lawns. Smaller pieces can be added to floral arrangements, centerpieces, or just set on a shelf as a natural sculpture.

Beach Glass

Beach glass is formed when broken pieces of glass are worn smooth by years of wave action pitching them about in the sand and rocks. They are shaped naturally and no two pieces are ever alike. Sea glass is used to make jewelry and for a variety of hobby and decorative purposes.

Clear glass turns into a milky white piece of sea glass through the polishing process. You will also find brown and green pieces. The rarest and most difficult pieces to find are blue.

Picking up sea glass is a redemptive process. It allows us to take something that has been discarded, and declared useless, and celebrate its transformation.

We carry the tiny bits home, for whatever decorative purpose we have chosen, hoping to preserve the memory of a lovely beach walk as well.

My daughter snubbed her nose at the pieces my granddaughters and I had accumulated noting, "It's just broken glass." "Yes," I agreed, "but in the same way a diamond is just a lump of coal."

**A brief pause on the rocks in Lexington Harbor before
continuing the quest for beach treasures**

Beacons Lighting the Way

> *"In the dark dreary nights*
> *when the storm is at its most fierce,*
> *the lighthouse burns bright*
> *so the sailors can find their way home again."*
> *Author unknown*

Thumb Lighthouses Standing Watch

Michigan has more lighthouses than any other state in the United States. Even with the advent of such modern navigational tools as global positioning satellites, lighthouses have lost none of their mystique. They remain monuments to the Thumb's maritime past and symbols of man's attempts to control his relationship with the often stormy Sweetwater Sea.

Old South Channel Range Lights

Located just off the southeastern tip of Harsens Island, these lights were built before Abraham Lincoln became president. They are unique in many ways. It takes both of them to guide the great freighters into the South Channel. The front light is thirty feet tall. The rear light stands forty feet tall. A ship's captain lined up the two lights and entered the channel just to the south of them. They opened the channel to twenty-four-hour shipping.

A second unique feature of the Old South Channel Range Lights is the man-made, mini-islands on which they stand.

Construction on the lights began in 1855 and was completed in 1859. The front light began to lean in 1875 and was repaired using the stone and timber crib from the original construction. In 1990 the light was again leaning, and a steel cell filled with limestone was placed around its base to offer additional temporary support. In 1996 a permanent seawall was constructed around the front light.

The rear light, even though constructed in the same manner and from the same materials, managed to withstand the elements better than the front light, although it now needs major foundation work. The rear light had a keeper's house standing next to it until 1930, when it succumbed to vandalism, age, elements and general deterioration.

Once described as "The Toughest Little Lights on the Lakes," the lights are on the National Register of Historic Places. Restoration efforts are being undertaken by a hard-working, non-profit staff to save these marvelous pieces of history. You can see additional pictures, read a history, and see an eight-minute video about these fascinating lights by going to *www.soschannellights.org*.

South Channel Lights
Photo Courtesy of Chuck Brockman

The Peche Lighthouse in Marine City

Peche Island Rear Range Lighthouse

Now located on the coastline in Marine City, this lighthouse was originally built in 1908 off Peche Island, Ontario at the head of the Detroit River. It marked the narrow passage from Lake St. Clair into the river. It served from that location for three quarters of a century.

In 1983 the lighthouse was scheduled for decommission and demolition. That same year a group of historic-minded citizens stepped in to halt the destruction and move the lighthouse to the waterfront in Marine City. The move required a healthy dose of imagination and an even greater degree of tenacity. The job was completed successfully in spite of the fact that the lighthouse weighed thirty-five tons, stood sixty-six feet tall and was fourteen feet in diameter.

The lighthouse has no current utilitarian function but adds charm and interest to the waterfront. It is a piece of preserved maritime history.

The Huron Lightship

Anchored just south of the Blue Water Bridge, the Huron Lightship is a museum open to the public. It is also a floating lighthouse. During its active days it could be anchored in any area where it was too difficult (too deep, expensive, or impractical) to construct a more traditional lighthouse.

The light was displayed at the top of the mast and the ship was equipped with fog signals consisting of bells, whistles, trumpets, sirens, and horns.

The Huron Lightship was built in 1920 by the Consolidated Shipbuilding Company of New York. It became a National Historic Landmark in 1989.

The Huron Lightship was stationed at various places in Lake Michigan for the first fifteen years of its service and then transferred to Lake Huron, where for thirty-six years it guided ships around the Corsica Shoals in Lake Huron into the narrow St. Clair River.

In 1972, after fifty years of service, the lightship was retired and local residents of Port Huron acquired it and enshrined it in the water across from Pine Grove Park.

The Fort Gratiot Lighthouse

Fort Gratiot Lighthouse

Located at 2800 Omar Street in Port Huron, just north of the Blue Water Bridge, the Fort Gratiot Lighthouse is the oldest operating lighthouse on the Great Lakes. It was built in 1825. It was named after the engineer in charge of its construction. The tower is eighty-six feet above the lake level. The keeper's cottage and the fog whistle house are painted red. The lighthouse is red brick painted white. It is a classic example of early nineteenth century lighthouse style. The tower collapsed in 1828 due to shoddy workmanship. It had to be rebuilt in 1829. Additional rebuilding was required in 1861.

The Storm of 1913 nearly washed the lighthouse off its foundation. Captain

Kimball, the keeper at the time of the storm, said he watched waves as high as thirty and forty feet pounding on the lighthouse, and he believed if the storm had lasted as much as an hour longer, the lighthouse would have washed away. The next year a retaining wall was built to offer greater protection from violent storms.

The city of Port Huron has applied to take over the ownership of the lighthouse under the National Historic Lighthouse Preservation Act. Significant restoration is taking place. The land on which the lighthouse sits is part of the existing Lighthouse Park. Tours can be arranged by calling (810) 982-3659.

The Port Sanilac Lighthouse

Port Sanilac Lighthouse

This lighthouse is currently a private residence, but you can still see it from the street or the parking lot that runs along its south side. The lighthouse was constructed in 1886 and sent out its first beams into the night on October 20, 1886. It originally burned kerosene but was electrified in 1929. Although privately owned, the eight-sided tower continues to provide light to ships navigating the area. The house attached to the tower is red brick covered with ivy. It is worth a drive down Lake Street in Port Sanilac to catch a glimpse of this architecturally interesting lighthouse.

Harbor Beach Breakwater Lighthouse

Constructed in 1885, this lighthouse is still active, although automated. It has a visibility of twenty-one miles. The best place to observe the lighthouse is from Trescott Pier. Upon entering Harbor Beach on M-25, turn right on Trescott

The Harbor Beach Breakwater Lighthouse

and drive to the end of the street. The lighthouse is beyond the fishing pier and sits on a freestanding crib off the long breakwater. It is not attached to land at either end so there is no way to walk or drive to it.

The Harbor Beach Lighthouse was constructed to provide additional safety for ships traveling from the St. Clair River to the Saginaw Bay. The Fort Gratiot Lighthouse sat at the south entrance to Lake Huron and the Pointe Aux Barques Lighthouse sat at the bay. In between was over a hundred miles with no harbor of refuge. Big freighters, confounded by storms in this open area, were forced to tough it out. This situation was responsible for many shipwrecks and the federal government, acknowledging the danger, set about easing the problem by erecting a lighthouse midway between them.

The initial decision was whether to locate a lighthouse in Port Hope or Harbor Beach. It was estimated it would take three thousand more feet of breakwater to construct it at Port Hope, so Harbor Beach got the lighthouse. The first beacon went out in 1875 and could be seen from thirteen miles.

The Harbor Beach breakwater is 8,200 feet long. Construction consumed over 1,000,000 tons of iron, 15,000,000 board feet of lumber and 48,000 cords of stone. The first year it was open the harbor provided shelter to over one thousand ships.

The Pointe Aux Barques Lighthouse

President Polk ordered this lighthouse built in 1857 to help ships navigate through some of the most treacherous shoals of the Great Lakes. Many ships met with disaster trying to "cut the corner" into the Saginaw Bay. The lighthouse was automated in 1957 and is still in service. It stands eighty-nine feet tall and has

103 cast iron steps to the top. Its flashing white light can be seen from eighteen miles out. The keeper's residence is now a museum in the lovely Lighthouse Park. There is also a gift shop.

The Pointe Aux Barques Lighthouse Historical Society has been instrumental in the upkeep and preservation of this lighthouse.

The first lighthouse keeper was Peter Shook, who took that post when the lighthouse was completed. Shook was married, and he and his wife Catherine had eight children. One evening Peter went to fetch a doctor to attend Catherine, and as Peter and the doctor made their way back to the lighthouse both men were drowned. Peter's body was never recovered. Catherine took over as keeper and filled the post for three years during which time she was able to feed, clothe and educate her eight children on her $350 a year keeper's salary.

Soon after she took over as keeper, there was a fire that burned the keeper's house. It was the dead of winter, and when officials arrived several days later, Catherine and her family were surviving in a lean-to, but the light had never flickered. She retired from service due to poor health and has recently been nominated to the Michigan Women's Hall of Fame.

It is rumored that the keeper's house is visited by the spirit of a woman, but there is no suggestion it is Catherine. (See related ghost story in Part Two.)

Port Austin Reef Lighthouse

The lighthouse was constructed in 1878 and abandoned in 1953. It began to deteriorate rapidly. It is now under lease to the Port Austin Lighthouse Association until the year 2020. The group managed to evict the resident flock of more than five hundred pigeons that were wreaking havoc with its interior. The association has reroofed and bird-proofed the lighthouse in their attempts to preserve its heritage.

The reef lighthouse is located two and a half miles north of the Village of Port Austin and two miles offshore at a point marking the tip of Michigan's Thumb. Ships headed northbound used it as a guide to turn into the Saginaw Bay. The lighthouse originally rested on an octagonal pier. The shape of the pier was modified in 1899 and the station was rebuilt to its present configuration. It stands sixty feet tall. It was decommissioned in 1984.

Charity Island Lighthouse

To get to this lighthouse you take a one-hour cruise to Charity Island from Caseville. It is located in the Saginaw Bay, thirty-four miles off the mouth of the Saginaw River. It was built to help ships avoid a number of shoals extending from the northern and southern shores of the island. The island is a 322-acre chunk of stone that creates a danger to navigation. The first light beamed out into Lake Huron shortly after May 26, 1857, the date the lighthouse keeper arrived.

The lighthouse is a thirty-nine-foot-tall brick tower located on a slight rise. It provided a thirteen-mile range of visibility.

It was a very difficult lighthouse to maintain because its location in the middle of a rock island left it so vulnerable to the elements. Of all of the lighthouses included in this chapter, it is in the worst condition. There is a Charity Island Preservation Committee attempting to stabilize and preserve the lighthouse. Interestingly, the lighthouse and the keeper's house are on two different parcels of land. The house was owned by individuals who finally had it demolished because it attracted too many curious visitors and was not in proper condition to accommodate safety. The preservation attempts are only for the lighthouse.

Lighthouse Preservation

Michigan is the only state that supports lighthouse preservation, and most lighthouses receive assistance from dedicated volunteers interested in preserving these historical treasures. It is definitely worth visiting the lighthouses that are open to the public and even worth taking a peek from the outside at the ones that are not. Along the way, if you meet any of the dedicated volunteers, let them know you appreciate their efforts.

Barns

"It will not always be summer; build barns."
Hesiod, 8th century BC

Dotting the Thumbscape

Powerfully symbolic of the Thumb's agricultural heritage, barns represent a tradition of hard work and promise. Many times the barn was built before the house because sheltering livestock and crops was essential to a farmer's success.

In Europe, farmers erected several smaller buildings for separate agricultural functions. American barns gathered everything under one roof.

Often that roof was a hip roof with a hay loft or haymow and wide side doors so tractors could drive in to unload fresh bales.

In addition to sheltering the domestic animals, the barn was also a workshop, a place for storing grain, and a place where machinery and tools could be kept when not in use. When its busy day was done, the barn often became the center of social functions as neighbors gathered for threshing parties and dances.

Silos stood next to many barns. These tall cylindrical towers were used for storing silage. Silage is grass or other crops harvested during the summer months. When stored in a silo these crops ferment naturally, basically becoming pickled. Cattle and sheep prefer silage to dry hay. It also has a higher nutritional value to help get them through Michigan's cold winter months.

Dairy barns had cow stanchions for "locking" a cow's head in place during milking. Some barns had stalls for horses.

Most Midwestern barns are red. Or at least they started that way. Red was a cheap pigment used to protect the barn against weathering. It also had nice "curb

Hip Roof Barn

appeal" when paired with a traditional white clapboard farm house.

There is a theory that barns are red because some farmers added blood from their most recent slaughter to the linseed oil they used to seal their barns. As the paint dried, it turned from a bright red to a darker burnt-orange red. That may have been the case in Europe many years ago, but it does not seem to be the ready explanation for red barns in the Thumb. In the Thumb farmers may have added ferrous oxide (rust) to the oil mixture. The ingredients of rust were plentiful on farms, and it is a poison to many fungi, including mold and moss, which often grow on barns. Adding the ferrous oxide was meant to slow down the decaying process.

Many barns are no longer red. With the decline of the small family-farm, many have been left to weather naturally and have fallen into a state of disrepair. Others have been torn down for the wood. Old barn wood became a decorating trend as builders reclaimed the history-steeped planks.

Today when people need lots of storage, they turn to the metal pole barn or building. It is practical and economically much cheaper to build than a traditional barn. It is estimated that a typical timber-framed barn could cost over $250,000 to build at today's current construction costs. Many of the massive barn beams used in traditional barns were cut from the hearts of virgin timber the size of which would not even be available today.

The historic barns of the Thumb are a treasure. As you drive the Thumb you will see them everywhere. Turn up a country side road and you will not drive a half mile without spotting one. Many barns have taken on a new life. The barn below houses antiques.

Perhaps the most interesting barn in the Thumb is the Octagonal Barn near Gagetown. (See picture in Gagetown listing of Part One of this guide.)

Country Village Antiques near Bad Axe

Hip Roof Barn near Kinde

Old Barn Near Croswell with Silo

Barn with Double Silos on Germania Road

Weathered Double Barn near Croswell

Weathered Barn

Aging but Dignified Barn near Sebewaing

Ghost Stories

> *"Ghosts,... all waiting their dismissal*
> *from the desolate shore,*
> *all turning on him eyes that were changed*
> *by the death they had died in coming there."*
> *-Charles Dickens*

Tales for Around the Campfire

Few things inspire our imaginations like a good ghost story, and Michigan's Thumb has its share. In the following eerie and sometimes downright ghoulish stories – from the convoluted tale of the Morrow Street Bridge Ghost to the timeless love-gone-bad story of the ghost of Minnie Quay and through to the Pointe Aux Barques' heroic ghost – you will hear the Thumb's chilling tales. They are told in about the same order you may encounter their ghosts lurking along your path as you drive from New Baltimore to Caseville.

The Ghost of the Morrow Street Bridge

A stranger and more contrary tale you will not read in these pages. This is the tale of "Annie Smith," although her true name has never passed the lips of any storyteller.

Annie was a mere sixteen years old, but her soul was much older. She could still remember her mother: the smell of her lilac soap and the sparkle of her eyes when she laughed. Annie was only nine years old when that laugh was extinguished and her mother's life came to a crashing end. Annie became mother to Emma, her youngest sister, born the same day their mother died. The mother's death also left Annie responsible for two brothers and another sister, all born sometime between Annie and Emma.

Without his wife, Annie's father became distant and unapproachable to his young family. Annie did what she could to keep the family together and provide the love her younger siblings needed.

When she turned fifteen, Annie thought her life would get easier. Her sisters were old enough to help her with household chores, and her brothers could take care of themselves. Annie even had dreams that she might soon have a life of her own and smiled thinking of the red-headed, freckled farm boy about a mile down the road.

It was late March, and the mean Michigan winter visited one final snowstorm on the little Algonac community where Annie and her family lived. Two soldiers, heading south from Port Austin to join up with Grant at Appomattox, were forced to seek shelter for the night. Annie's father treated them like visiting royalty and brought out his best moonshine. The men talked about Mr. Lincoln, the country, and farming. Annie smiled, watching her father more animated than she had seen him since her mother's death. He ordered her to bring out their extra blankets and make a pallet for their guests in front of the fireplace. She was pleased to do as she was bid.

It took only a few hours for Annie's happiness to turn sour. She was awakened in the middle of the night to the smell of nasty, liquored breath on her face. A rough, calloused hand covered her mouth and whispered softly that if she was quiet no one would get hurt. Annie barely had time to think of her sisters sleeping soundly in a single bed only a few feet from her own.

It was over in an hour-long minute. Annie lay in silence until dawn. Then she boiled a pan of water and tried to wash away the filthy feeling that clung to her like her ripped and sweat-soaked nightgown. The soldiers were already gone.

In 1865, hers was a story best borne in silence – a memory best suppressed. Annie's life might have returned to a semblance of normalcy had her belly not begun to grow. It was not a situation she could share with her father. She began corseting her waist and wearing ever looser clothes. No one paid much attention.

It was late November and the weather was warmer than normal. The full moon intermittently peeked out from dark clouds that threatened a menacing squall. Her first pain came at 9:30 pm, but everyone in the house was asleep. A farm family's day was charted by the rising and setting of the sun.

Snoring loudly from the soothing effects of alcohol, Annie's father could sleep through a storm, or the agonizing screams of childbirth. But, unlike their father, Annie knew that her siblings would awaken to any sound she made. She silently put on her high-top shoes without lacing them completely and grabbed her raggedy coat and tied it about her with a length of rope. She also picked up a small knife and a tiny embroidered blanket and made her way into the woods. For the next five hours she suffered the pain alone – unless you counted the random owls and hawks that occasionally checked her progress. When the final push brought her new daughter into the world, Annie used the small knife to cut the cord.

She whispered the name Annabelle and wrapped the child in the tiny blanket she had so lovingly and furtively stitched over the past year. She held the baby close for a few moments, then laid the precious bundle under a tree and headed home.

The infant's crying weakened as Annie put distance between them. When the whimpering was almost inaudible she could stand it no longer and retraced her steps to reclaim her child. But, before she reached Annabelle, the crying had stopped. The clouds now completely covered any illumination from the sky and her frantic search was in vain.

Annie's physical pain was masked by anguish of the incomprehensible act she had committed. Annie took the rope she had used to tie her coat about her and hung herself at the foot of Morrow Bridge.

The next morning, Native Americans hunting in the area were the first to see her corpse swaying in the wind. They cut her down and took her body into the village to return to her family.

When settlers, including Annie's father, arrived at the village, they presumed the Native Americans had murdered the young girl. Her blood-soaked dress was all the evidence they needed to conclude this was not a natural death. The settlers began firing on the band of Native Americans, killing many.

Over the years there have been reports of green, glowing orbs in the area of the bridge and also sightings of a bloody woman, beseeching anyone coming near to help her find her baby. There are stories that if you go on the bridge and honk your horn three times you will hear a baby cry beneath the bridge. There have been reports of the ghost of a woman seen through flames of fire on the road nearby.

One version sets forth most of the details recounted above, but it does not include the rape. Perhaps it was just the boy down the road who fathered the child? Many variations are told, mixing and matching alleged facts.

Undoubtedly, the most interesting attempt to get at the truth was offered by Francis Sampier, who made the ghost the subject of a film about the Morrow Street or Morrow Bridge Ghost. Here is what he said, "The legend was really started around the 1950s, when a donkey was seen running through the woods. People rumored it was a monster, so the old folks called it, 'The Morrow Road Monster.' Then it was rumored to eat babies. Somehow over decades the mother was added to the story and it became her baby that was eaten. Next it morphed into a ghost on the road looking for her child. And that is what it remains today. All because a donkey was on the loose."

Believe what you will!

The Harsens Island Ghost

What's a man to do when ghosts inhabit his house? Call *Ghost Busters*, of course. Or, in this case, invite them to bid on the chance to spend a night and investigate.

That is what Bob K. did. Bob owns a house on Williams Street on serene and peaceful little Harsens Island.

He has owned the residence for thirty years and lived in it for twenty. He has several sons, a daughter, and a wife, all of whom have experienced the ghost's presence in the home. After he and his wife moved out, one of his sons lived there for a few years. This son reported seeing shadowy people folding clothes and described sleep paralysis and night terrors. He felt that one upstairs bedroom increased his "desires," including that for alcohol.

After the son and subsequent tenants moved out, the house remained unoccupied for several years. Apparently the last renters before its abandonment could not contend with the unexplained lights, burning smells, mysterious electrical malfunctions, and loud echoes that came with the place. They decided to get out while the getting was good, so to speak.

Bob K., not knowing what to do with a haunted house that he could not even rent, decided to bring in professionals. He ran an ad on e-Bay that brought several responses from psychics or mediums willing to pay for the opportunity to investigate the paranormal activity in the house. The Michigan Ghost Society provided the winning bid.

As for what made the house so angry, these ghost busters claim to have contacted three spirits that may shed some light on the situation:

Isabella is the spirit of a woman who worked for a family that owned the house before Bob. Since Isabella did not actually live or die in the house, it is unclear why her spirit remains there.

Timmy is the ghost of a four-year-old boy who was killed by an automobile in front of the house. He was innocently riding his trike when the tragedy befell him. It is relatively easy to see why he might be unhappy.

The third ghost has no name but is believed to be Timmy's uncle – and the person who accidentally ran his car over poor little Timmy. Obviously, the uncle could be contending with a lot of guilty feelings and anger. Maybe he is shunned in the afterworld.

There may be additional ghosts residing at the Williams Street address, but those are the ones identified by the ghost hunters of the Michigan Ghost Society. During their investigation they described sensations of being choked in the upstairs bedroom. One member of the society contends she was scratched by one of the ghosts. She was wearing a T-shirt and a jacket, and yet claims she sustained a scratch that went from the base of her neck all the way down her spine. She suffered several smaller scratches as well.

The Michigan Ghost Society used everything from high-tech photography equipment (said to have revealed interesting white spots) to spirit sticks in trying to figure out what is happening inside the house.

One thing appears clear, these ghosts are not the mild mannered Casper types. They want no one in the house and have even been heard whispering that visitors should get out.

You could not pay most people to spend the night in that house!

The Spirit of the Sauk Warriors

At one time the Sauk were a major tribe of Native Americans in the Thumb area. Their name can be translated as "People of the Yellow Earth." The word Saginaw means "Place of the Sauk" and many roads, streets, and businesses in the Thumb, as well as a city are named Saginaw.

The Sauk inhabited a large settlement on the banks of the Black River near what is now Port Huron. The Sauk were known for their fierceness and warlike disposition towards other tribes of the area.

The Chippewa, Pottawatomie, Menominee, and Ottawa banded together to battle their menacing common enemy. They chose to attack at a time when they knew the Sauk men were off hunting. They crept into the village and massacred the women and children. The Sauk warriors returned to a decimated settlement and were immediately filled with inconsolable grief.

However, being outnumbered, these Sauk warriors could not engage in a full frontal attack on the tribes that had wreaked havoc on their village. Instead they made periodic forays into the villages of the tribes responsible for the attack. They slipped in during the dark of night and burned a single hut or killed a single enemy and then slipped out under cover of blackness.

The Chippewa were convinced that the ghosts of the dead Sauk had returned to haunt them. Who can say that the anguished Sauk did not have assistance from the spirits of their deceased loved ones?

A Ghostly Tale of Mistaken Identity in the Lawrence House

Are our friends in Canada less superstitious? Do they actually have fewer ghosts and ghost stories? Or are they just unwilling to talk about them? No one seemed to have a ghost story to share. There is one exception:

One of the women working at the Lawrence House admitted there are stories about a ghost who resides in the lovely old Victorian Gallery and makes mischief with the elevator. Since the house has been turned into an art gallery showcase, it has undergone some updating including an elevator that now reaches between floors. This elevator has been known to act quite contrary. Doors will open and shut spontaneously, and it will travel from floor to floor without anyone pushing a button.

One morning the poor woman went to work quite early and found she was alone in the beautiful old house. She was working on the first floor so did not need to use the obstinate elevator. But from her vantage point behind the desk she could see the elevator doors opening and shutting. The elevator was clearly in one of its moods. She heard the elevator go up a floor and then she heard it come back down. The doors opened, but still she saw no one inside.

Unable to tolerate it, she shouted, "OK, ghost, come on out."

You can imagine her surprise when the "ghost" responded, "It's OK, ma'am. I'm the repairman and I'm just fixing the elevator."

Apparently the repairman was standing to the side and behind the control panel where he could not be seen.

The Lost Souls of Lexington

Lexington lore is replete with Ghost stories:

The Cadillac House's George

The Cadillac House's George is its restless resident ghost. He tries to unnerve staff by rattling pizza pans, drinking beers, and otherwise being a nuisance. Still, you must feel a bit sorry for George as he seeks his unrequited and cheating love.

Sitting with his sweetheart in the first booth from the door on a rainy April morning, George had business to attend. Fearing that his lady-love was seeing his best friend, it was with a heavy heart that George left Lexington to make the trip to Croswell.

When he returned that evening, earlier than expected, the innkeeper (the Cadillac House was formerly a hotel) grinned and pointed up the stairs. George bounded up and opened the door to his love's room. As he had feared, she was not alone. Catching her in such a compromising position broke George's heart. His best friend broke George's neck by pushing him off the balcony, or so the story goes.

George still wanders the Cadillac House hoping to convince his lover of the error of her ways.

Captain's Quarters

A seafaring captain is said to be drawn to the nautical motif and familiarity of this lovely little B&B. Perhaps it reminds him of his ship or maybe it just feels like home. There may also be a second ghost residing at Captain's Quarters. There have been reports of a little girl staring out from a front window. Some stories suggest she either lived there or stayed there for a night. No more details are known about either of these mysterious ghosts. Most guests enjoy the stories and it seems clear these ghosts mean no harm.

Lost Sailors

If you decide to walk the beach near Lexington Harbor by moonlight, you may sense a disturbing presence. Try as you may, at first you will see nothing but the million shimmering diamond-like reflections of the moon on the black water. Look even closer and it is said you may see wisps of white rising from the sea. Listen very carefully and you may even hear the mournful wailing of sailors whose ships went down in the Great 1913 Storm. Several freighters sank that night and pieces of their ships were scattered for miles along the Lexington beaches. Sailors lost in time are said to still be trying to make it home to the loved ones who waited for them on shore that fateful night.

Ghost Ships that Haunt the Thumb

No chronicle of ghost stories would be complete without mentioning the phantoms of ships and sailors that have gone down in the waters of Lake Huron. A "ghost ship" generally refers to a ship that vanishes at sea only to be later spotted through mists and storms. Not all ships that sink return to sail again, and not all send up spirits to haunt the living. But the next few stories tell of ghost ships that do:

The Griffon

The Griffon may be the first ship on Lake Huron to be designated a ghost ship. Some argue she is the first ship to go down in the Great Lakes, but others claim that dubious honor goes to the *Frontenac*, lost in Lake Ontario in early 1669. If the *Frontenac* went down earlier, the *Griffon* may be the first big ship to vanish in Lake Huron. The *Griffon* was built by La Salle and weighed forty-five tons and had five guns. She was on her maiden voyage in 1679 and had sailed across Lake Erie, Lake Huron, and Lake Michigan. She picked up a load of furs and was headed back through Lake Huron on her return trip when she went down with all six of her crew members. She has been followed to the depths by thousands more ships but perhaps because the *Griffon* was first, her crew is the angriest. Or, perhaps it is the persistent rumors of mutiny that makes her rest uneasy.

Look into the mist some foggy morning and you may see her sail by.

The Nashau

The Nashau vanished in the Saginaw Bay in 1892. Her captain and thirteen unlucky crewmen went down with her. The gale winds that came from nowhere plunged this propeller-driven steamship to the depths, but she refuses to stay put. On treacherous nights when the devil can be heard shrieking in the tempest, she is still seen trying to find her way to port and safety.

The Erie Board of Trade

The Erie Board of Trade was taken down by a ghost and herself became a ghost ship. It is a story best told in the words of one who was there. The following account was carried in the *Saginaw Courier* in 1883, by an unknown author. This is the exact, unedited story told by the mystery writer as he described it in the words of a sailor who was there:

> *Down in the lower part of South Street the other day, an old sailor sat on an anchor stock in front of a ship chandler's store. He was an intelligent-looking man and was fairly well-dressed for one of his calling. Other sailors were seated on a bale of oakum, on a wide-mouth pump without a plunger, and on the single stone step of the store. The ship chandler and a young friend sat in*

chairs just inside the door. The group was talking about ghosts. One of the men had just told his experience.

"You're a sorry dog," said the ship chandler to him. "You were drunk, and the spirits you'd taken within made you see the spirits without. It's always that way."

The old sailor threw one leg over the anchor stock, faced the ship chandler, and said: "You know I never take no grog, don't you, captain?"

The ship chandler nodded.

"Well, I saw a ghost once. I saw it as plain as ever I saw anything. The captain of the schooner I was on and the man in the waist both saw it, too. There wasn't a drop of liquor on board. It happened up on the Lakes, and I reckon you know the captain. It was the talk of the docks the whole season."

"I know a Captain Jack Custer of Milan. He's the only fresh-water captain I'm acquainted with," said the ship chandler.

"He's the man. I heard him speak of you once. It was a little over ten years ago. I was before the mast then. It was at the opening of the season, and I was in Chicago. I'd been through the canal from Toronto on one of these little canallers. What with tramping through mud with a line over my shoulder and taking turns around snubbing posts every time the schooner took a notion to run her nose into the bank, I'd got enough of canal schooners.

"I heard at the boarding house that some men were wanted on a three-masted schooner called the Erie Board of Trade. The boys gave her a pretty hard name, but they said the grub was good and that the old man paid the top wages every time, so I went down and asked him if he'd got all hands aboard. He looked at me a minute, and then asked me where my dunnage was. When I told him, he said I should get it on board right away.

"The Board of Trade was as handsome a craft as ever floated on the Lakes. She'd carry about 45,000 bushels of corn. Her model has as clean lines as a yacht. As I came down the dock with my bag under my arm, I had to stop and have a look at her. The old man saw me at it. He was proud of her, and I thought afterward that he rather took a fancy to me because I couldn't help showing I liked her looks.

"The first trip around to Chicago every man but me got his

dunnage onto dock as soon as he was paid off. I'd seen worse times than what we'd had, and when I got my money I asked the old man if he'd want anyone to help with the lines when the schooner was towed from the coal-yard to the elevator. He said he reckoned he could keep me by if I wanted to stay, so I signed articles for the next trip there.

"When we were getting the wheat into her at the elevator we got the crew aboard. One of them was a red-haired Scotchman. The captain took a dislike to him from the first. It was a tough time for 'Scotty' all the way down. We were in Buffalo just twelve hours and then we cleared for Cleveland to take on soft coal for Milwaukee. The tug gave us a short pull outside the breakwater, and we had no more than got the canvas onto the schooner before the wind died out completely. Nothing would do but we must drop anchor, for the current, settling to the Niagara River, was carrying us down to Black Rock at three knots an hour.

"When we'd got things shipshape about decks, the old man called Scotty and two others aft and told them to scrape down the topmasts. Then he handed the boatswain's chair to them. Scotty gave his chair a look and then turned around, and touching his forehead respectfully, said, 'If you please, sir, the rope's about chafed off, and I'll bend on a bit of ratlin' stuff.'

"The captain was mighty touchy because the jug had left him so, and he just jumped up and down and swore. Scotty climbed the main rigging pretty quick. He got the halliards bent onto the chair and sung out to hoist away. I and a youngster, the captain's nephew, were standing by. We handled that rope carefully, for I'd seen how tender the chair was. When we'd got him up chock-a-block, the young fellow took a turn around the pin, and I looked aloft to see what Scotty was doing. As I did so he reached for his knife with one hand and put out the other for the backstay.

"Just then the chair gave way. He fell all bunched up 'til he struck the crosstrees, and then he spread out like and fell flat on the deck, just forward of the cabin on the starboard side. I was kneeling beside him in a minute, and so was the old man, too, for he'd no idea that the man would fall. I was feeling pretty well choked up to see a shipmate killed so, and I said to the captain: 'This is pretty bad business, sir. This man's been murdered,' says I.

"When I said that, Scotty opened his eyes and looked at us. Then, in a whisper, he cursed the captain and his wife and children, and the ship and her owners. It was awful. While he was* *still talking the blood bubbled over his lips, and his head lurched over to one side. He was dead.*

"It was three days before the schooner got to Cleveland. Some of the boys were for leaving her there, but most of us stayed by, because wages were down again. Going through the rivers there were four other schooners in tow. We were next to the tug, and some lubber cast off the towline without singing out first. We dropped our bower as quick as we could, but it was not before we'd drifted astern, carrying away the head gear of the schooner next to us and smashing in our own boat under the stern.

"There was a fair easterly wind on the Lake, and as we had got out of the river in the morning we were standing across Saginaw Bay during the first watch that night. I had the second trick at the wheel. The stars were shining bright and clear and not a cloud was in sight. In the northwest, a low, dark streak showed where the land was. Every stitch of canvas was set and drawing, though the booms sagged and creaked as the vessel rolled lazily in the varying breeze.

"I had just sung out to the mate to strike eight bells when the captain climbed up the companionway and out on deck. He stepped over to the starboard rail and had a look around, and then the lookout began striking the bell. The last stroke of the bell seemed to die away with a swish. A bit of spray or something struck me in the face. I wiped it away, and then I saw something rise up slowly across the mainsail from the starboard side of the deck forward of the cabin. It was white and all bunched up. I glanced at the captain, and saw he was staring at it too.

"When it reached the gaff near the throat halliards, it hovered over an instant, and then struck the cross-trees. There it spread out and rolled over toward us. It was Scotty. His lips were working just as they were when he cursed the captain. As he straightened out he seemed to stretch himself until he grasped the maintop mast with one hand and the mizzen with the other. Both were carried away like pipe-stems. The next I knew the ship was all in the wind. The square-sail yard was hanging in two pieces, the top hamper was swinging, and the booms were jibing over.

"The old man fell in a dead faint on the quarter deck, and the man in the waist dove down the forecastle so fast that he knocked over the last man of the other watch. If it hadn't been for the watch coming on deck just then, she'd rolled the sticks out of her altogether. They got the headsails over, and I put the wheel up

without knowing what I was doing. In a minute it seemed we were laying our course again. The second mate was just beginning to curse me for going to sleep at the wheel, when the mate came along and glanced at the binnacle.

"'What the heck is this?' he said. 'Laying our course and on the other tack?'

The young man by the ship chandler had listened with intense interest. "Here," he said. "That story is true. I was there. I'm the captain's nephew you spoke about. I was reading in the cabin that night. As the bell began to strike, I felt a sudden draft through the cabin, and my paper was taken out of my hands and out of the window before I could stop it. I hurried out of the cabin after it, but as I got my head up through the companionway I heard the crash of the falling masts. When the schooner began to go off on the other tack, I saw a bit of waterspout two miles away to the leeward, and..."

The ship chandler laughed.

"Did you find your paper?" he asked.

"No!" said the young man.

"I thought not," said the ship chandler.

"Well," said the old sailor, "the main facts in this story can be easily verified. The next voyage the schooner was sunk. The insurance company resisted payment on the grounds that she had been scuttled by her captain. During the trial of the case, the story of the death of Scotty and the loss of her topmasts under a clear sky was all told under oath. Anybody who doesn't believe it can see a copy of the printed testimony by applying to Roseburg & Barker, the ship chandlers at 1789 Central Wharf, Buffalo."

The Ghost of Ada Loop Harrison

Port Sanilac is a beguiling village and thanks to Captain Stanley Harrison who donated the Loop Harrison Mansion to the Historical Society in 1976, it has one of the finest museums in the Thumb. Behind the walls of the elegant Victorian, however, not all is as placid and serene as the exterior suggests. The tormented ghost of Ada Loop Harrison wanders the twenty antique-filled rooms finding no peace.

Ada lived a life of privilege, at least by Port Sanilac standards. Her father was Dr. Joseph Loop, the well-respected and beloved physician who ministered to the local population. He treated their ills, listened to their problems, delivered their babies, and in some cases tried futilely to stave off death. Dr Loop often took his medicine to his patients by horse-drawn buggy. The museum today holds many of his physician's instruments and some early carriages.

Dr. Loop built his spectacular home in 1875 and it was magnificent by any standards, but compared to the log cabins and small homes of most of the populace, it was truly a mansion. Ada lived almost her entire life surrounded by opulence. After her marriage, she and her husband lived there. In the music room she taught piano lessons to youngsters so thrilled to see the inside of the grandiose house that they accepted Ada's stern demeanor and obediently practiced their boring scales.

In 1925 the Model T Ford arrived in Port Sanilac. The contraption called the Tin Lizzie was produced from 1908 to 1927 and is credited with "putting America on wheels." It has also been credited with taking Ada's life. There are several versions of the story, and one describes Ada crossing the street to collect rents from a tenant of the Loops. Another says she was leaving a party, dressed in an exquisite, flowing green gown. A third version dismissed the Model-T and claims Ada was killed by an out-of-control buggy. All variations end with her being struck by a careless traveler riding along after dark without the benefit of lights. All agree the driver felt a sickening thump and got out to investigate. What he found was the dying Ada; her lifeblood seeping into the dirt of what is now M-25. She was immediately rushed inside the Loop home, but nothing could save her.

Since becoming a museum, the Loop Harrison Mansion has seen its share of contractors doing repair work to the residence. These workers have described seeing Ada pacing back and forth in the upstairs bedroom she had slept in as a child. She appears to be contemplating the spot where she met her death. As she walks, her movements create a lingering chill in the air. It was enough to scare the jeepers out of the bravest man on the crew.

Sometimes Ada is seen haunting the grounds, and in recent years she has become fond of the Barn Theatre which now stands next to the mansion. Theatre-goers describe feeling her touch them. They turn to see no one nearby. Theatre workers have experienced the signs of her playfulness with a cup or a pen taken or moved. Ada apparently enjoys the performances at the Barn and only the most uncharitable would begrudge her a slight diversion from the drudgery of her otherwise unsettled life.

The most bizarre stories about Ada, however, are those involving current-day motorists who report seeing a wisp of a woman ahead of them on the road at the exact spot Ada was killed nearly a century ago. They experience a thud and immediately screech to a stop, certain they have just killed someone. The poor drivers rush to local homes to report the accident and secure help, but when they return to the site, there is no body. Ada has returned to her home.

The Ghost of Minnie Quay

This is a double ghost story. Both stories are founded in fact, not fiction. In the 1800s, Forester, Michigan was a place of promise. It boasted more than four hundred residents, a pier that brought shipping to the town, and the lovely Tanner House Hotel to provide rooms for visitors. Its citizenry was a hard-working, decent sort – albeit a bit meddlesome. Forester was expected to flourish and grow ever richer.

That did not happen. Today, Forester is a ghostly shadow of its former self. The lumber industry burned up in the Great Fires. The shipping industry was lost when the piers were washed away in the Storm of 1913. Today, Forester's population is a mere handful, and the most viable business is the saloon.

But, there is another ghost in Forester. Young Minnie Quay continues to walk the beaches as she has for more than a hundred years. She is the long-suffering ghost of this near ghost town.

In 1876, farming and mill work in the Thumb were hardscrabble means of existence. Fourteen-year-old Minnie Quay could hardly be blamed for seeking diversion from her otherwise dull but demanding life. To the naïve young girl, the sailors who docked at Forester seemed worldly and wise. They were cloaked in the aura of mystery and seemed to offer the promise of dreams about to be fulfilled.

Like the heroine of any good Greek tragedy, Minnie lost her heart to a particularly handsome young seaman. As he readied to depart the little village he kissed away her tears with the promise he would return for her. Rumor of Minnie's relationship, or perhaps in her eyes it could even rightly be called an engagement, was quickly repeated by local gossips to Minnie's parents, James and Mary Quay.

Minnie's parents were less enamored with the affair than their love-struck young daughter. She was still a child. Minnie's parents were certain that when she was a bit older she would find a more suitable partner – if not love – in a local, responsible, hard-working farm boy. Mr. Quay forbade his daughter to continue the liaison. Mrs. Quay was overheard ranting to her daughter that she would rather see her dead than married to a sailor.

When the sailor's ship was due back in port, the elder Quays, not trusting their headstrong daughter would obey their orders, locked her in the house and stood guard, refusing to permit her any opportunity to yield to temptation.

Minnie was heartsick as she considered ways to join her young man, but it was not meant to be, and from the failed tryst, things only got worse. Her lover's ship vanished in stormy Lake Huron waters. At least eight ships sank in Lake Huron storms that year. One such ship, *the Port Huron*, was lost near Lexington. Others went down near Port Austin and Harbor Beach. Regardless of which ship her love rode to his death, Minnie was left disconsolate.

Because of her parents' arbitrariness, Minnie had not even had the opportunity to say goodbye or to explain why she had not been at the dock to greet her love as she had promised she would be.

On April 26, twenty-eight days short of her fifteenth birthday, Minnie's parents needed to make a trip to Port Sanilac. They decided to leave the grieving Minnie home with her younger brother Charles. The other Quay children went along for the trip.

Minnie estimated the time of their return then tucked her little brother in for a nap, believing her parents would return soon.

Then, with her pain unendurable, Minnie tied her long blonde hair in red-velvet ribbons, donned her gauzy, white, go-to-church-on-Sunday dress, and walked deliberately to the pier. She waved at a few neighbors sitting on the front porch of the hotel. She gave them no cause to suspect what was about to happen.

She stood for only a few moments contemplating the choppy waves that she knew would take her to her love. April is a cold month to test the waters of Lake Huron, but it made no difference to Minnie. It was easy to slip into the whitecaps that promised to reunite her with her sailor.

Several people were close enough to witness Minnie's tragic suicide and there was a rush to the water with many hands grappling to reach her before she drowned. Unfortunately her body eluded those hands for an hour, plenty long enough to preclude retrieving young Minnie alive.

Maybe Minnie's sweetheart was married. Maybe he was merely toying with her naïve and youthful affections. Or maybe he never understood why she was not at the pier when he arrived to see her.

Whatever the reason may be, if Minnie thought their spirits would be reunited by the icy waters of her Great Lake, she was as disappointed in death as she had been in life. Now it is the solitary figure of Minnie Quay who haunts the beach

Minnie Quay lies buried with her parents and brother Charles

near Forester and cries to young maidens she chances to meet on her walks, urging them to forsake this world and join her in the hereafter. Or, as the last verse of a local ballad goes:

> *"But, Minnie Quay is not at rest,*
> *Or so the people say.*
> *Her ghost still walks the lonely shore,*
> *And you can see her to this day."*

The dock from which Minnie Quay plunged into the water was destroyed in the Storm of 1913; any remaining wooden vestiges have long since rotted. A few of the rock piling supports can still be seen today. At night, if you walk this stretch of beach, you may see Minnie's ghost bobbing back and forth between them.

The Ghost of the Hunter Savidge

The bones of the schooner *Hunter Savidge* lie in nearly two hundred feet of water northeast of Pointe Aux Barques, hurled there by convulsive winds that sprang from nowhere. It was late Sunday afternoon, August 20, 1899. It had been a sweltering, muggy day that made clothes stick to one's body and the smallest patch of shade seem a blessing. The *Hunter Savidge* had waited for hours, every sail set and prepared, as the crew hoped to catch just the slightest puff of a breeze to ease them along their journey.

The two-masted schooner *Hunter Savidge* had been built for the prosperous, lumbering Savidge family. The "Hunter" came from Mrs. Savidge's maiden name. Captaining the ship that unfortunate day was Fred Sharpstein. He had brought along his wife, Rosa, whom he affectionately called "Ma." One of their twin sixteen-year-old sons, John, had hired on for his first trip as a crewman. Also aboard was Mary Muellerwies, wife of the ship's current owner, and the couple's six-year-old daughter, Etta. Mary and Rosa had joined the voyage for a pleasant summer outing on the beautiful lake. The schooner had delivered a load of coal to a buyer in Sarnia, Ontario and was now sailing empty back to Alpena. The ship's first mate that day was Tom Duby.

Without warning the air that had been so stagnant and calm turned ferocious and caught the crew and passengers unprepared for the wind's ravaging blows.

Captain Sharpstein, fearing the worst as the storm bore down on them, sent the women and young Etta below to the cabin where he hoped they would be safe. The last thing he needed was for one of them to blow overboard during the squall. The storm hit with such might that it tipped the vessel on its beam ends. The women were trapped in the cabin. Visibility was limited in the roiling sea, thoughts were confused, and time was short – all factors that worked against Rosa, Mary and Etta extricating themselves from their eventual tomb.

As the ship capsized, the men on deck were all thrown into the water where at least they had a fighting chance of survival. Most were able to swim to the surface and grab the sides of the now overturned wreck. Tom Duby, however, drowned. John Sharpstein managed to break the surface and called to his father. Fred swam towards his panic-stricken son who was floundering; John's heavy boots and clothing pulling him under. The stricken father watched helplessly as his child was swallowed by angry waves a mere few feet in front of him.

It was only minutes before the steamer *Alex McVittie* reached the site of the wreck and picked up survivors. Captain Sharpstein asked the captain of the *McVittie* to take the *Hunter Savidge* in tow, but the captain of the *McVittie* was hurrying north and denied the request. To avoid losing any more time he put the crew of the *Hunter Savidge* aboard the southbound *N. E. Runnels* which took them to Sand Beach (now Harbor Beach). He was not inclined to squander precious time searching for people he believed were already dead.

Captain Sharpstein was horrified. He had seen the aft section of the boat still afloat just before rescue by the *McVittie* and he believed that trapped air might afford the missing women and child a chance of survival for at least a short time after submersion. In fact, Fred was convinced Ma was still alive. He had seen similar situations before and knew of sailors who had lived to tell him about it.

At Sand Beach Captain Sharpstein hired a tug, the *Frank W* to take him back to the spot where the *Hunter Savidge* had gone down, but no trace of the wreckage or missing women could be found. A subsequent search by the life saving station crews failed to find any sign of the vessel either, despite reports from other ships claiming to have seen the schooner floating up to four days later.

For months Captain Sharpstein was said to walk the shoreline, searching vainly for his wife and muttering, "Ma's out there somewhere," to anyone who would listen. Sigmund Freud published his famous landmark book *The Interpretation of Dreams* two months after the wreck of the *Hunter Savidge*, but it took no expert to figure out the cause of the nightmares Mr. Sharpstein endured each evening. Unable to gain closure and bury his beloved wife, it is easy to empathize with his nearly inconsolable grief.

For years afterward sightings were reported by sailors who insisted they witnessed the ghostly stern of the vessel still suspended by the air trapped in the cabins and hull. Sometimes when the fog settles in they see the *Hunter Savidge* floating aimlessly with the winds. And, they believe "Ma" Rosa Sharpstein is still out there… somewhere waiting to be found.

Well-known Great Lakes diver and wreck finder, David Trotter began searching for the remains of the *Hunter Savidge* in 1980 and finally found her in 1988 – almost a century after she sank. Trotter dove the site for nearly a month before finding the nameplate that definitively identified her. Subsequent divers have tried to find the bones of the missing women and child, but with no success.

One diver found a white porcelain cup buried in the sand of the wreck site and when he gently picked it up, he noted the delicate handle had not even been broken. A few feet away lay the matching porcelain teapot, another civilized reminder of more genteel moments during the trip. It was a capricious storm that could kill innocent travelers but leave bone china without a chip.

The Heroic Spirit of Pointe Aux Barques

Old lighthouses seem perfectly suited for the spirits of the restless dead. Many lighthouses reportedly have ghosts. The stories usually revolve around a ship that crashes because of some misfeasance or malfeasance on the part of the lighthouse keeper. It is usually the stairs to the tower where the spirits seem to be felt, as though a ghost tries to recreate the scene of the keeper's failure and maybe urge him to move more quickly to send out the signals that will somehow reverse the tragedy and save the dead man's life. The following story is a twist on the lighthouse ghost theme:

On April 10, 1916, at age fifty-four, Captain Henry Cleary died of pneumonia. He had been a crew member of the old Pointe Aux Barques lifesaving station. There are at least two stories suggesting that Mr. Cleary, who had played the role of hero in many rescue operations during his lifetime, was not willing to abandon his good works after death.

The First Story:

In 1966 the *Daniel J. Morrell* went down near Port Austin and all but one member of the crew perished. The sole survivor, Dennis Hale, allegedly told the story of an apparition that appeared to him as he lay near freezing in his life raft. The ghost had long hair and loomed rather unkempt before him.

Hale's own beard was heavy and white with ice. Twice he started to eat the ice from his beard, and twice the figure appeared and warned him that if he did so, he would die of pneumonia. Hale heeded the advice and was later rescued.

The Second Story

The second story involves a sixteen-year-old girl. It is she who, in her later years, came to believe that the ghost both she and Hale witnessed was that of Captain Cleary.

The young woman was home alone for a weekend while her parents were in Sault Ste. Marie. They mistakenly believed she had invited three friends to stay with her. The keeper's cottage for the Pointe Aux Barques Lighthouse was less than two hundred feet from the young woman's family home.

During the middle of the night she was startled awake to find a milky, translucent image standing at the foot of her bed. She tried to scream, but no words came out. She observed the intruder's dark, neat, almost military-style of clothing. She noted his handlebar mustache. But, it was his piercing eyes that transfixed her. As he stood there she heard a man's deep voice, whether from him or inside her head, telling her she needed to get up and quickly go downstairs and lock the door. With that the solitary specter vanished.

With his departure her body was released from whatever immobilizing force had paralyzed her. She scurried downstairs where she found the front door unlocked. She turned the bolt and then lay down on the couch and tried to get back to sleep. She was too frightened to consider, even for a moment, going back upstairs to her bedroom. About 3:00 am she heard someone trying to turn the handle of the front door. There was a thudding against it. The sound was definitely not a knock intended to awaken anyone, but more like a hard push with someone's strong shoulder.

Scared out of her wits though she was, she managed to force her trembling legs to carry her to a side window which offered a view of the enclosed front porch on the other side of the door. There stood a stranger she had never seen before. She later described him as looking like Charles Manson. This one was no ghost. She screamed at him to "get out of here!" He returned her look and after a few long moments of obvious deliberation, he turned and walked out the porch door.

The young girl never saw him or the ghost again. Upon hearing the story of Dennis Hale and coupling it with some research of the lighthouse and the lifesaving crew she believed she could identify their ghost as that of Captain Cleary.

The Ghost of the Frank Murphy House

In Harbor Beach the Frank Murphy House is a local tourist attraction by day. Frank Murphy, the well-known and popular politician who was raised in that small city, merits lots of attention. The family house, as well as Murphy 's law office, are open to the public and contain significant family artifacts.

By night there may be something else going on. The museum is operated by volunteers, and one of them believes that Murphy's younger sister haunts the place. The volunteer telling the story has received phone calls from local Harbor Beach residents telling her that lights are on in the house at night – long after the museum has closed.

These calls always result in a rush to the house to extinguish the source of such illumination. Yet upon arrival, the house is found to be completely dark and a quick check of all of the switches and lamps reveals nothing amiss. There are also times when caretakers arrive to find the outside doors to the master bedroom suite open, in spite of the fact that they had been deliberately and tightly bolted. Snow covers the floor and the air holds a feeling of unrest.

Maybe the existence and extent of this haunting will become clearer in the future.

The Days the Thumb Burned

You don't have to put out the fire
when all is burned out.
Unknown

The Great Fires of 1871 and 1881

In the late 1800s the Thumb was ravaged and forever changed by two cataclysmic fires a decade apart. When these infernos finished their savagery, everything in their paths lay in ruins. Counting the dead and calculating the loss was left to the survivors. The rich lumber industry had died and turned to ash, and Michigan's Thumb would never be the same.

In the early days of its recorded history, Michigan was one giant forest. Timber was the Thumb's most valuable resource. It seduced lumber barons, timber prospectors or timber lookers intent on seeking their fortunes. Many that fell under its spell were not disappointed. Indeed, their success rates were markedly better than those of gold prospectors who stampeded San Francisco at about the same time. More money was made on Michigan timber than from all of the gold mined in Alaska during the Yukon Gold Rush.

Dozens of saw mills dotted the landscape along the rivers and tributaries of Sanilac, Huron, and Tuscola counties. Small towns devoted to lumbering sprouted on the shores of the Great Lake herself. As you have undoubtedly seen from reading the histories of the small towns included in this book, lumbering was the lifeblood of their early economies, and the mill was the heart pumping that blood.

Although it was a time when the white pine was king, numerous farms had been cleared and cultivated. When the final flames of the two great fires were extinguished, most of the farms had been razed.

The Fire of 1871

Everyone has read a historical account of the Chicago Fire of 1871, but most are unaware of the tragedy that befell Michigan's Thumb beginning that same day. Both fires started on October 8, 1871. That day and the next will always be known in the Thumb as the "Days Michigan Burned."

August and September that year had been unseasonably dry. Not a drop of rain had fallen in two months. The precipitation that normally marked summer's end was conspicuously absent. The severe drought was superimposed on Michigan's irresponsible and greed-inspired lumbering practices. The conflagration that roared into the Thumb demanded payback for man's imprudence. The fire began on the west side of the state, and by October 9 it was out of control on the eastern shores.

Before it became the massive wall of fire that rolled across the entire width of Michigan, the fire had modest beginnings. Many small brush fires were burning. Gradually they multiplied and ran together, their proliferation fed by the dry air from over the land rather than the moist air from Lake Huron. The wind changed direction often and each time carried chips of burning wood and sparks from these smaller fires to start new blazes. Eventually it became one huge sheet of flames.

It was called a "tree top" fire because it was fueled by massive piles of tree tops left behind as lumbering operations took the valuable trunks and left the useless tops to litter the forest floors. The small limbs and pine slash had been collecting and drying for years. It became tinder to fuel the relentless fire. The accumulated needles and twigs held heavy amounts of resin, and when combined with the leaves, tree tops, and other dried organic matter, this mixture burned with intense heat.

Fed by this fuel, these fires burned hottest at ground level and destroyed everything in their path. At some spots that path seemed arbitrary, as the flames jumped a house here or a barn there and picked up again on the other side. Just as often as not, when the wind changed, the flames returned and consumed what they missed the first time.

The fire reached the Thumb about midnight on October 8 and by the next day was in full reddened splendor. Farmers, who had been awakened to screams of "fire," struggled to hold back the onslaught. Some gave up and scrambled out of harm's way, looking back to see their homes, livestock, and meager possessions going up in smoke. Still others succumbed to the smoke and flames and left only their charred remains to attest to their deaths.

The holocaust sent people from Forester and other lakeside villages into the water. Those fortunate enough to salvage a boat embarked on the lake and covered themselves with wet clothing and quilts. Their only hope, their only salvation, was that their lake would stop the devil-driven hell.

Some desperate farmers tried to outrun the firestorm. One family climbed into their wagon and covered themselves with wet blankets and headed for a stream a half mile away. They arrived seconds before the wagon began to burn. They dove into the shallow water, again covering themselves with wet blankets to squelch the burning embers that rained down on them. There was nothing more to do but wait for the inferno to recede and pray they would be alive when it did.

It took Forester a mere half hour to burn to the ground. Some people stood at the lake's edge contemplating their choice of death – drowning or burning.

At Sand Beach, currently the city of Harbor Beach, William Mann was awakened by a neighbor with news that fire was coming. Mann and his wife began making desperate attempts to bury some of their most critical tools, hoping to save them for the daunting task of rebuilding that they knew they would face if they escaped this furnace alive.

Mann's farm reached all the way to Lake Huron. When it became clear their lives were in danger, he sent his children to the shore, instructing them to wade in the water and remain there until it was safe to come out. Mrs. Mann remained to help her husband battle the blaze. The oldest Mann child was Rachel, aged seven. She carried the baby on one hip and the others tagged along as their father had ordered.

The children were not the first to arrive at the lakeshore. Several other neighbors were already standing in the waves, soaking their clothes and hoping to escape death since the flames could not follow them into the water. However, the waves were also ferocious that night, riled by the same gale force winds that spread the fire. Some women and children were unable to stand in the face of the water's rush and were thrown repeatedly back against the beach.

Mr. Jim Huxtable arrived at the shore dragging a large open boat. With his family safely aboard, he prepared to shove off and head for open water where they might all breathe a little easier. The smoke was becoming almost as dangerous as the fire. Seeing the terror in the eyes of the young Mann children, he took pity on them and loaded them aboard.

The little group rowed out only a short distance before everything on land disappeared behind the dense smokescreen. During the night, the wind picked up and Mr. Huxtable tried to row closer to shore so that the waves would not capsize his crowded little vessel, but the shore was not where it was supposed to be. Huxtable shouted out to anyone who might be on the beach, but got no reply.

When the sun finally came up on a new day, Huxtable found himself far out into the lake and could see no land in any direction. One child had died during the night. The ship and its twelve survivors carried no food and everyone was drenched and cold. For three days they continued to drift.

On the morning of October 12· Mr. Huxtable thought he could see land in the distance. He managed to row to the Canadian shore, and there, in a town called Goderich, they buried the dead child.

It was feared that Mr. and Mrs. Mann were dead, but a local newspaper carrying the pathetic story reached the Mann parents who, it turned out, had miraculously survived. The Manns and their children were joyously and tearfully reunited in Port Huron in one of the few happy outcomes of the tragedy.

Thousands of acres of valuable lumber were gone by the time the fire burned out. It is estimated that the dwellings, barns, household goods, winter provisions, grain, and livestock of between four and five thousand people were destroyed.

The Fire of 1881

The horror the Thumb residents believed was behind them returned almost exactly a decade later with even greater magnitude and intensity. The conditions were very similar. The area was rain-deprived and parched. There had been no measurable rainfall in two months.

This time the Thumb was more densely populated. In retrospect, it seems as though the first hideous fire was merely a prelude. The aftermath of the first blaze turned the attention of farmers to the land being sold by struggling lumber companies at bargain-basement prices. In spite of the drought conditions, many of these farmers spent time clearing their land of trees and stumps and the new growth that had sprouted after the earlier fire. They were aided in their task by shovels, picks, handsaws, and matches. Of those tools, matches were the most effective. Brush fires were built to clear the timber, and in a situation clearly reminiscent of the 1871 fire, these smaller fires got out of hand. Dry kindling and gale winds again made a lethal combination.

In many places the Fire of 1871 had merely deadened the green timber, allowing it to dry out and become tinder for this second, even more hellish fire. There is an old proverb that says wood already touched by fire is not hard to set alight. Nowhere did that have more literal translation than in the Thumb of Michigan in 1881.

On September 5, a month and four days short of the ten-year anniversary of the 1871 fire, this second conflagration took only four hours to travel across the entire width of the Thumb, leaving 150 people dead in Sanilac County alone.

More than 14,000 people living in the Thumb were left destitute; 1,521 homes were destroyed; 1,480 barns were reduced to rubble; 51 schools were nothing more than ashes. When the remaining county death tallies were added to Sanilac's, the final figure rose to over three hundred. Many more died later from smoke inhalation or complications from their burns. The number of seriously injured or blinded was staggering.

The flames of the inferno advanced with such speed that they overtook galloping horses. The fire was so scorching hot that it burned buildings and trees completely to the ground, so that the only trace they ever existed was a powdery ash residue covering the scarred earth. Horrified onlookers described the blaze as soaring a hundred feet high.

Some hapless victims of the Thumb had warning before the flames showered down on them; blinding smoke filled the air long before the flames were visible. Lamps were lit mid-day due to the smoky darkness.

Stories abound of the victims' desperate survival measures. Families crowded into wells and remained huddled there for several hours before summoning the courage to crawl out; some never survived long enough to crawl out.

One such tragedy befell the Freiburger family living in Austin Township. Desperate to escape the raging fire, they jumped into their shallow well, where searchers later found their suffocated bodies. A local cemetery marks their deaths with eight headstones.

In Wheatland Township, six bodies were found on a burned-out farm. Neil and Mary Erhart and their newborn baby daughter were among them; the infant's future extinguished before the flames could be put out.

Parisville, barely a dot on the map, contributed twenty-eight victims to the final death toll. Yet just east of this small village the Lemanski family surprised the blaze by doing the only thing that seemed to make sense in such a catastrophe. They dropped to their knees and asked God to spare them. They later described a miracle; the flames parted and went around them. Out of gratitude the family erected a cross at the site.

In Bad Axe the winds began at noon. By 1:00 pm the city was enveloped in darkness. Residents then heard a strange roar. It was the sound of the approaching flames that would soon storm down from heaven. As the fire swept into town, people were lifted into the air and set back down again by winds created from the intense heat. Four-hundred people huddled in the new brick courthouse and watched as the buildings around them were turned to rubble. A group of about thirty men inside the courthouse sanctuary made frantic trips to the pump for water to keep the walls and floors of the building wet. When the first group was overcome by smoke and exhaustion, a second shift of men took over. They watched in horror as the darkened hardware store across the street suddenly burst into a bright red glare as kerosene and gunpowder ignited. The fire moved so quickly that it traveled from Bad Axe to the Lakeshore in less than two hours.

Amidst the holocaust, postman Ira Humphrey took the words "the mail must go through" to a new and fatal level. Despite the inferno blazing in the Thumb, he continued to make his daily rounds – even after being warned by several people that the area was too dangerous. His reply was that he was delivering the mail and he had to go on. He finally came to a spot where the onlookers were adamant that he stop. He unharnessed his horse and proceeded a short way to get a better look. He reported to the group that he thought he could make it, and with that, he began walking in the direction of danger. His clothes caught fire. He removed his vest and jacket and rolled in a field trying to extinguish the flames. Another wave of fire surged towards him. When rescuers recovered his body, the crystal of his watch was melted. His horse found its way to a local farm where the owner was fighting his own heroic battle against the fire. He could not personally deliver the sad information about Mr. Humphrey's unfortunate demise to the waiting Humphrey family. He wrote a note, attached it to the horse's neck, gave the horse a swat on the rump, and sent it home carrying the grave news.

One local farmer recalled that a neighbor's team of oxen came through the fire alive but lost their hooves. Another neighbor turned six hogs loose and the only trace he later found of them was six large grease spots several yards from where he had set them free.

Perhaps the most ill-advised actions of the disaster were those of a man, who believing his death was imminent, slit the throats of all of his livestock to spare them suffering. He then took his shotgun and placed the barrel in his mouth ending his own life. The fire passed all around his place and left his buildings untouched.

Surely the most poignant image to come out of the of the fire was that of a young mother, her charred remains found in a crouching position on the ground, with her five children kneeling and encircling her. One hand of each child rested in her lap.

After the fire subsided, William Bailey, a sergeant in the U.S. Army Signal Corps, was sent to the area to take an accounting of the situation. He talked to the survivors and shortly after the fire wrote this description:

> *The flames came rushing on, sometimes in huge, revolving columns, then in detached fragments that were torn by the winds from the mass, and sent flying over the tops of trees for a quarter of a mile to be pushed down to the earth again. Flames were seen to leap many feet higher than tall pines, and everywhere over the burning country sheets of flame were flying in every direction. The flying sand and smoke blinded people who walked, in the gathering darkness, into fire-traps. Those who escaped were blind for weeks. Half naked creatures made their way into village streets, often bearing the charred remains of the dead with them. Many found refuge from the fires in the lake, and even there they were suffocated by the smoke blown from the shores. The cinders, falling in the water, made a lye, so that it was necessary to go down several feet under the surface for drinking water.*

Bailey also noted that sailors felt the uncomfortable heat seven miles out on chilly Lake Huron. The heat withered leaves on trees two miles from its path and cooked vegetable patches of corn, potatoes, and onions turning them to stew, in fields otherwise untouched.

Even for those fortunate enough to have walked, limped or crawled out of the ravaged area, life was a shambles. They were homeless. The forests, which in the past had always offered lumber to build, or rebuild, their homes was gone. The crops which they had recently harvested were destroyed. The water was unsafe to drink. They had no source of food, and winter was fast approaching. Many needed medical help which was not available. Even the air was polluted with the stench of dead animals rotting and awaiting disposal.

It took a while for the enormity of the disaster to reach the outside world. All telegraph lines were down and the railroad tracks so littered with debris that no trains could pass. When the staggering circumstances became known, headlines across the country told story after horrible story:

"Tremendous fires in Sanilac and Huron Counties," "Richmondville Destroyed," "Deckerville Reported Burned," "Many People Horribly Burned," "Wholesale Devastation," "Entire Townships Become Roaring Furnaces," "Counties Left in Ashes", and *"Survivors Fled to the Lake to Escape Inferno".*

There was no other news worthy of telling during the next few weeks.

The damage estimates rose above two million, and that was at the value of the 1881 dollar. Two-thousand square miles, more than a million acres of forest, were reduced to cinders in an afternoon. Entire villages had vanished. The hours of 11:00 am to 4:00 pm on Monday, September 5 saw the brunt of the damage, but the fires refused to die until rain finally came on September 7. Those rains helped save the village of Lexington which had been fighting vigorously to hold back the blaze.

Relief committees were set up to deal with the devastation. The American Red Cross was just getting organized in New York. Clara Barton sent her agent, Julian Hubbell, to Port Huron to investigate what could be done. In response to his report, Ms. Barton began coordinating aid efforts by the fledgling organization. She raised money and sent food, bedding, medical aid, lumber, farm equipment, and other supplies to the victims. Her effort was small in comparison to that of local agencies, but the long-term importance to Barton's organization was great. The need for an organization ready to step in and be available to raise money and supplies in time of disaster was apparent. The American Red Cross, now respected and relied upon worldwide, first offered its assistance to the victims of the Thumb Fire of 1881.

Thumb lumbering had barely survived the fire of 1871. In many areas that earlier fire had burned only the tree tops, killing the underlying trees, without reducing them to ashes and soot. Lumber mills managed to stay in business by harvesting the trees that had survived and by cutting up those that died but had not yet rotted. The second, more deadly fire of 1881 sealed the fate of mills and lumbering in the Thumb. The King was dead.

The Big Blow / The Storm of 1913

They might have split up
or they might have capsized,
They may have broke deep
and took water.
And all that remains
is the faces and the names,
of the wives and the sons
and the daughters.
-Gordon Lightfoot

The Chippewa have a legend that explains November's fury. They attribute the whims of the winds to two spirits: Gitchee Manito and Matchie Manito.

Gitchee Manito is a good wind spirit that favors Ningabianinodin, the pleasant and steady West Wind. Gitchee Manito also loves the gentle South Wind, Jawaninodin that brings the pleasant summer breezes.

Matchie Manito, on the other hand, is an evil wind spirit that favors Kiwedininodin, the terrible North Wind and Wabaninodin, the evil East Wind that breeds so many of the lake's tempests.

When the winds become schizophrenic and seem unable to find their direction, the Chippewa believe it is the two spirits competing to test their wind-summoning strengths. During the maelstrom of 1913, Lake Huron was their playing field. At some point, as in many sporting competitions, the game got out of hand.

During that November weather aberration a dozen or so long ships became Gitchee Manito and Matchie Manito's playing pieces.

Settlers in the Thumb area, oblivious to the legends of Gitchee Manito and Matchie Manito, spent November 9 in their own houses of worship. When they entered their churches, the weather was an unseasonably warm 80 degrees. Mother Nature could not decide if she was headed to December or retreating to August. Perhaps some worshipers were considering a late season picnic after the service. The heat, so uncharacteristic of November, just begged a last day at the beach. First they had to give thanks and ask God's continued blessings.

As they sat in their pews singing "How Great Thou Art," the music was drowned by sounds like that of ricocheting buckshot. It turned out to be pellets of ice, snow and sleet peppering their handsome stained-glass windows; the temperature had dropped at least 50 degrees as their pastors took up collection.

On the lake, two days earlier, one seasoned captain had predicted a white hurricane, but crews of other ships were ignorant of his warning. Captain

George Holdridge captained the steamer *Robert W. Bunsen*. On November 7 he was downbound on Lake Huron. His crewmen believed the unseasonably hot weather and placid waters were the lake's signal that she was cooperating with their efforts to get their last haul of the season behind them.

Captain Holdridge saw it differently. He had been a sailor all of his life. He had sailed the salt waters of the China Sea, where he developed the internal barometer that told him with no uncertainty what was coming. On this November morning, as his ship briskly traversed the glassy Huron waters, Holdridge grew concerned about what his internal weather equipment was predicting.

The sky was copper-colored and although the sun's rays were visible, he could not distinguish the familiar round orb. The world was cloaked in surrealistic garb. When the *Bunsen* was just off Harbor Beach, Holdridge announced to a crewmate, "Boy, you're going to see a storm such as you never saw before!" The Captain then called down to the engine room and told his chief to give it all he could; they needed to get out of there. He knew the storm was coming; he just was not sure when she would strike.

About the same time as church was letting out, the *James C. Carruthers*, the *Wexford* and the *Hydrus* were entering Lake Huron headed downward. They ignored the warning flags and lights that had been hoisted in accord with maritime procedure. These ships had endured rough seas on Superior and were hoping Huron would afford them better conditions.

At the far end of the lake where the St. Clair River gives way to the big lake's open water, the *Charles Price*, the *John A. McGean,* and the *Isaac Scott* charted a northern course at daybreak. Warnings in both Sarnia and Port Huron signaled the folly of their actions. With heavy gale warnings flying in a hundred ports as early as the preceding Friday morning, it may seem foolhardy that ship captains blithely ignored the threat, but they were used to November storms, and they needed to make every minute count before the close of navigation for the season. Big chances were taken. For many it was the last run of the year and they were anxious to be on their way.

The storm started out no more threatening than many wild November squalls originating on Lake Superior. By the time it reached Huron two days later it had mutated into a witch's brew beyond anything seen before or since. It was birthed by an unusual and horrific confluence of factors.

A massive low pressure system had spawned in the Aleutians and moved steadily over the Canadian provinces on a path headed for Superior. A second low pressure system, born in the Rocky Mountains, was beating a northeasterly path from lower Minnesota to join the first. The marriage of these two colossal fronts brought savage and sustained winds and rough seas. The fickle gusts would start from the east; turn in minutes to the south, or north or even west, as though they could not make up their minds from which direction they wanted to pummel the sea.

All of this was bad, yet predictable. What came next was beyond bad, and entirely unprecedented. A third low pressure system originating in the Gulf of Mexico swept northward from Georgia in an abnormal path. This diabolical third front covered the east coast with record-breaking snowfalls and battered it with hurricane-strength winds.

Straight out from the docks of lower Lake Huron, the three fronts converged, creating a cataclysm like no other. The lake convulsed and churned under the assault. The snow raged down and sideways in eighty and ninety-mile-per-hour gusts that lasted for at least twenty-four hours.

Lake Huron lies in a geographic area where cyclonic storms can and do come up quickly – often without warning. The lake also has its own peculiar and distinctive danger spots. One of the foremost is the Six Fathom Bank that lies almost due east of the Black River and Port Huron. It is in the center of the lake and not too far from what would normally be considered by ship captains to be a fair "up lake" or "down lake" course. Yet even the earliest explorers, like Father Hennepin, received warnings from local Native American tribes to avoid that area and stay close to the coast, because the sands made navigation dangerous when they were disturbed by any high wind.

During the storm of 1913, ship captains were operating blind. The storm reduced visibility in most parts of the lake to a mere few feet. Captains gave up trying to stay on course and fought courageously to simply stay afloat and avoid collisions.

In one instance their efforts may have been sabotaged by a lighthouse keeper's unwillingness to authorize a payment of $25. It is one of the unnecessary horrors that always come out of such natural disasters. During foul weather, ship captains depended on the lightship stationed offshore at the mouth of the St. Clair River to guide them safely from Lake Huron into that narrow river channel. By midday on Sunday, November 9, seventy-five-mile-per-hour winds had dragged the lightship and her anchors two miles east and two miles south, leaving her up against the Canadian shore. By some cruel, quirk of fate, her light and fog signal continued to operate, guiding unsuspecting ships into the waiting trap of the Corsica Shoal. This tragic circumstance claimed the *Northern Queen* and the *Matthew Andrews*.

Captain Joseph Lampoh had successfully brought the *Andrews*, loaded with iron ore, down the length of Lake Huron through the early hours of the vicious storm. Relying on the signals from the lightship, he then steered her aground at Kettle Pointe, Ontario.

The operator of the lightship had been offered the services of a Canadian tug to tow her back to her assigned station. The keeper balked because he was not authorized to make the $25 expenditure.

In fairness, both the *Northern Queen* and the *Matthew Andrews* were forced ashore by misdirection but although these vessels sustained heavy damage, the

crews lived to tell the tale of the Storm of 1913. The crews of ten others (two in
Lake Michigan) did not. What we know of their ordeal is speculation supplanted
by the accounts of vessels, like the *Hanna*, that passed them as she headed to
shore and relative safety.

We love tales of adventure, and there will always be a romanticism connected
with sailing the seas and braving its dangers. But on Sunday, November 9 and
Monday, November 10, 1913, it can be said with absolute certainty that no
captain or crewman considered himself (or herself, since a couple of women
went down too) caught in a tide of romantic circumstances. Theirs was a raw and
ugly struggle for survival and, unlike sentimental formulaic plots, there would
be no triumphant happy ending.

Romance was starkly absent as these terrorized men clutched slippery
railings with numbed fingers and fought desperately to keep from going over.
Giant sheets of ice, intent upon capsizing their colossal freighters, repeatedly
swamped them. Romance must have been miles from their minds as they sought
last minute reprieves from a God who seemed to have momentarily lost track
of them but with whom they were intent on making final peace. Their every
gesture and attempt at saving themselves were nothing but meaningless and
futile efforts.

They were going down. On shore some of their distress calls were heard but
there was no possibility of sending assistance. Aboard, they got out the life rafts
and vests, both useless and trivial protection against a sea that sent waves thirty-
five-feet high exploding over them, waves capable of taking a flat bottomed ship,
over five hundred feet in length or nearly twice the length of a football field and
weighing several hundred tons, and flipping her turtle-style to the bottom.

The best they could hope for was an easy death. Perhaps for a few lucky
victims death was instantaneous, a blow to the head by flying debris. For others it
may have been blessedly brief as they gasped for two or three minutes to suck in
fresh air but got only angry water to fill their straining lungs. For the remainder
it meant freezing to death in a horror beyond description. Floating around them,
the last earthly sights they would witness, was carnage from their ships and the
bodies of their mates.

The morning it all ended a farmer saw what appeared to be several men,
covered with ice, walking out of the water. Upon closer inspection they turned
out to be frozen corpses bobbing upright in the waves, held in that position by
their useless life jackets.

Altogether eight long-ships vanished in Lake Huron that wretched night.
So spiteful was the storm that two of Huron's ships have not been located to
this day. The last to be found was the *Wexford,* which remained in an unknown
grave site until 2000. The final resting places of the *James C. Carruthers* and the
Hydrus are still a mystery.

When the white hurricane ended, it fell to the living to pick up her pieces.

The final death count from the Big Blow is estimated at 248. One hundred and seventy-eight of those perished in the original Sweet Water Sea, Lake Huron. These numbers are considered fairly accurate, but back then ship rosters were not kept in a precise manner. Many crewmen were not listed by their full or legal name. Local cemeteries where they are buried honor them only as "Skip" or "Red." Some may never be acknowledged at all.

The number of victims would have been much greater if the ships had carried passengers. These were cargo ships and the crew of the largest numbered twenty-eight. Two sets of twin ships perished: the *Charles S. Price* and her sister ship the *Isaac M. Scott*, and the *Argus* and her sister ship the *Hydrus*.

The eight ships that perished in Lake Huron during the storm of 1913:

Vessel	Lives Lost	Length in feet	Capacity in tons	Value in 1913
Charles S. Price	28	524	9,000	$340,000
Isaac M. Scott	28	524	9,000	$340,000
James C. Carruthers	19	550	9,500	$410,000
Wexford	17	270	2,800	$125,000
Regina	15	269	3,000	$125,000
John A. McGean	23	452	7,500	$240,000
Argus	24	436	7,000	$130,000
Hydrus	24	436	7,000	$130,000

The *H. M. Hanna Jr.* and the *Matoa* were also deemed total constructive losses, but because they had made it to shore there was no loss of life.

The following is the best account available of what happened to each of the great ships that vanished:

The Charles S. Price

The *Charles S. Price* was seen by Captain A. C. May of the *H. B. Hawgood* on Sunday afternoon, November 9. Captain May had steered his ship some distance up Lake Huron before he realized the enormity of the weather conditions. He then hauled around and started back for the relative safety of the St. Clair River. Near Harbor Beach he saw the *Price*. She was headed north and into the worst of the storm.

It is clear that at some point the *Price* also turned around, because her remains were found close to the entry to the St. Clair River at Port Huron. Observers felt that if she had managed to get an additional fifteen miles behind her, she might have been a survivor. As it turned out, she was one of the great ships to "turn-turtle."

On Monday morning, November 10, Captain Plough of the Lakeview Lifesaving Station above Port Huron searched the tossing water with his telescope and suddenly spied what appeared to be the hull of a vessel. There were no masts or smoke stack. Plough called Captain Tom Reid of the Reid Wrecking Company in Sarnia who, in turn, sent a big tug to investigate. Reid confirmed that a huge, flat bottomed freighter was turned completely upside-down. The bow was about thirty feet out of the water but the stern was submerged. It was not possible to tell the length of the ship nor could its identity be established, as the hull looked exactly like the hull of many other ships.

For six days she remained a mystery ship amid speculation that it was the *Regina*, the *James C. Carruthers*, or the *Wexford*. Finally, William Baker, a diver from Detroit, plunged into the icy waters, worked his way around the hull clutching the railings above him, and found the nameplate. He checked it twice to be sure. There was no indication of a collision and there was no other vessel trapped under its bow. It turned out that the wrecked boat's peculiar position was caused by trapped air that was escaping in a tiny, slow stream of bubbles. All doubt was gone. It was the *Charles S. Price*.

The *Price* finally sank from sight on November 17, eight days after she had been flipped completely by the monstrous sea.

For one woman awaiting the news identifying the mystery ship it was the end of uncertainty but also the end of hope. She was the wife of second mate, Howard Mackley, and she finally knew her husband's fate. When the ship had passed Detroit early on Sunday morning her husband had posted a letter to her, and when the *Price* was abreast of their home in St. Clair, he pulled the whistle in customary salute. Mrs. Mackley was there waiting to wave a response greeting. She watched his ship travel upriver until it was out of sight, unaware it was the last time they would perform their loving ritual.

For assistant engineer Milton Smith, who had looked at the weather forecast in Cleveland and decided to sit this one out, there was the relief of simply being alive. He had felt uneasy about the trip for days and had tried to talk his friend and neighbor, wheelsman Arz McIntosh, into leaving with him, but McIntosh insisted he needed the money.

Of all of the ships that went down that terrible night, it was the *Price* that caused the most concern. No one believed a bulk freighter, with its wide flat-bottom could possibly be flipped over and sunk like a toy boat in a bathtub.

The Isaac Scott

The Isaac Scott was also spotted by Captain A. C. May, as he headed for safety at the foot of the lake. Captain May encountered the *Isaac Scott* about five or six miles north of the Port Huron Lighthouse at approximately 3:30 pm Sunday afternoon. May later described his feeling that the *Scott's* captain had been a fool to leave the St. Clair River, the very destination for which May was headed. It seemed inconceivable that the *Scott's* captain would make for the open waters of the storm-churned lake.

The *Scott* foundered farther up Lake Huron, near Pointe Aux Barques. Relatively little sign of her was immediately found, other than one empty lifeboat with its canvas covering still intact. The lack of drifting bodies and artifacts suggested she capsized quickly, without providing the crew enough warning to make even pitiful attempts at avoiding certain death.

The James C. Carruthers

The James C. Carruthers was a Canadian ship making only her third voyage. Because the captain's name was William H. Wright and the manager of Marine Affairs for the company owning her was also named Wright, the boat was nicknamed the "All-Wright boat." For three days after the storm, panicked family members and the ship's owner waited for the final word that the *Carruthers* was lost. Evidence began slowly drifting in: a lifejacket, an oar, a piece of debris believed to have been part of her cabin. When the bodies began appearing, lingering hopes were quashed. The ship's owner predicted they would never find Captain Wright, who under any and all circumstances would go down with his ship. More astonishing, perhaps, is the fact that the *Carruthers,* herself, has never been found.

One amazing story of survival did come out of the sinking of the *Carruthers*. Days after the storm, Thomas Thompson was summoned to Goderich by his daughter, Mrs. Edward Ward of Sarnia. She told her father that she had just identified the body of her brother, John Thompson. The elder Mr. Thompson arrived, and like his daughter, identified his son's body. The waters may have been a bit unkind but there was no mistaking the J. T. tattoo, the scars on his nose and leg, and the two deformed toes. It was definitely his son. Father and daughter set about making funeral arrangements.

Meanwhile, in Toronto, John Thompson was surprised to read about his death in the newspaper. Without calling, he hopped a train for Sarnia and arrived in time to crash his own funeral! He "survived" only because he had not been aboard the ill-fated *Carruthers*.

The Wexford

The Wexford spewed bodies and cargo on the Canadian shores. Even after the snows melted, the beaches were white with her 96,000 bushels of spilled grain. Still, the *Wexford* herself remained invisible for eighty-seven years until she was finally discovered in 2000 near Grand Bend, Ontario.

Out of every natural disaster, there always seems to be one story of someone lucky enough to have missed a train, a plane, or in this case, the ship that goes down. During this storm it was James McCutcheon, a sailor on the *Wexford*. He was among the small army of people who rushed to the lake shore to assist in identifying the bodies. He told of missing the train that was supposed to carry him to Sarnia where he would have boarded the *Wexford*. McCutcheon had been late and missed his ship on only three occasions in his life. On the first occasion the ship he had intended to board caught fire and sustained heavy casualties. The second time he missed a departure, the ship was wrecked and again there was the heavy loss of lives. As he stood surveying the bodies of his dead shipmates he uttered the understatement of the disaster, "I'm the luckiest guy alive."

The Regina

The *Regina* went down in mystery and speculation. The bodies of crewmen from the *Price* and the *Regina* floated to shore together. Sometimes the waves threw them into each others arms. Twelve men, later identified as being from the crew of the *Price*, were found wearing the life jackets of the *Regina*. The explanation that makes the most sense is that the two ships collided before sinking, and in those moments before they went under, men slipped and slid from the deck of one doomed ship to the other. Perhaps believing one ship might survive, some crewmen may have jumped to the more stable of the two. During the pandemonium that must have broken out, men likely grabbed whatever life preservers were available with no consideration for which ship it came from.

If a collision did take place, one of the ships had to limp for many miles before going completely under, since the *Price* was found in Port Huron and the *Regina* was found thirty miles farther up the lake between Lexington and Port Sanilac.

The *Regina* may have been the most ill-equipped vessel to venture forth and vanish in the Great Storm. When it was all over, it would not have made a difference.

She was making her last trip for the season and Captain McConkey was anxious to get home to his wife and two daughters. At Sarnia he picked up a heavy load of iron pipe that was lashed to his deck. He then headed into Lake Huron. His ship's broken communication equipment prevented him from knowing how severe the storm warnings were. It is believed that the ship made it as far as the Saginaw Bay when the brutal winds forced her to turn back.

Water began to freeze everywhere on the ship. The crew put on life preservers and readied the lifeboats. By 11:00 pm the captain was the only man left on the ship. People on shore heard his mayday pleas, but in the face of ninety-mile-an-hour winds and thirty-five-foot waves, they were helpless to offer any assistance. The captain was a frightened thirty-four-year-old husband and father who only wanted to see his family again. His body was found nine months later, along with his watch and his diary. He was the last of the crew to be found. His ship was not found for seventy-three years.

Missing from the *Regina* when she sunk was George Gosby. Three weeks earlier Gosby stumbled over a hatch cover and fell into a hold as the *Regina* was being loaded. Initially feeling sorry for himself for having to sit out the remainder of the season, he had reason to consider himself very fortunate.

The John A. McGean

The *John A. McGean* floundered and sunk about seventy-five miles north of Port Huron and slightly north of Harbor Beach. The *McGean* was captained by the colorful Dancing Chauncey Ney, who, as his nickname suggests, loved to dance. He liked to be in port on Friday and Saturday nights so he could catch the local dances. He never left the dance floor until the band played its last tune.

One of the *McGean's* life rafts drifted onto the beach with its gruesome crew of three dead men lashed to it. A second *McGean* raft carried a single body. The frozen bodies of most of the remaining crew were found washed ashore and scattered about randomly along the sand and rocks. A few remained bobbing in the water. All were accounted for except Chauncey Ney whose last dance partner was an angry Lake Huron.

The Argus

The *Argus* was the only ship to sink that day before the eyes of horrified witnesses. Captain Walter C. Iler of the steamer *George C. Crawford* was fighting his own battle on the rogue and rampaging sea when he witnessed a scene he would remember forever. Captain Iler was attempting to turn his huge vessel around, but meeting with little success, when a temporary lull in the wind helped him right his ship and escape the raging waters. Sometime late Sunday afternoon, between snowy whiteouts, he caught sight of the *Argus* laboring strenuously beneath her heavy load of coal. Her bow and her stern appeared suspended by huge waves going in different directions, leaving the cargo-heavy midsection unsupported in the gap between the waves. Iler watched her crumble like an eggshell and disappear.

Captain Paul Gutch of the *Argus* washed ashore with no lifejacket. Mrs. William Walker was a second cook on the *Argus*. When her body floated out of the water she wore the lifejacket marked "Captain" – likely an unselfish act of heroism but all for naught. No life jacket could protect against the whirling white waters made foamy by ice and snow.

The Hydrus

The *Hydrus*, twin sister ship to the *Argus*, was probably, of all the ships recovered, the one with the worst recovery rate for bodies. Several are believed to have washed onto the rocky shores of the Saugeen Native American Reservation. Speculation suggested that the Native Americans, because of their religious beliefs, were hesitant to touch the bodies. Eventually, shifting winds and currents may have carried some of the dead to places where no one would ever find them. At least two lifeboats with bodies of seamen from the *Hydrus* were recovered. No one has found the wreckage of the *Hydrus*.

In the storm's aftermath, several bodies washed to shore with watches still on the victims' wrists. Many of the watches stopped between 8:00 pm and 11:00 pm on Sunday, November 9. The weather bureau reported that the highest winds on Lake Huron came between 6:00 pm and 8:00 pm that evening.

While Lake Huron buried many secrets beneath her turbulent waves that awful night, she did give up another. Near Harbor Beach, fishermen found a body and wreckage from a tug, the *Searchlight*, which had vanished with all hands aboard in 1908. The violent storm had unearthed the watery grave.

Less than a year after the big storm, the Great Lakes offered a possible demonstration of how those freighters were capsized in November 1913. On May 8, 1914 the *Kirby* sank in a relatively modest storm. The *Kirby* was regarded as completely seaworthy, but she sank almost without warning. The subsequent investigation revealed that a great wave had come over the port bow, submerging the deck. The weight of the water pushed the bow downward and tipped the stern high in the air. Before the Kirby could right herself, a second wave came at her and stood the boat in a position with her hull poised out of the water. A third deadly wave then caught her from beneath. She heaved upward, stood motionless for thirty seconds and then plunged to the bottom.

Captains of the ships that managed to get ashore during the Storm of 1913 reported their vessels being struck by waves coming from all directions.

Immediately after the Storm of 1913, the death count and human suffering was foremost on everyone's mind. Eventually, it became apparent that the white hurricane had also destroyed one of the Thumb's major industries. Docks were destroyed at Harbor Beach, Lexington, Forester, and Port Sanilac. They were never rebuilt, and the great cargo freighters no longer stopped at these small towns. The transportation of many goods moved inland to the railroad. The face of shipping and transportation in the Thumb had changed forever.

Today, meteorologists would call the Storm of 1913 a weather bomb. To many of the Thumb's people it, quite simply, was the end of the world.

Index

A

B

M

About the Author

Julie Albrecht Royce was born and grew up in Michigan's Thumb. She attended elementary and high school in Sandusky, Michigan and received a Bachelor of Arts from Michigan State University. She attended graduate and law school at the University of Cincinnati where she received an M.Ed. and a J.D. After graduation she returned to her home state and practiced law for twenty-five years in Lansing. Ms. Royce was a First Assistant Attorney General to Frank Kelley for several years and to Jennifer Granholm when Ms. Granholm was Attorney General.

After retirement Ms. Royce and her husband, Bob, moved to Lexington, Michigan where they live today. In 2004, Governor Granholm visited Lexington and spoke of the need to promote the unparalleled magnificence of Michigan's lakeshores. Ms. Royce took her former boss's words to heart and authored *Traveling Michigan's Thumb*. She and her husband enjoyed the project so much that she wrote a second guide, *Traveling Michigan's Sunset Coast*.

Michigan's Thumb remains her home and her first love. Having the option of living anywhere, she chooses to live three blocks from where she was born.

Map of the Thumb Route

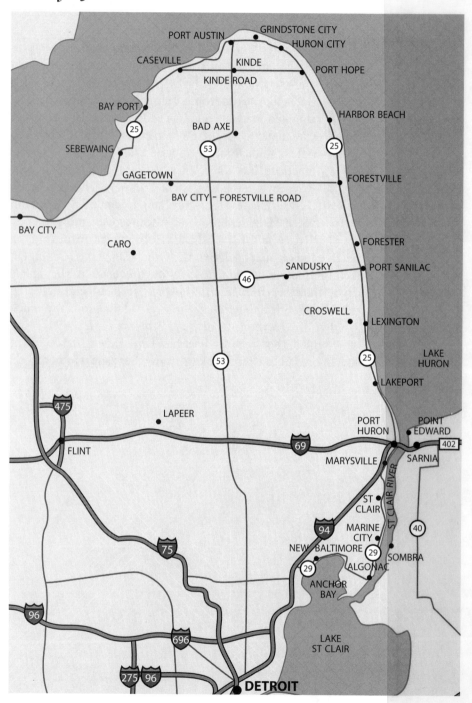